BRITISH BROADCASTING

BRITISH BROADCASTING

A Study in Monopoly

BY

R. H. COASE

Reader in Economics
in the University of London

THE LONDON SCHOOL OF ECONOMICS
AND POLITICAL SCIENCE

(University of London)

LONGMANS, GREEN AND CO
LONDON · NEW YORK · TORONTO

LONGMANS, GREEN AND CO LTD
6 & 7 CLIFFORD STREET LONDON W I
ALSO AT MELBOURNE AND CAPE TOWN

LONGMANS, GREEN AND CO INC
55 FIFTH AVENUE NEW YORK 3

LONGMANS, GREEN AND CO
215 VICTORIA STREET TORONTO I

ORIENT LONGMANS LTD
BOMBAY CALCUTTA MADRAS

First Published *1950*

*The books in this series are published by the London
School of Economics and Political Science, but the
authors alone are responsible for the views expressed
in them.*

Made and Printed in Great Britain by The Garden City Press Ltd., Letchworth, Herts.

CONTENTS

PART III.—PUBLIC DISCUSSION

ACKNOWLEDGMENTS

It is a pleasure to record the helpfulness with which all my requests for information have been met. I am especially indebted to the British Broadcasting Corporation and to the Post Office. The British Broadcasting Corporation gave me access to their archives for the period up to 1926 and allowed me to use their valuable collection of Press cuttings. The Post Office allowed me to consult the unpublished Minutes of Evidence of the Sykes Committee of 1923 and of the Crawford Committee of 1925. The officials of both the Corporation and the Post Office have also been of the greatest assistance in answering my many questions. But it is essential that I make it clear that I alone am responsible for the accuracy of the facts as I have stated them and for the opinions I have expressed.

Among the many individuals who gave me information, I am especially grateful to Lord Reith, who spared himself no trouble to be of service to me and whose comments on my drafts were most helpful. I have also to thank Mr. H. L. Beales, Mr. E. S. Byng, Mr. Tom Clarke, Mr. P. P. Eckersley, Sir Frank Gill and Mr. A. W. Maton, all of whom gave me valuable information. Information was also very kindly given to me by Broadcast Relay Service, Ltd., the *Daily Mail*, the International Broadcasting Company, the Marconi Company and the Newspaper Proprietors' Association.

I am grateful to my friends, Mr. R. S. Edwards and Mr. Walter Taplin, who both read the whole of the manuscript and whose candid comments have given this book such readability as it possesses.

It is fitting that I should here record my indebtedness to Professor Sir Arnold Plant. I came under his guidance some seventeen years ago while an undergraduate at the London School of Economics and from the intellectual stimulus I then received I continue to benefit in all my work.

There are two other debts that I must acknowledge. The first is to the Economics Research Division of the London School of Economics which financed the research upon which this book is based.   The second is to Miss L. E. Levy, whose hard work, efficiency and enterprise as research assistant made this study possible.

Chapters 1 and 4 of this book represent revised versions of two articles, " The Origin of the Monopoly of Broadcasting in Great Britain " and " Wire Broadcasting in Great Britain " which appeared in *Economica* for August, 1947, and August, 1948, respectively.   I have to thank the Editorial Board of *Economica* for permission to reproduce them.

R. H. Coase.

September, 1948.

INTRODUCTION

In this book I set out to answer the following questions :

(1) How is it that broadcasting in Great Britain came to be organised on a monopolistic basis ?

(2) What has been the effect of the monopoly on the development of, and policy towards, competitive services such as wire broadcasting and foreign commercial broadcasting intended for listeners in Great Britain ?

(3) What are the views which have been held on the monopoly of broadcasting in Great Britain ?

The first question is answered in chapters 1, 2 and 3 ; the second in chapters 4 and 5 ; the third in chapters 6 and 7.

In chapter 8, " A Commentary," I examine the cogency and implications of the arguments by which the monopoly has been justified and I discuss the forces in society which have contributed to the widespread support which the monopoly has enjoyed.

It is not my aim in this book to come to a conclusion as to whether or not it is desirable that broadcasting should be organised on a monopolistic basis in Great Britain. But this study is presented in the hope that it will be of assistance in any reasoned discussion of this question.

I have divided the notes into two classes. Those which are references to sources or relate to points of detail or are expansions of the text have been placed as numbered notes at the end of each chapter. The others, which are intended to be read with the text, have been placed at the bottom of the relevant page.

PART I

THE ORIGINS

CHAPTER ONE

THE ORIGIN OF THE MONOPOLY

1. THE GENESIS OF BROADCASTING IN GREAT BRITAIN

SUCCESS in the transmission of speech and music by radio did not immediately lead to proposals for the establishment of a broadcasting service.[1] At first the transmission of sound by radio was regarded simply as a new means for sending messages and as its original name, wireless telephony, indicates, was considered to be a new kind of telephone. This point of view is well illustrated by the following quotation from what appears to be the first book published in Great Britain which was wholly devoted to wireless telephony. " The possible fields in which wireless telephony may be utilised are many and diverse, but those in which its commercial application is probable are relatively few. One reason at least for this statement is to be found in the competition of the old-established wire telephone, and in the much greater secrecy of wire communication over wireless. As a well-known writer has recently aptly put it : ' A wireless telephone talk is a talk upon the house-tops with the whole world for an audience.' The practical utilisation of wireless telephone methods is therefore confined almost entirely to cases where the wire telephone cannot be used, or is rendered unreliable from exterior causes. Wireless telephony's most important field is consequently for long distance, and especially trans-ocean work, and for communication with ships."[2] And this writer goes on to instance as especially important uses, amongst others, communication with moving railway trains and with aircraft.[3]

There were some who thought of other uses for wireless telephony. Mr. A. C. C. Swinton had drawn attention in November, 1918, to the possible distribution of news by this means. But what he had in mind was a service similar to that of the tape machine. He pointed out that it would be possible to receive and print news messages transmitted by special distributing stations. He also mentioned the possibility " in the near future " of a public speaker addressing " an audience of thousands, scattered, maybe, over half the globe." But there is no suggestion here of a broadcasting service. And the report of Mr. Swinton's talk in the *Wireless World* goes on to say : " But by far the most fascinating and important problem spoken of was that of wireless distribution of electrical energy in bulk." [4]

The idea of a broadcasting service must have occurred to some workers in this field. We know that David Sarnoff, then of the American Marconi Company, in a memorandum to the Managing Director written at a much earlier date (about November, 1916) envisaged the possibility of a broadcasting service, [5] and doubtless the same idea had occurred to others. But in general, even among the experts in the field, there seems to have been little, if any, awareness of the potentialities of the discovery of wireless telephony for use in transmitting news, talks, discussions, commentaries, plays and concerts to people in their own homes. [6]

The first major experiment in wireless telephony in Great Britain which had the character of broadcasting was that made by the Marconi Company early in 1920. [7] A transmitting station of 15 kilowatts was built at Chelmsford, and from February 23rd to March 6th there were two daily transmissions of speech and music. [8] The object was experimental—to obtain reports on the quality of reception from different places and with different types of receiving sets. [9] Although these transmissions had the character of broadcasting, the primary purpose was not to entertain or instruct the listeners. [10] The next event, and one which attracted considerable attention, was the broadcast by Dame Nellie Melba on June 15th, 1920. This was sponsored by the *Daily Mail* and the broadcast was made from the Chelmsford station of the Marconi Company. [11] During the summer of 1920 some additional transmissions were made. One experiment which was made in co-operation with the Press Association was a test of the efficiency of wireless telephony in the sending of news to newspaper offices. [12] But after the summer of 1920 wireless telephony broadcasts ceased. [13]

Why did these experimental broadcasts stop ? The reason appears to have been that the Post Office disapproved of them and refused to license further broadcasts. The Post Office derived this power to control wireless telephony in the early 1920's from the Wireless Telegraphy Act of 1904. In this Act it was provided that in order to operate apparatus either for transmitting or receiving wireless signals, it was necessary to have a licence and also that this licence might be in a form and with conditions determined by the Postmaster-General.[14] According to Mr. P. P. Eckersley, the Post Office wrote to the Marconi Company " and said that the experimental broadcasting transmissions must cease because they were interfering with important communications. . . ."[15] There is no official statement which is explicit about this matter. But in reply to a parliamentary question about experiments in the distribution of news by wireless telephony, after what appears to be a reference to the experiments carried out in collaboration with the Press Association, the Postmaster-General, Mr. A. H. (later Lord) Illingworth, added : " It was also found that the experiments caused considerable interference with other stations, and for the present the trials have been suspended."[16] This is presumably a reference to the Post Office's communication to the Marconi Company.

But broadcasting did not altogether cease in Great Britain. There was still the work of the amateurs. " In London district there had been few evenings in the week since 1920 without entertainment of some kind—all this, however, on low power and in so far as it was broadcasting, technically against the law."[17] And Mr. A. R. Burrows remarks, " the number of tests requiring the assistance of gramophone records seemed somehow to increase week by week."[18] By the end of 1921 " it was possible any evening in all parts of Great Britain to listen-in to well-known amateur stations at work." These included " frequent programmes of speech and music."[19] In addition, broadcast concerts from the Hague, which had started in May, 1920, and which continued throughout this period, were heard by the amateurs in Great Britain. And towards the end of 1921 concerts were broadcast from the Eiffel Tower which could also be heard in Britain.*

At the second conference of wireless societies called by the Wireless Society of London on March 1st, 1921,[20] one item on the agenda was " The possibility of regular telephone transmission from a high-power station to include all matters of interest to amateurs and to be on different definite wavelengths for calibration purposes." Mr. E. Blake, who was the Marconi Company's representative at the conference, said that the Marconi Company had applied to the Post Office for a temporary licence to carry out " a somewhat

* As an indication of the scale of the activities of the amateurs at this time, it should be noted that there were at the beginning of 1921 150 amateur transmitting licences and over 4,000 receiving licences. These figures were given by Captain F. G. Loring, the Post Office representative, at the second conference of wireless societies, March 1921.

humbler programme for amateurs than was suggested on the agenda." The Marconi Company's application had not been refused but " the Post Office required some very good evidence that such a programme would really be welcomed by amateurs and had suggested that the views of the Institution of Electrical Engineers or of the Committee of the Wireless Society of London should be obtained. . . . The intention of the Marconi Company was to transmit for a mere half-hour or so once a week." Mr. Blake said the Marconi Company did not feel justified in asking for more than that and explained that it was proposed that the transmissions should consist of both telegraphy and telephony.[21] This proposal received general support, although the President of the Wireless Society of London (Major J. Erskine Murray) remarked that " C. W. and the rest of the programme is very much more important than telephony, although the latter, perhaps, is more amusing."*

The attitude of the Post Office was made clear by Captain F. G. Loring, the Post Office representative at the conference. He said : " As to the possibility of regular telephone transmissions, that will be favourably considered by the Post Office when it is put forward, but we do not like it coming from the Marconi Company, as it puts us in rather an awkward position. It would come very much better from the Wireless Society. The Marconi Company's representative will, I am sure, understand what I mean. The application will be much easier for us to deal with if it comes from an organisation like the Wireless Society than from a firm. We cannot give the Marconi Company preferential treatment over any other firm, so that if they asked for permission to send out for half an hour every week, half a dozen other companies could come along, and we should have to give them similar permission, whereas if the Wireless Society were to apply it would make it much easier for us. The question of wavelengths is a very difficult one because at the present time it is not easy to find wavelengths which do not interfere with genuine work."[22]

Following this conference, fruitless negotiations continued for nine months between the Wireless Society of London and the Post Office.[23] It needs to be emphasised that these negotiations were not concerned with the establishment of a broadcasting service. The

* A note explaining these technical terms is perhaps required. Telegraphy is the transmission of messages by means of signals, e.g., the Morse code ; telephony is the transmission of sound ; C.W. (continuous wave) is used as a synonym for telegraphy.

licences granted to the amateurs (both for transmitting and receiving) were for experimental purposes. And the reason for setting up the proposed broadcasting station was to aid in their experimental work—although the motives of some, at least, of the amateurs were no doubt mixed. The Post Office agreed in August, 1921, to the transmission by the Marconi Company of signals by wireless telegraphy for amateurs but permission for wireless telephony was withheld.[24] While these negotiations were proceeding, amateurs (particularly those belonging to the provincial societies) became restive and letters began to appear in the *Wireless World* from September, 1921, onwards urging that telephony transmissions should be started in Britain. There was also at this time an appeal for subscriptions in order that the concerts from the Hague should not be discontinued. And this naturally strengthened the feeling that there ought to be telephony transmissions in Britain.

On December 29th, 1921, a petition signed on behalf of sixty-three wireless societies representing 3,300 members was handed to Post Office officials, asking for wireless telephony transmissions in Great Britain. It included the following passage : " We would point out that it is telephony in which the majority of our members are chiefly interested, this being the most recent achievement in wireless and that in which for moderate distances at all events, improvements such as avoidance of distortion, and the production of really articulate loudspeakers and such like, are most required.

It is therefore primarily to serve the scientific purpose of improving the receiving arrangements that we desire to have telephony included. . . ."[25]

When the petition was handed in at the Post Office, the representatives of the wireless societies " voiced a national resentment that public services such as wireless Time and Telephony should be left to our neighbours to provide, and that permission to transmit Weather Reports, news and music by wireless telephony should be refused to Companies competent and willing to do so without interference with the defensive services of the country."[26] This comment clearly refers to a service with aims wider than those mentioned in the petition.

As a result of the petition, the wireless societies were informed in a letter, dated January 13th, 1922, that the Postmaster-General " has now authorised the Marconi's Wireless Telegraph Company to include a programme of 15 minutes telephony (speech and

B

music) in the weekly transmission from their Chelmsford station for the benefit of wireless societies and amateurs." [27]   The first broadcast took place on February 14th, 1922. It was made from a station at Writtle (near Chelmsford) which was operated by the Marconi Scientific Instrument Company. Mr. P. P. Eckersley was in charge of the broadcasts and their character is well described in his book. [28] The station continued to give its weekly programme until January 9th, 1923. " This was to be the first broadcasting station in Great Britain to do regular and advertised transmissions." [29]

2. Proposals for a Broadcasting Service

The first regular broadcasting station in Great Britain was that set up at Writtle. But its main purpose was to assist amateurs in their experiments ; not to provide a broadcasting service. Furthermore, although the Writtle station preceded in point of time the establishment of a broadcasting service, it would probably not be true to say that the ultimate provision of such a service was made more likely or even brought forward to any considerable extent in time by the opening of the Writtle station. The most that can be claimed is that the practical example which the Writtle transmissions furnished may have had some effect in easing the course of the negotiations leading to the establishment of a broadcasting service. The position has been described by Mr. P. P. Eckersley :

" Many declare that if it had not been for Writtle, and the interest that Writtle stimulated, broadcasting would never have come to England.

" While I, as a worker at Writtle, and one who was responsible for the artistic and the technical side of the transmission, am much flattered by the suggestion, I am still unconvinced.

" Broadcasting came about because those interested came over from the States and pointed out what vast sums of money were being made there, what interest broadcasting was creating, and how England had got left behind. This I think was the great stimulant— American broadcasting. It had nothing to do with the then unhonoured and unsung transmissions, attracting no notice in the ordinary Press, and of which the general public was wholly ignorant. This is not false modesty, it is the truth, and while, of course, the Writtle transmission may have raised to fever pitch the enthusiasm of real wireless amateurs I think it did little to attract general notice."[30]

A simple study of dates confirms the truth of this analysis. The Writtle transmissions did not start until February 14th, 1922. Yet we know that already by March of that year (before any conclusions could be drawn from the experience of the Writtle broadcasts) a number of radio manufacturers had applied to the Post Office for permission to broadcast.[31] The reason for these applications is quite clear. Experience in the United States had shown that there was a large market for receiving sets once a broadcasting service had been provided.[32] Radio manufacturers were therefore anxious that a broadcasting service should be established in order to create a demand for their receiving sets. On April 3rd, 1922, the Postmaster-General announced in the House of Commons that the whole question was being referred to the Imperial Communications Committee in order to obtain the views of the other Departments.[33]

The next public move was a statement issued on April 19th, 1922, by Mr. Godfrey Isaacs, Managing Director of the Marconi Company.[34] He said that " they were only waiting for the necessary facilities—and he thought the Government were going to give them." The Marconi Company's programme was " to supply instruments to the householder on hire." They planned to set up broadcasting stations in different parts of the country and to transmit on particular wavelengths, " if we get assistance, as I have no doubt we will, from the authorities " so that only those hiring the particular receivers would hear the programmes. Mr. Godfrey Isaacs' reason for preferring the hiring of instruments was that " Modifications would be introduced from time to time in the apparatus, and once a man had bought his property, he would not feel happy if soon after he had to buy something better." He added that if the public wanted to buy the apparatus they could do so.* A noteworthy omission in Mr. Isaacs' statement is that he makes no reference to the repercussions which the Marconi Company plan would have on those of the other companies which desired to start broadcasting or to the problem of how the wavelengths would be allocated between the various companies. It may be that he

---

* I have been informed by the Marconi Company that an important activity at this time of the Marconi Marine Company was the hire and maintenance of wireless apparatus for ships and that this arrangement was preferred by shipowners to outright sale. This probably had some influence on Mr. Isaacs' views.

thought it impolitic to refer publicly to these questions at that stage. Or perhaps he imagined that, in the event, the Marconi Company would be bound to undertake the operation of all the broadcasting stations. This would not have been an unreasonable expectation. The Marconi Company was the only British company with experience in the operation of broadcasting stations and was, in fact, operating the only broadcasting station at work in Great Britain. Furthermore, the Marconi Company claimed to control many master patents in connection with broadcasting. [35]

This Marconi Company plan brought a letter of protest in *The Times*.[36] The writer (Mr. H. H. Brown) objected to the " reception of telephony so controlled that the hire or purchase of the instruments of a particular firm was an almost essential preliminary." And he went on to say : " I suggest that rather than place one firm in a privileged position, they should raise the annual charge for a ' receiving ' licence sufficiently to defray the cost of a ' broadcasting ' station."

In the meantime, the Wireless Sub-Committee of the Imperial Communications Committee held its first meeting on April 5th, 1922. A further meeting of this Committee was held on April 22nd, 1922.[37] The report of this Committee was not published but its main terms can be gathered from a speech of the Postmaster-General, Mr. F. G. Kellaway, in the House of Commons on May 4th, in which he stated that he was adopting the recommendations of this Committee, and also from two articles by Sir Henry Norman, Chairman of the Wireless Sub-Committee of the Imperial Communications Committee, in *The Times* for May 8th and May 9th, 1922.

The main recommendations of the Committee appear to have been :

(1) Broadcasting stations should be set up in Great Britain.

(2) The wavelength band of from 350 to 425 metres should be allocated for this purpose.

(3) The country should be divided into the areas around London, Cardiff, Plymouth, Birmingham, Manchester, Newcastle, Glasgow or Edinburgh (but not both) and Aberdeen and one or more broadcasting stations should be allowed in each of these areas.

(4) The power of the stations should be $1\frac{1}{2}$ kilowatts.

(5) Only bona fide British manufacturers of wireless apparatus should be allowed to broadcast. For this they should pay the Post Office an annual fee of £50.

(6) No advertising should be allowed. Mr. Kellaway makes no mention of this in his speech. But Sir Henry Norman says in his article : " Of course every big retail house would like to shout the merits and low prices of its taffetas and tulles, its shirts and shoes. There is no room for this." [38]

(7) Those possessing receiving sets should pay an annual licence fee of 10s. Sir Henry Norman says that " This is necessary in order to locate apparatus in times of need and so that the user knows the conditions with which to comply." There is no suggestion that the licence fee should be used to pay the costs of the broadcasting service.

(8) There would have to be regulations regarding the news that the broadcasting stations would be allowed to transmit.

Mr. Kellaway said in his speech on May 4th : " What I am doing is to ask all those who apply—the various firms who have applied—to come together at the Post Office and co-operate so that an efficient service may be rendered and that there may be no danger of monopoly and that each service may not be interfering with the efficient working of the other." This corresponds with the statement by Sir Henry Norman that "the commercial firms are to arrange amongst themselves how to share sites, times and wavelengths."

What is clear is that at this time there was no publicly expressed view that there ought to be a monopoly of transmission in the case of the British broadcasting service. Sir Henry Norman envisaged the possibility of there being ultimately a State broadcasting station. But that was clearly something for the future which did not affect the immediate arrangements. At the beginning of May, 1922, it appeared, at least to those outside official circles, that the broadcasting stations were to be operated independently by various firms manufacturing radio receiving sets. [39] Sir Henry Norman, who must have been very well informed on Government policy, said of the companies, " Each will announce its own service and there will be a natural rivalry to furnish the most attractive programmes, since hearers may conclude that the firm supplying the best entertainment in the clearest manner is the most likely to make good apparatus." [40]

3. THE NEGOTIATIONS

It was not only radio manufacturers who wished to establish broadcasting stations. The *Daily Mail* had proposed (probably early in May, 1922) that a *Daily Mail* Marconi Company broadcasting service should be set up. This " came to nothing because of Post Office opposition."[41] The applicants for permission to set up broadcasting stations also included some of the large department stores.[42] But the Post Office decided that only bona fide manufacturers of wireless apparatus should be considered.[43] Consequently, only representatives of radio manufacturers appear to have been invited to the meeting which the Postmaster-General had foreshadowed.

This meeting took place at the General Post Office on May 18th, 1922. It was attended by the representatives of 24 firms[44] which had applied for licences to broadcast. The Chairman of the meeting was Sir Evelyn Murray, Secretary of the Post Office. He explained that it would be impossible to grant all the applications which had been made and the firms " were asked to arrive at some co-operative scheme among themselves."[45] Whatever the impression may have been earlier as to how broadcasting was to be organised in Great Britain, it was made clear at this meeting that the Post Office was in favour of a single broadcasting company.[46]

The larger firms, however, divided themselves into two groups.[47] One group comprised the Marconi Company, the General Electric Company and the British Thomson-Houston Company. The other group consisted of the Metropolitan-Vickers Company together with the Western Electric Company* and the Radio Communication Company.† It must have become apparent at this first meeting that it would prove difficult to bring these two groups to agree on a single scheme. For the official statement issued after the meeting, in spite of the desire of the Post Office for a single scheme, had as its concluding section : " The best means of attaining these objects seemed to lie in co-operation among the firms concerned, and it was suggested that one or probably two groups should be formed which should become responsible, both financially and otherwise, for the erection and maintenance of the stations and the provision of suitable programmes. In accordance with these suggestions it was

---

* Now Standard Telephones and Cables Ltd.

† It should be noted that the Metropolitan-Vickers Co. Ltd. were associated with the American Westinghouse Company, and the Western Electric Company were associated with the American company of the same name.

arranged that the representatives of the various firms should collaborate in the immediate preparation of a co-operative scheme, or, at the most, of two such schemes, for consideration by the Post Office authorities." [48]

On May 23rd the representatives of the firms met at the Institution of Electrical Engineers, the Chairman of the meeting being Mr. (later Sir Frank) Gill of the International Western Electric Company. [49] At this meeting a smaller Committee was appointed to draft a scheme. The discussions on this Committee do not seem to have gone very smoothly. But whatever the detailed course of the discussions may have been, the final result was that the two groups failed to come to any agreement for a single broadcasting company and " they reported to those who appointed them that one broadcasting company appeared impossible but that two broadcasting firms could probably be formed which would operate independently." [50] The differences which caused the negotiations to break down " were other than technical differences," [51] and it can therefore be presumed that they concerned the conditions on which the Marconi Company would be willing to furnish its patents to the other companies. [52] The Postmaster-General was informed of this failure to reach an agreement by a deputation—presumably at the meeting on June 16th. [53] The Postmaster-General stated at this meeting that he would be willing to license the two groups of manufacturers but not more—and no doubt he made it clear that he hoped the manufacturers would in the end be able to agree on a single broadcasting company.* The scheme for independent working which the Post Office would have been willing to sanction was that in London there would be one station belonging to each group, but that the rest of the country would be divided between them. [54]

Following the meeting with the Postmaster-General a sub-committee was appointed consisting of Mr. (later Sir Archibald) McKinstry (of the Metropolitan-Vickers Company) and Mr. Godfrey Isaacs (of the Marconi Company). The task of this sub-committee was to draw up an agreement on matters of common interest such as, for example, the allocation of wavelengths. " During the protracted discussion of this sub-committee the difficulties of operating two companies became so apparent that negotiations for

---

* Mr. Kellaway said in his speech on August 4th in the House of Commons : " . . . there may be two ; I hope myself, in the interests of broadcasting, there will be only one. . . ."

the formation of one company were carried on between the two members, resulting in their being able to report to their respective groups a basis for the formation of one company, which was ultimately agreed to." [55]

There is no question that the difficulties in formulating these common conditions must have appeared formidable. But there were other factors at work which helped in bringing about the agreement to form a single broadcasting company. First of all there was the evident desire of the Post Office, a Department with which all firms must have wanted good relations, that there should be a single broadcasting company. Secondly, there is little doubt that the Marconi Company was itself in favour of a single company.[56] And no doubt this made it willing to make concessions on the points which had led to the breakdown of the earlier negotiations. Thirdly, it must not be forgotten that the main interest of the manufacturers was not in broadcasting as such. Their aim was to sell receiving sets and they wanted a broadcasting service to be established in order to be able to do this. Consequently the interest of the groups in preserving their independence in the case of the broadcasting service was not particularly great.

The agreement to form a single broadcasting company was reached on August 11th, 1922.[57] At the end of August a draft of the Articles of Association was sent to the Post Office.[58] On September 12th, 1922, a meeting was held at the Post Office to discuss the Postmaster-General's suggested modifications to the draft Articles of Association.[59] By October all differences had been resolved and on October 18th a meeting, at which representatives of about 200 firms were present, was held at the Institution of Electrical Engineers to ratify the draft Articles of Association. At this meeting the Chairman, Sir William Noble,[60] was able to say that there was " complete agreement with the Postmaster-General."[61] The British Broadcasting Company was registered on December 15th, 1922. The Licence to broadcast was not, however, issued to the Company until January 18th, 1923.[62] The delay appears to have been due to difficulties in negotiating an agreement with the Press on the question of news broadcasts. [63]

But the start of broadcasting in Great Britain did not wait for the conclusion of these lengthy negotiations. The delay in setting up a service had caused considerable dissatisfaction and in consequence it was decided to begin broadcasting before all the details of the scheme had been worked out and agreed. The date fixed for the official start was November 14th, 1922. On that day broadcasting began from the Marconi Company's station at Marconi House, London. On November 15th it began from the Metropolitan-Vickers Company's station at Trafford Park, Manchester. Both these stations had been operating on an experimental basis during the summer.[64] On the same day, broadcasting began in Birmingham from a station operated by the International Western Electric Company for which the General Electric Company had provided space in their works at Witton.[65] This station had been set up in October at Oswaldestre House, London, by the International Western Electric Company for experimental purposes and was later removed to Birmingham when it was decided to start broadcasting.

4. THE BROADCASTING SCHEME OF 1922*

The broadcasting scheme was built around the British Broadcasting Company. The capital of this Company was to be subscribed by British radio manufacturers—and they alone could be members. Each member agreed not to sell any apparatus for listening to broadcasts unless the components were British made, and they also agreed to pay the Company, according to a scale laid down in the agreement, a royalty on the sales of all sets and certain of the main components.[66] Any British radio manufacturer could become a member of the Company by subscribing for at least a £1 share and by entering into the Agreement with the Company. The licence which the Post Office issued for receiving sets required the listener to use a set manufactured by a member of the British Broadcasting Company and 50 per cent. of the licence fee was paid over to the Company. Thus the funds that the company had at its disposal came from three sources : the subscribed share capital, royalties on sets and components, and 50 per cent. of the licence

* The broadcasting scheme was embodied in (i) the Memorandum and Articles of Association of the British Broadcasting Company, (ii) the licence granted to the company by the Postmaster-General, and (iii) the agreement made between the company and its members. For the licence and agreement, see *Wireless Broadcasting Licence* (Cmd. 1822), 1923. It was provided in the licence that the Articles of Association could not be altered without the consent of the Postmaster-General ; the important clause in the Memorandum could not be altered except in accordance with a clause in the Articles which requires the consent of the Postmaster-General ; and the agreement was incorporated as a schedule to the licence. In consequence, no substantial change in the arrangements was possible without the agreement of the Postmaster-General.

fee.[67] There is no question that the willingness of the manufacturers
to subscribe the capital of the broadcasting company and to pay
the royalties was dependent on their expectation of obtaining
profits from the sale of receiving sets.[68] As Mr. A. McKinstry said :
" The position is that the British Broadcasting Company was formed
by the manufacturing firms merely to broadcast in the hope that the
interest created by broadcasting would make the public buy
receiving sets, and they are looking for their profit, not from the
British Broadcasting Company, but from the sale of sets."[69] To make
sure that the demand for receiving sets which would follow the
institution of the broadcasting service would increase the sales of
members of the British Broadcasting Company, it was provided that
the listener could only use sets manufactured by members of the
Company and these in their turn had to use British components.[70]
All members of the Company agreed to pool (without payment)
all patents needed for broadcast transmissions.[71]

The scheme was very ingenious ; and so too were the arrangements which regulated the relations of the six main companies[72] to
the others. The share capital of the Company consisted of 100,000
£1 cumulative ordinary shares, on which the maximum dividend
that could be paid was 7½ per cent. per annum. The six firms
which had been primarily concerned with initiating the broadcasting scheme each subscribed for 10,000 shares and it was provided
that they could not hold, in total, more than 60,006 shares. Any
application from another firm had to be granted in full. If the
granting of all applications would bring the issued share capital
above 100,000 shares, all holdings in excess of ten shares were to be
reduced *pro rata* to make the total of holdings equal to 100,000
shares.   The provisions regarding the directors were similarly
detailed. The number of directors was to be not less than six or
more than nine ; six were to be appointed by the six main firms
and two could be appointed by members of the Company other
than the six main firms ; and the directors could also appoint an
additional director who would be permanent Chairman of the
Company.*

The Licence which was granted to the Company ran from
November 1st, 1922, to January 1st, 1925, and gave the Company
permission to operate eight broadcasting stations. The Company
had " to transmit efficiently " from each of these stations on every

* Lord Gainford, a former Postmaster-General, was appointed the first chairman.

day (including Sundays) " a programme of broadcast matter to the reasonable satisfaction of the Postmaster-General." The Licence also laid down the hours of broadcasting (which could be any hour on Sunday and between 5 and 11 p.m. on week days), the wavelengths (which had to be from 350 to 425 metres), and the power (which was to be fixed by the Postmaster-General but was not to exceed 3 kilowatts). The Postmaster-General had the right of inspection of any apparatus ; and the Company was compelled to transmit, if requested by a Government Department, any " communiqués, weather reports or notices issued as part of any programme or programmes of broadcast matter." The Postmaster-General also had the power to take possession of the stations in an emergency.

There were in the Licence two important limitations on what the Company might broadcast. The first concerned the transmission of news. It was provided that the Company should not broadcast any news or information in the nature of news " except such as they may obtain from one or more of the following news agencies, viz. : Reuters Ltd., Press Association Ltd., Central News Ltd., Exchange Telegraph Company Ltd., or from any other news agency approved by the Postmaster-General."[73]

The other limitation concerned advertising. The clause in the Licence ran : " The Company shall not without the consent in writing of the Postmaster-General receive money or other valuable consideration from any person in respect of the transmission of messages by means of a licensed apparatus, or send messages or music constituting broadcast matter provided or paid for by any person, other than the Company or person actually sending the message. Provided that nothing in this Clause shall be construed as precluding the Company from using for broadcast purposes without payment concerts, theatrical entertainments or other broadcast matter . . . given in public in London or the provinces." The exact legal force of this clause is rather obscure. It is clearly aimed at preventing advertising. But in fact it was not interpreted as prohibiting sponsored programmes ; and a programme sponsored by Harrods was broadcast in 1923.[74] Lord Riddell, who gave evidence to the Sykes Committee on behalf of the Newspaper Proprietors' Association, doubted whether this was legal.[75] But the British Broadcasting Company clearly thought that it was and it is unnecessary here to unravel the legal problem.

So far nothing has been said about the nature of the legal monopoly granted to the British Broadcasting Company. The reason is a simple one—the Company had no legal monopoly and there was nothing to prevent the Postmaster-General licensing another broadcasting company. Now this was not the view of the directors of the Company at the time it was formed. They believed that they had been granted an " exclusive licence."[76] The evidence to the Sykes Committee[77] of the Solicitor to the Post Office in which he pointed out that there was no legal monopoly caused some annoyance to the directors of the Company. They explained that when in the course of the negotiations they had wanted to include a clause in the Licence which specifically said that they were to have an exclusive licence, the Solicitor to the Post Office had replied that they " were already sufficiently protected."[78] They also recalled the very great efforts which the Post Office had made to bring about a single broadcasting company and claimed that this gave them a " moral monopoly."[79] It was made clear that if another broadcasting company was allowed it would not be able to derive any revenue either from the British Broadcasting Company's share of the licence fee or from the royalties paid by the manufacturers.[80] Furthermore, it was doubtful whether any other company could broadcast at all without the use of patents controlled by members of the British Broadcasting Company ; and there seems little reason to suppose that they would have been willing to allow a competing broadcasting company to use their patents.[81] So whatever the legal position may have been, it must have appeared, when the British Broadcasting Company was formed, that for practical purposes a monopoly had been granted. And so it was to prove.

5. POST OFFICE POLICY

It is broadly true to say that the establishment of the broadcasting service in Great Britain as a monopoly was the result of Post Office policy. The attainment of the monopoly was no doubt made easier by the necessity for some agreement as between the radio manufacturers on the question of patents and by the fact that the manufacturers' main interest was not in the operation of a broadcasting service but in the sale of receiving sets. But the obvious desire of the Post Office for a single company was decisive.* There can be no question that if the Post Office had wanted to bring about competing broadcasting systems it would have been possible to do so. Although the two groups may, at the end of their long negotiations, have preferred to have a combined system, they would have been willing to operate independently if the Post Office had wanted them to do so.† I shall therefore examine in this section the basis of Post Office policy towards broadcasting and attempt to discover the reasons which led it to favour a monopoly.

At first the Post Office thought of wireless telephony, as did others, simply as a new method of transmitting messages and therefore as requiring co-ordination with other means of communication and particularly with wireless telegraphy. Thus, the Postmaster-General in an answer to a parliamentary question on wireless telephony on April 20th, 1920, said : " I am giving every possible facility for its further development, but its progress must be co-ordinated with that of wireless telegraphy."[82] And later in the same year, in the answer in which the Postmaster-General alluded to the suspension of the Marconi Company experiments in broadcasting, he goes on to add : " Experiments are, however, being made to test the practicability of using high-speed wireless telegraphy for news and commercial services, and promising results have been obtained,"[83] Much the same attitude was shown in 1921.[84]

That wireless telephony was considered to have only limited uses and therefore to be of no particular importance, would itself be sufficient to explain the Post Office's lack of encouragement to experiments in broadcasting. But there is, I believe, another factor which should be taken into account. The allocation of wavelengths

---

* Compare the evidence of Sir William Noble on May 8th, 1923, to the Sykes Committee, question 279 : " It was the desire of the Post Office that we should have one company, and one company only, and we fell in with the view and eventually the two sides which were in opposition to each other agreed to the view of the Post Office to have one company. . . ."

† See the evidence of Sir William Noble to the Sykes Committee on May 8th, 1923, question 353 : " *Mr. Trevelyan*—The groups would have been content rather than not start at all to have each had a broadcasting licence at the start. The actual arrangement for a single company was really thrust on you by the Post Office. *Sir William Noble*—That is so." It is true that had the Post Office insisted on independent operation, this would have happened. And consequently the fact that the Post Office favoured a monopolistic organisation was decisive. But the statement that the " arrangement for a single company was really thrust " on the radio manufacturers is too sweeping. The Post Office at one stage agreed to independent operation and suggested the outline of such a scheme. Subsequently the firms concerned agreed to a combined scheme ; and in reaching this decision the preference of the Post Office for a single company was only one of the factors at work.

was the responsibility of the Wireless Sub-Committee of the Imperial Communications Committee. On this Committee there were three Service representatives, one Post Office representative and the representatives of certain other Departments. It was, therefore, a Committee on which the Services were strongly represented.[85] Now we know that it was with reluctance that the Services agreed to wavelengths of 325 to 450 metres being allocated to broadcasting (and then only with restrictions on the hours of service).[86] It seems clear that their opposition would have been very much stronger at an earlier date. The Post Office would have had to exert considerable pressure on the Service Departments to obtain wavelengths for broadcasting—and this they were probably unwilling to do.

But in the spring of 1922 came the applications from the manufacturers. These had been influenced by events in the United States. But so, too, was the Post Office. Mr. F. J. Brown, Assistant Secretary of the Post Office, had spent the winter of 1921-22 in the United States ; he had taken a great interest in broadcasting developments, had discussed the subject with many of the leading authorities in the United States and had attended some of the meetings of Mr. Hoover's first Radio Conference. In the United States at that time there was no effective regulation of the number of broadcasting stations. It seems that the only regulation was of the wavelength on which stations could broadcast—and the only wavelength then allowed was, for most stations, 360 metres. The need for some regulation of the number of stations was evident ; and Mr. F. J. Brown was impressed by this as well as by the great strides broadcasting was making in the United States.[87]

The way in which this question was treated in Great Britain led some to conclude that a monopoly was needed in order to prevent interference. Consider the following argument taken from a speech in the House of Commons by Mr. Kellaway, the Postmaster-General. " . . . it would be impossible to have a large number of firms broadcasting. It would result in a sort of chaos, only in a much more aggravated form than that which has arisen in the United States of America, and which has compelled the United States, or the Department over which Mr. Hoover presides, and which is responsible for broadcasting, to do what we are now doing at the beginning, that is, proceed to lay down very drastic regulations indeed for the control of wireless broadcasting.

It was, therefore, necessary that the firms should come together if the thing was to be efficiently done. You could not have twenty-four firms broadcasting in this country. There was not room . . . and it was suggested to them that, for the purpose of broadcasting information, whatever it might be, they should form themselves, if possible, into one group, one company."[88]

Mr. Kellaway did not say that it was necessary to have a monopoly in order that there should not be interference ; but the wording would be very liable to cause the incautious listener to imagine that this was so. Certainly many at that time seem to have been confused by the way the problem was presented. For example, a witness before the Sykes Committee[89] having said " It is arguable that there must be one central Broadcasting Authority," was immediately answered by Lord Burnham in the following words : " Is it not a fact ; already it is common knowledge ; that in America the want of regulation has meant very chaotic conditions." [90] And there are many other examples.[91]

But we cannot, of course, assume that the Post Office officials shared this view. It was obvious to them that the possibility of interference made necessary not a monopoly but a limitation in the number of broadcasting stations. Why then was it Post Office policy to bring about a monopoly ? Mr. E. H. Shaughnessy, who was Engineer in charge of the Wireless Section of the Post Office, was asked, when giving evidence to the Sykes Committee, about the necessity for a monopoly in transmission. He first referred to the problem of the Marconi Company's patents. But he went on to say that " if they were prepared to license people, then you would have a very large number of firms asking for permission probably, and some of them might be sufficiently wealthy to put up decent stations—most of them would not—you would have a very great difficulty in acquiescing, you could not acquiesce in all demands. And then you would have the difficulty of selecting the firms which the Post Office thought were most suitable for the job, and, whatever selection is made by the Post Office, the Post Office would be bound to be accused of favouring certain firms. So that the solution of the problem seemed to be to make all those firms get together to form one Company for the purpose of doing the broadcasting." [92] There can be little doubt that here we have the main reason which led the Post Office to favour a monopoly. One way out of the difficulty would have been for the Post Office itself to undertake the service.

But this it was unwilling to do.[93] If there was to be a broadcasting service in Great Britain it would have to be run by private enterprise ; and the Post Office could avoid the problem of selection only if a monopolistic organisation was set up. The difficulty of selection if there was not a monopoly must have been in the minds of Post Office officials for some time. It was this problem, as we have seen, which caused the Post Office early in 1921 to prefer to deal with an application from the Wireless Society of London rather than with one from the Marconi Company. Captain F. G. Loring, the Post Office representative, then said : " We cannot give the Marconi Company preferential treatment over any other firm, so that if they asked for permission . . . half a dozen other companies could come along, and we should have to give them similar permission, whereas if the Wireless Society were to apply it would make it much easier for us." [94] This point of view was reaffirmed when, in April, 1923, the *Daily Express* applied to the Post Office for a broadcasting licence. Of this, Mr. F. J. Brown said : " The answer which the Postmaster-General caused to be sent to that application was this. That he did not want to give facilities to one particular newspaper or organisation which he could not give to other newspapers and organisations and he asked the *Daily Express* how they would propose to meet that difficulty."[95]

There can be no question that there was a very real danger of creating monopolistic conditions in other fields if broadcasting licences were granted to particular firms. The nature of this danger was made evident when the Marconi Company, in April, 1922, proposed to set up broadcasting stations. And Mr. F. J. Brown has said : " It was . . . contrary to the policy of the British Government to grant a monopoly of broadcasting to one, or even to two or three, manufacturing firms, as this would place them in a superior position to their competitors for pushing the sale of their goods." [96] This aspect of the question seems to have been constantly in the mind of the Post Office. A large number of the modifications to the draft scheme which were put forward by the Postmaster-General during the course of the negotiations seem to have had as their aim the protection of the interests of the smaller firms.[97]

But it so happens that the plan for independent operation by the two groups which was evolved in the course of the negotiations was one which avoided this particular difficulty. All radio manufacturers would have been free to join one or other of the groups ;

none could have been penalised by the existence of independent broadcasting companies. Yet the Post Office still preferred that there should be a monopoly. The reason is fairly clear. There would still have remained the problem of the allocation of wavelengths and districts between the two groups. And the Post Office could not have avoided responsibility for the solution of these difficult problems. And there is also reason to suppose that the Post Office considered that it would be more economical to have one company instead of two or more.[98]

I have described the arguments which led the Post Office to favour a monopolistic broadcasting organisation. The Post Office did not itself wish to operate the broadcasting service. Consequently the only solution was to attempt to establish a single broadcasting company. But the problem to which a monopoly was seen as a solution by the Post Office was one of Civil Service administration. The view that a monopoly in broadcasting was better for the listener was to come later.

NOTES ON CHAPTER I

[1] For an historical account of the inventions which led to broadcasting, see H. M. Dowsett, *Wireless Telegraphy and Broadcasting*, 1923, Vol. I, pp. 1-53.

[2] P. R. Coursey, *Telephony Without Wires*, 1919, p. 356.

[3] *Op. cit.*, p. 357.

[4] For the section of Mr. Swinton's address dealing with wireless telephony, see the *Journal of the Royal Society of Arts*, November 22nd, 1918, pp. 14-15. A report of this talk (and the comment given in the text) appeared in the *Wireless World* for April 1919, p. 32.

[5] See G. L. Archer, *History of Radio to 1926*, pp. 112-113, where Mr. Sarnoff's memorandum, which foreshadowed the main features of a modern broadcasting service, is reproduced.

[6] See, for example, W. T. Ditcham, " The Progress of Wireless Telephony," *Yearbook of Wireless Telegraphy and Telephony*, 1920, p. 922.

[7] The earlier experiments were concerned with transmissions which were directed to particular places. The intention was not to broadcast.

[8] See A. R. Burrows, *The Story of Broadcasting*, pp. 47-48.

[9] See Frank P. Swann, " A High-power Wireless Telephony Installation," *Wireless World*, May 1st, 1920, p. 79 ; and P. P. Eckersley, *The Power Behind the Microphone*, p. 37.

[10] Compare P. P. Eckersley, *op. cit.*, p. 38.

[11] For an account of how this broadcast came to be given, see Tom Clarke, *My Northcliffe Diary*, pp. 150-151. For an account of the broadcast itself, see the *Daily Mail*, June 16th, 1920.

[12] See *The Times*, July 20th, 1920, and the *Wireless World*, August 7th, 1920, p. 396.

[13] The latest experimental telephony broadcasts by the Chelmsford station to which I have been able to find a reference are those on August 28th, 29th and 30th, 1920. See the *Wireless World*, October 2nd, 1920, p. 490. In the *Wireless World*, October 16th, 1920, p. 518, there is a reference to " Chelmsford's inability to transmit speech."

[14] See the evidence of Mr. R. W. Woods, Solicitor to the Post Office, on May 2nd, 1923, to the Sykes Committee.

[15] P. P. Eckersley, *op. cit.*, p. 38. Compare also B. L. Jacot and D. M. B. Collier, *Marconi—Master of Space*, where it is said, after a reference to the Melba concert, that the Postmaster-General " sent a protest, deploring that a national service such as wireless telegraphy should be put to such a frivolous purpose " (p. 123). A contemporary comment ran as follows : " Opinion among airmen is practically united against a continuance of the ' concerts ' given to the world at large by the Chelmsford Wireless Station. A few days ago the pilot of a Vickers Vimy machine belonging to the Instone Air Line was crossing the Channel in a thick fog and was trying to obtain weather and landing reports from Lympne. All he could hear was a musical evening !

" A technical comment on this is that one of these days there will be a serious crash or a machine will be lost at sea through a pilot coming over in bad weather, trusting in the wireless, only to find that it is being used as a toy to amuse children ! " See *The Financier*, August 25th, 1920.

[16] See Parliamentary Debates, House of Commons, November 23rd, 1920.

[17] " History of the Wireless Society of London," *Wireless World*, November 25th, 1922, p. 257.

[18] See A. R. Burrows, *op. cit.*, p. 57.

[19] See H. M. Dowsett, *op. cit.*, Vol. II, p. 171.

[20] This account of the conference is based on the minutes published in the *Wireless World*, April 16th, 1921, pp. 42-52.

[21] See Wilfred Goatman, " The Beginnings of British Broadcasting," *London Calling*, October 10th, 1946, for some further details about the Marconi Company's proposal. The first approach to the Post Office to begin regular transmissions was made on December 28th, 1920, authority being sought to transmit on medium waves a weekly half-hour of speech, music and continuous wave telegraphy. The authorities were not convinced that there was need for such a service, although it was acknowledged that " transmissions of music would no doubt interest and entertain the recipients."

[22] See the *Wireless World*, April 16th, 1921, p. 51.

[23] See the *Wireless World*, January 21st, 1922, p. 665.

[24] See the *Wireless World*, March 4th, 1922, p. 754.

[25] See the *Wireless World*, January 21st, 1922, p. 665.

[26] See the *Wireless World*, January 21st, 1922, p. 649.

[27] See the *Wireless World*, March 4th, 1922, p. 754.

[28] P. P. Eckersley, *op. cit.*, pp. 41-43.

[29] P. P. Eckersley, *op. cit.*, p. 40.

[30] P. P. Eckersley, *Captain Eckersley Explains, a Reply to his Numerous Correspondents* (1923), p. 2.

[31] See F. J. Brown, " The Story of Broadcasting in England," *Radio Broadcast*, June 1925, p. 176, and " Broadcasting in Britain," *London Quarterly Review*, January 1926 ; and also Mr. F. J. Brown's evidence to the Sykes Committee, May 2nd, 1923.

[32] The first regular broadcasting station in the United States appears to be that established by the Westinghouse Electric and Manufacturing Company in Pittsburgh. This station started operating in November 1920. During World War I the Westinghouse Company had set up two experimental stations, one at the plant in Pittsburgh and one at the home of Dr. Frank Conrad (an employee of the Company). After World War I, Dr. Conrad continued his experiments. He sent out interesting programmes (largely gramophone records) and his station was considered to be one of the best amateur stations in the United States. An advertisement of a local department store in a Pittsburgh newspaper for radio receivers which could be used to receive the programmes sent out by Dr. Conrad attracted the attention of Mr. H. P. Davis, of the Westinghouse Company. It resulted in the decision (made early in 1920) to build a broadcasting station at Pittsburgh ; the return for the outlay coming from the sale of receiving sets and the advertisement for the Westinghouse Company. Other stations were opened by the

Westinghouse Company late in 1921 and other companies followed suit. See H. P. Davis, " The Early History of Broadcasting in the United States," in *The Radio Industry, the Story of its Development*, pp. 189-225 ; and G. L. Archer, *History of Radio to 1926*, pp. 199-242. Visiting Englishmen were greatly impressed by the " broadcasting boom." Mr. F. J. Brown, in a letter written in February 1922 from the United States, said of the Westinghouse Company : " They . . . are stated to be selling receiving sets (varying in price from $30 to $150) at a rate of 25,000 a month, and are quite unable to meet the demand. Other people are following suit, and it is likely that there are now between 200,000 and 300,000 receiving sets in use." See F. J. Brown, " The Story of Broadcasting in England," *Radio Broadcast*, June 1925, p. 175. In his evidence to the Sykes Committee on May 2nd, 1923, Mr. F. J. Brown stated : " Before I left," which was in March 1922, " the number was said to have increased to 500,000. . . ." In an article in *The Times* of May 8th, 1922, Sir Henry Norman stated that the number of receiving sets in the United States was believed to be 750,000.

[33] See Parliamentary Debates, House of Commons, April 3rd, 1922.

[34] See *The Times*, April 19th, 1922, p. 12.

[35] See A. R. Burrows, *op. cit.*, p. 64. Compare also the evidence of Mr. E. H. Shaughnessy (at that time engineer in charge of the Wireless Section of the Engineer-in-Chief's Department, General Post Office) on June 14th, 1923, to the Sykes Committee : " . . . in order to establish a transmitting station for broadcasting ; I think one must necessarily use some of the Marconi Company's patents. Whether these patents are valid or not, they have not been fought in the courts, and I think they must use them ; so that in this country, at any rate, the transmitting stations would be a monopoly of the Marconi Company." Mr. Shaughnessy went on to point out that it could cease to be a Marconi Company monopoly only if they were prepared to license others.

[36] See *The Times*, April 25th, 1922.

[37] See Parliamentary Debates, House of Commons, August 4th, 1922.

[33] This is in accord with the view of a Post Office official returning from the United States in a statement to *The Times* on April 7th. " Such an important service was not to be drowned by advertising chatter or used for commercial purposes that could be quite well served by other means of communication."

[39] Compare H. de A. Donisthorpe, *Wireless at Home*, which must have been written about this date : " The authorities are now granting licences to various companies so that they may erect wireless telephony stations . . ." (p. 8).

[40] Mr. F. J. Brown's statement that " The Committee (that is, the Imperial Communications Committee) recommended that an endeavour should be made to induce the various manufacturing firms to co-operate in the establishment of a single broadcasting company " in " The Story of Broadcasting in England," *Radio Broadcast*, June 1925, p. 176, appears to me to be inconsistent with this view expressed by Sir Henry Norman, who, as Chairman of the Wireless Sub-Committee, can be presumed to know what the recommendations were.

[41] See Tom Clarke : *My Northcliffe Diary*, p. 874. Mr. Tom Clarke informs me that the attitude of the Marconi Company was also lukewarm.

[42] Information furnished by the Post Office. See also the account of an address delivered by Lord Gainford on June 2nd, 1927, in the *Annual Report of the Royal Cornwall Polytechnic Society*, 1928, and the *B.B.C. Yearbook* for 1928, the section entitled " The Press and Broadcasting." I had earlier been puzzled by a sentence in this section of the *B.B.C. Yearbook* for 1928 which seemed to imply that the newspapers agreed at this time not to operate broadcasting stations. (See R. H. Coase, " The Origin of the Monopoly of Broadcasting in Great Britain," *Economica*, August 1947, p. 198, footnote 3). But the revised version of this sentence which appeared in the *B.B.C. Yearbook* for 1930 (p. 183) makes it clear that there was no such implication.

[43] Information furnished by the Post Office. This was, of course, in accordance with the recommendation of the Imperial Communications Committee.

[44] Other accounts give the number as 19, 20 or 23 firms. But 24 is the figure given by the Postmaster-General. See Parliamentary Debates, House of Commons, August 4th, 1922.

[45] See the evidence of Mr. F. J. Brown to the Sykes Committee, May 2nd, 1923.

[46] See the evidence of Sir William Noble to the Sykes Committee on May 8th, 1923, question 237.

[47] *B.B.C. Archives.*

[48] This is taken from the statement as issued by the Post Office. In *The Times*, May 19th, 1922, the phrase " probably two groups " appears as " possibly two groups."

[49] Not Mr. Godfrey Isaacs, Managing Director of the Marconi Company, as reported in *The Times*, May 24th, 1922.

[50] See paragraph 5 of the statement submitted on behalf of the British Broadcasting Company to the Sykes Committee, May 8th, 1923, by Sir William Noble and Mr. (later Sir Archibald) McKinstry.

[51] Evidence of Mr. A. McKinstry to the Sykes Committee, May 8th, 1923.

[52] Compare A. R. Burrows, *op. cit.*, p. 64 : " . . . the delicacy of the situation was not generally understood—quite apart from the desire of the Government and the Post Office that broadcasting should be free from the irregularities so apparent in America, the patent situation required much clearing up, as the Marconi Company claimed to possess many master patents governing wireless telephony."

[53] See Mr. Kellaway's statement, Parliamentary Debates, House of Commons August 4th, 1922.

[54] Compare *Nature*, August 5th, 1922, p. 197.

[55] See paragraph 9 of the statement submitted on behalf of the British Broadcasting Company to the Sykes Committee, May 8th, 1923, by Sir William Noble and Mr. McKinstry.

[56] Compare the statement of Mr. Godfrey Isaacs, *The Broadcaster*, August 1922, p. 18.

[57] See *The Times*, August 19th, 1922.

[58] See *The Times*, August 24th, 1922.

[59] See *The Times*, September 13th, 1922.

[60] Sir William Noble had been Engineer-in-Chief of the Post Office and, on retiring, had joined the General Electric Company. He had become Chairman of the Committee in the summer of 1922, when Mr. Gill went to the United States.

[61] See *The Times*, October 19th, 1922. According to Sir William Noble's statement, submitted to the Sykes Committee, May 8th, 1923, " about 400 representatives were invited." In the Sykes Committee report it is stated that 300 attended (p. 8) as against the 200 mentioned in *The Times*.

[62] The Postmaster-General who actually signed the licence was Mr. Neville Chamberlain, Mr. Kellaway having resigned on October 19th, 1922. Later Mr. Kellaway joined the Board of the Marconi Company. There followed in April 1923 a curious argument as to which Postmaster-General had been responsible for the scheme. Sir W. Joynson Hicks (who had become Postmaster-General after Mr. Neville Chamberlain) said in the House of Commons that Mr. Kellaway had made the agreement. Mr. Kellaway thereupon wrote to *The Times* saying that the agreement was made by Mr. Chamberlain three months after he had left the Post Office. Mr. Chamberlain replied in a speech that " this was a transparent quibble. He had only put his name to it and not altered a word." Mr. Kellaway then wrote another letter to *The Times* in which he claimed that " this involved the most startling evasion of responsibility." See *The Times* for April 21st, 23rd, 24th and 26th, 1923.

[63] *B.B.C. Archives.*

[64] See A. R. Burrows, *op. cit.*, p. 68, and *The Times*, November 14th and 15th, 1922. The dates on which broadcasting started from the various stations are given in Appendix II to the Crawford Committee Report, 1926 (Cmd. 2599).

[65] The date given in Appendix II of the Crawford Committee Report for the opening of the Birmingham station is November 16th, 1922. But Mr. A. E. Thompson, who was engineer-in-charge of the Birmingham station, has informed me that broadcasting began there at 3 p.m. on November 15th.

[66] The scale of royalty payments was as follows : on each crystal set, 7s. 6d. ; on

each microphonic amplifier without using valves, 7s. 6d. ; on each crystal set and one valve, £1 7s. 6d. ; on each crystal set and two valves, £2 2s. 6d. ; on each one-valve set, £1 ; on each two-valve set, £1 15s. ; on each set adapted for more than two valves a further sum for each additional valve holder of 10s. ; on each telephone ear piece, 3d. ; on each loud speaker with or without trumpets, 3s. ; on each valve, 2d.

[67] It is not certain at what stage the idea was conceived of using the licence fee (or part of it) to finance the broadcasting service. Mr. F. J. Brown said, in his evidence to the Sykes Committee on May 2nd, 1923 : " I do not quite know where the suggestion first came from, the papers do not show definitely. . . ." The first reference I have been able to find is in a letter to *The Times* of April 25th, 1922, by Mr. H. H. Brown. The suggestion was also put forward in another letter to *The Times* of June 6th, 1922, by Captain W. H. M. Marshall. It was advocated by Sir D. Newton in the House of Commons on June 16th, 1922. It was clearly under discussion before the decision to form a single broadcasting company was reached. See *Nature*, August 5th, 1922, p. 197.

[68] The running costs for the eight broadcasting stations were estimated at £160,000 per annum. The number of receiving sets which would be sold within 12 months was commonly estimated at 200,000. See the evidence of Mr. F. J. Brown to the Sykes Committee on May 2nd, 1923. Fifty per cent. of the licence fee of 10s. on 200,000 sets would yield the company £50,000, or just over 30 per cent. of the running costs. The remainder of the running costs and all the capital expenditure would have to be contributed by the manufacturers. It is not possible to estimate the amount which the royalty payments would yield without specifying the type of set used. But if 90 per cent. of the sets were crystal sets, if the other 10 per cent. were equivalent (on an average) to a two-valve set, if two head-phones were purchased with each set and if a loud-speaker were purchased with each valve-set, then the yield from the royalty payments would be just over £110,000, or enough to make up the total of the running costs. But on this basis, if the running costs of the second year were to be covered, about 150,000 sets would have to be sold in that year. (Fewer sets would have to be sold in the second year, since the licence revenue would again accrue from the sets sold in the first year.) The six main firms gave an undertaking to the Post Office that if the three sources of funds mentioned (licence fees, royalties and share capital) were not sufficient to cover the expenses of the company during the two years of the licence, they would themselves furnish the necessary money. This was not included in the licence ; it was an " honourable understanding." See the Minutes of Evidence to the Sykes Committee, questions 287-291 and 638-640.

[69] See his evidence to the Sykes Committee on May 12th, 1923, question 589.

[70] The decision that for a period of two years licences should contain a provision that only British apparatus should be used was taken early in July. See *The Times*, July 12th, 1922. But it was also decided that those who constructed their own receiving sets should not be subject to this condition. See Parliamentary Debates, House of Commons, July 27th, 1922. This was incorporated in clause 25 (3) of the licence. This provision was to have very important consequences not foreseen at that time.

[71] This provision was in the agreement.

[72] These were : the Marconi Company, the Metropolitan-Vickers Company, the Western Electric Company, the General Electric Company, the British Thomson-Houston Company and the Radio Communication Company.

[73] The news agencies had early been concerned to safeguard their interests following the introduction of broadcasting. See, for example, the statement of Colonel Joseph Reed, chairman of the Press Association Ltd., *The Times*, May 10th, 1922. Various meetings were held which resulted in this clause being included in the licence. See Sir William Noble's evidence to the Sykes Committee on May 8th, 1923, question 395.

[74] The broadcast sponsored by Harrods is referred to in the evidence to the Sykes Committee, questions 1555 and 1556.

[75] In his evidence to the Sykes Committee on May 29th, 1923, question 1556.

[76] See paragraph 10 of the statement submitted on behalf of the British Broadcasting Company to the Sykes Committee by Sir William Noble and Mr. McKinstry.

[77] On May 2nd, 1923.

[78] See the evidence of Sir William Noble to the Sykes Committee, May 8th, 1923, question 237.

[79] See the evidence of Sir William Noble to the Sykes Committee, May 8th, 1923, questions 274-279.

[80] See the evidence of Mr. F. J. Brown to the Sykes Committee on May 2nd, 1923, and of Sir William Noble on May 8th, 1923, question 240.

[81] See the evidence of Sir William Noble to the Sykes Committee, May 8th, 1923, question 238.

[82] Parliamentary Debates, House of Commons, April 20th, 1920.

[83] Parliamentary Debates, House of Commons, November 23rd, 1920.

[84] See the comments of a " high official of the Post Office " on Colonel Carty's experiments, *The Times*, April 13th, 1921, and an answer to a Parliamentary question by the Postmaster-General, Parliamentary Debates, House of Commons, July 11th, 1921.

[85] See the evidence given by Mr. E. H. Shaughnessy on June 14th, 1923, to the Sykes Committee.

[86] See Sir Henry Norman's statement regarding this in the Minutes of Evidence to the Sykes Committee, May 31st, 1923, question 1909.

[87] See the articles by Mr. F. J. Brown already referred to in note [31] above. Mr. Brown was greatly impressed by the views expressed by Mr. Hoover, including those on the part which advertising should play in broadcasting. Mr. Brown quotes Mr. Hoover's words in his article in the *London Quarterly Review* : " It is inconceivable that we should allow so great a possibility for service, for news, for entertainment, for education, and for vital commercial purposes to be drowned in advertising chatter, or to be used for commercial purposes that can be quite well served by our other means of communication." (Page 28). It was obviously Mr. Brown who repeated these words in a statement to *The Times* on his return from the United States (see note [38] above). It is interesting to think that the views of Mr. Hoover and his advisers, which seem to have made little impression in the United States, may have had a decisive effect on the evolution of broadcasting policy in Great Britain.

[88] Parliamentary Debates, House of Commons, August 4th, 1922.

[89] Mr. F. W. Challis, of the Electrical Importers and Traders Association.

[90] See the Minutes of Evidence of the Sykes Committee, May 29th, 1923, questions 1394 and 1395.

[91] The witnesses who appeared before the Sykes Committee on behalf of the National Association of Radio Manufacturers agreed that to avoid unnecessary confusion, broadcasting licences should be granted to one body only. When this was questioned, Mr. G. Burney replied : " We have had a little knowledge of what has happened in the States ; it is for that reason that we think it should be under one Authority." See the Minutes of Evidence of the Sykes Committee, May 15th, 1923. Another example is to be found in C. A. Lewis, *Broadcasting from Within* (1924). Mr. Lewis was Deputy Director of Programmes in the British Broadcasting Company. He says : " It may be asked, why did the Postmaster-General give an exclusive right to one company only to broadcast ? The reason for this is a purely physical one. Assuming the stations to be of a given power and range, it is found it is impossible to operate more than eight stations without causing interference between them. The chaotic state of affairs in America, where a large number of stations are transmitting on a narrow band of wavelengths and no form of control exists, was an object lesson in what *not* to do, and consequently the control was put into one company's hands. . . ." (pp. 15-16). This is in line with a statement issued by the British Broadcasting Company on April 17th, 1923, in which it was said that the initiative which led to the formation of the Company came from the Post Office " knowing that if the chaos in the United States was to be avoided one broadcasting authority was essential." See the *Manchester Guardian*, April 18th, 1923.

[92] See his evidence to the Sykes Committee, June 14th, 1923, question 3095.

[93] See Mr. Kellaway's statement, Parliamentary Debates, House of Commons,

June 16th, 1922 : " I do not regard it as desirable that the work should be done by the Government, and I do not contemplate a condition of things under which the Post Office will be doing this work."

[94] The *Wireless World*, April 16th, 1921, p. 51.

[95] See his evidence to the Sykes Committee, May 2nd, 1923. The account given in the *Daily Express* of April 14th, 1923, of the Postmaster-General's reply is in almost the same words.

[96] See " The Story of Broadcasting in England," *Radio Broadcast*, June 1925, p. 176.

[97] *B.B.C. Archives.*

[98] See F. J. Brown, " Broadcasting in Britain," *London Quarterly Review*, January 1926, p. 30. " Moreover, it was clear that if the stations were to be efficient, and if their programmes were to be satisfactory, a very large expenditure would be necessary ; and that if the stations duplicated one another there would be great waste of money." It will be remembered that it was part of the plan for independent operation that the two groups should each operate a broadcasting station in London.

CHAPTER TWO

THE SYKES COMMITTEE

1. Reasons for the Inquiry

THE broadcasting scheme described in the preceding chapter did not meet with universal approval. At a very early stage of the negotiations, fears were expressed that the proposed company would be a combine controlled by the large firms and protected against foreign competition by the prohibition of the use of imported parts and sets. It was this view of the scheme which led to complaints that a monopoly was being established ; but what the critics had in mind was, of course, a monopoly in the manufacture of radio equipment. [1] A suggestion in July, 1922, that a select committee be appointed to inquire into the proposed broadcasting scheme was rejected by the Government. Mr. Neville Chamberlain stated that this would delay arrangements, and added " I have not seen any indication of a demand either from those who would provide the services or those who would use them for a committee." [2] None the less, events so fell out that an inquiry was held within a few months of the start of broadcasting in Great Britain.

The agreement into which members of the British Broadcasting Company were to enter was not published until the beginning of March, 1923. Shortly afterwards, the Postmaster-General received a deputation of manufacturers and traders to protest against the terms of the agreement. [3] Later in the month another deputation saw the Postmaster-General in order to ask for a revision of the agreement. [4] And finally, early in April, there came an attack on the principle of monopoly in transmission, and a series of articles in the *Daily Express* called for the abolition of the broadcasting monopoly. [5]

But the broadcasting inquiry was precipitated by difficulties which arose between the British Broadcasting Company and the Post Office. One of the conditions of the licence to be taken out by those who had radio receiving sets was that these sets should be manufactured by members of the British Broadcasting Company. The Postmaster-General had, however, stated that those who made

30

their own sets would be granted an experimenter's licence ; and in the case of this licence there was no restriction concerning the parts which could be used. It had, of course, been expected that the number of people who would be able to make their own sets would be few. But parts were offered for sale (some manufactured in Great Britain and some manufactured abroad) which it was comparatively easy to assemble at home to make a receiving set. The crystal set period was beginning. The number of experimental licences issued was relatively great. Between November 1st, 1922, and the end of the year, 6,000 experimental licences were issued as against 12,000 ordinary licences.* In consequence, the British Broadcasting Company approached the Post Office about this question in January, 1923. It was decided to suspend the issue of experimental licences for the time being and to grant them only in those cases in which the Post Office was reasonably sure that the applicant was making his own set and not simply assembling ready-made parts. The Company and the Post Office then considered what should be done. The Post Office proposed that there should be a third form of licence, a constructor's licence. This was agreed by the British Broadcasting Company (after consultation with the Radio Society of Great Britain) and they suggested that the annual fee in the case of the constructor's licence should be 20s., of which the Company would receive 15s. But the Postmaster-General, Sir William Joynson-Hicks (later Lord Brentford), would not agree to a fee higher than that of the existing licences, which was 10s. Ultimately, the Company agreed to accept a 10s. fee, but only on condition that all the components used bore a mark which indicated that they had been made by a member of the British Broadcasting Company. The Postmaster-General was unwilling to accept this condition and in consequence he decided to refer the whole question to a Committee of Inquiry.[6]

This Committee, the terms of reference of which were very wide, was appointed on April 24th, 1923, the Chairman being Sir Frederick Sykes.† It was able to report on August 23rd, 1923. The investigations of the Committee were extremely thorough ; evidence was given to it by all the chief personalities concerned with broadcasting : and from a study of the report and of the evidence given to the Committee, it is possible to derive a clear picture of the

* For the statistics of the number of licences issued, see Appendix I.
† For the composition of this Committee, see Appendix II.

state of informed opinion at that time on broadcasting in Great Britain. I propose to review the report and evidence given to the Sykes Committee under two heads : first, the immediate difficulties which had arisen in carrying out the broadcasting scheme, and second, the problem of the future organisation of broadcasting, particularly in relation to the monopoly.

2. THE IMMEDIATE DIFFICULTIES

The main problem with which the Sykes Committee had to deal was that created by the home constructor. But there were also the complaints which some of the smaller firms (manufacturers and traders) had made against the broadcasting scheme. I shall consider these first.

It appeared to some of the smaller manufacturers that they were being forced to join an organisation the policy of which would be controlled by their large competitors. And they feared that the power of the British Broadcasting Company to inspect their books would be used in such a way as to disclose their trade secrets to the large firms. They also objected to certain other features of the agreement ; notably to the provision which required every member of the British Broadcasting Company to make a deposit of £50 with the Company.[7] The complaint by the small manufacturers about the Company's power to inspect books was met in one of the early meetings of the Committee. The representatives of the British Broadcasting Company indicated that they were quite willing that any inspection of the books in order to verify a firm's returns should be made by an independent auditor.[8] The other complaints were not answered directly (for the main evidence of the British Broadcasting Company was given before that of the associations of small manufacturers and traders) but certain of the evidence undoubtedly took the edge off these criticisms. It was pointed out that the Marconi Company did not dominate the British Broadcasting Company as had been implied in some of the criticisms[9] ; and that the Company had an independent Chairman, Lord Gainford, who had stated that he would not be a party to any arrangement which gave one firm an unfair advantage over another.[10] The Sykes Committee commented that " whilst it is true that the scheme gives the British Broadcasting Company unusual powers, we have had no proof that the Company have made any improper use of their position." [11] Nevertheless, they recommended that the £50 deposit should be abolished.[12] But the representatives of the smaller firms made it clear that even if their complaints about the way in which the scheme was administered were overcome, there would still remain another feature to which they strongly objected—the system of royalty payments.[13] However, this is a question which cannot be dealt with separately from the main problem which the Sykes Committee had to consider, that created by the home constructor.

The Company obtained the money for running the broadcasting service from royalties to be paid by members on the sales of sets and certain of the main components and from the Company's share in the licence fee. In addition, there was the capital subscribed by the radio manufacturers. The $7\frac{1}{2}$ per cent. which might be earned on the share capital would not have induced the manufacturers to establish the broadcasting service since part of the income of the Company came from the manufacturers themselves in the form of royalty payments. What the manufacturers had in mind was the increased profits which would accrue as a result of the sale of receiving sets. It was therefore natural that they should have been reluctant to set up the broadcasting system until they were assured that the demand for receiving sets would not be satisfied by foreign manufacturers. It was therefore part of the bargain that the Postmaster-General should make it a condition of the ordinary licence that only sets made by the members of the British Broadcasting Company could be used.

The home constructor threatened the financial basis of this scheme in various ways. He avoided paying the royalty on the complete sets ; and the parts he used were either not subject to a royalty payment or (except for valves) could be so sub-divided as not to be subject to the royalty tariff of the Company. And in so far as the parts bought by the home constructor were of foreign manufacture, they did not yield any profit to the British manufacturers. But the home constructor affected the scheme in another way. There were two licences available. The first, the ordinary licence, was for those buying their sets from members of the British Broadcasting Company ; the second was for the experimenter. But the home constructor was not qualified to take out an ordinary licence and in the majority of cases could not be classified as an experimenter. There was, therefore, no licence which met his case. In consequence, there was widespread evasion. It was estimated in April, 1923, that there were 200,000 persons with radio receiving sets who had not taken out licences.[14] The home constructor not only avoided the royalty payments ; because only the ordinary and experimenter's licences were available, he was unable legally to contribute by paying a licence fee. And in addition, in so far as the apparatus which he used was of foreign manufacture, the profits which the British manufacturers had expected to receive to recompense them for the costs of establishing the broadcasting service did not accrue to them. It was this situation which led the British Broadcasting Company to support the proposal for a constructor's licence, on condition that the main components were manufactured by members of the Company.

The Sykes Committee state in their report that they have been " impressed by the general objections to the system of marking and royalties, and by the practical difficulties attending its operation." And the report goes on to say : " We do not consider it feasible or desirable to prevent the construction of wireless sets from ready-made parts. Yet it would be obviously unfair that users of ready-made sets should pay royalty to meet the cost of the broadcasting service while users of home-made or home-assembled sets should escape. The marking of all the minute parts of a set would be impracticable ; but a suggestion has been made that about ten of the principal component parts should be marked ' B.B.C.' and should pay royalty. We have examined these parts and have satisfied ourselves that nearly all of them could easily be subdivided into two or more smaller parts, which could be sold without marking or royalty. It seems clear, therefore, that just as difficulties arose in the system of marking of sets through the use of unmarked parts, so difficulties would arise in a system of marking of component parts through the use of smaller unmarked parts." [15] This argument led to the conclusion that royalty payments should not be used to finance the broadcasting scheme. But it was equally fatal to the condition which the British Broadcasting Company wanted to attach to the constructor's licence.[16]

The Committee then proceeded to examine the various possible methods of finance.[17] The first was for the cost to be met out of the public funds. It had been suggested to the Committee that " broadcasting might be regarded as a public entertainment service, in the same way as the provision of music in the public parks." Another proposal was that " the cost of the service should be charged

to the Education Vote." The Committee commented : "If practically every taxpayer were a ' listener ' there might be no injustice
in meeting the cost of broadcasting out of taxation. But under
existing conditions it would not, we consider, be right that the
general body of taxpayers should be required to pay for the daily
service which only those possessing wireless receiving sets can enjoy."

The second method was to use customs and excise duties. The
Committee concluded from the evidence given on behalf of the
Customs and Excise Department that " it would be impracticable to
identify and tax all the numerous small parts which may be used in
the construction of a wireless set, and that it would be necessary to
restrict the duty to complete sets and to the principal component
parts." But this would lead back to the difficulty which the Committee had encountered in connection with marking, as the duty
could then be avoided by subdivision. There was also the fact that
many of the parts used in the construction of radio receiving sets were
also used for other purposes and it would be difficult " to levy or waive
a duty according to the use eventually made of the apparatus." The
collection of excise duties would also involve the licensing of manufacturers and the inspection of their factories. In view of all these
objections, this method of finance was rejected by the Committee.

The third method of finance was to use the proceeds from
licence fees to be paid by manufacturers and dealers in radio
equipment. This was also rejected by the Committee. The Customs
and Excise Department pointed out that the costs of administration
would be rather heavy. But the factors which seem to have weighed
more with the Committee were that " any system of licensing,
especially when applied to retail trade, is in itself objectionable on
the ground of its restrictive character " ; that there would be
considerable evasion; and that "legislation, which could scarcely
fail to be contentious, would be necessary."

The fourth method to be examined was the finance of the broadcasting service by means of revenue from advertisements. The
representatives of the newspapers had urged that the prohibition of
advertising should be maintained and strengthened, " mainly on the
ground that it would seriously affect the interests of newspapers
which rely largely on advertising revenue." The Committee's views
on advertising were as follows : " We attach great importance to
the maintenance of a high standard of broadcast programmes, with
continuous efforts to secure improvement, and we think that

advertisement would lower the standard . . . would tend to make the service unpopular, and thus to defeat its own ends. In newspaper advertising the small advertiser as well as the big gets his chance, but this would not be the case in broadcasting. The time which could be devoted to advertising would in any case be very limited, and, therefore, exceedingly valuable ; and the operating authorities, who would want revenue, would naturally prefer the big advertiser who was ready to pay highly, with the result that only he would get a chance of advertising. This would be too high a privilege to give to a few big advertisers at the risk of lowering the general standard of broadcasting." But they go on to say : " We consider, however, that there would be no objection to the operating concern being allowed to accept the gift of a concert and to broadcast a preliminary announcement giving the name of the donor ; and also to broadcast the name of the publisher and the price of a song which is about to be broadcast." That is to say, the Committee objected to the raising of revenue by the broadcasting of advertisements but they saw no reason why sponsored programmes should not be allowed ; although they do not seem to have considered that this should be the main source of the income of the broadcasting authority. Similarly they thought the broadcasting of commercial information in code to subscribers should be allowed " under suitable safeguards " if " it is necessary to find supplementary sources of revenue."

It was the view of the Sykes Committee that the cost of broadcasting should be borne by the listener and not by the taxpayer. But, as we have seen, they rejected as means of financing the service royalty payments, customs and excise duties and licence fees for radio manufacturers and dealers, and they considered that sponsored programmes and the broadcasting of commercial information should only be used as a means of supplementing the income of the Company. The only method which remained was to use the proceeds from the licence fee on the receiving set. And this seems to have been considered by the Committee to be a very suitable method of financing the service. It was paid for by the listener and, according to the Committee, had the additional advantage that the possibility of increasing the revenue of the Company through a growth in the number of listeners provided an incentive for those running the broadcasting service to make improvements. If marking was to be abandoned, this ruled out the possibility of there being a constructor's licence with conditions as to the parts which could be used. But it also made it unnecessary to distinguish between the ordinary licence and the experimenter's licence. The Committee therefore recommended that there should be a uniform receiving licence " and that it should be placed on sale at Post Offices and issued on payment of the fee without any formalities or questions." [18]

To make up for the loss of income which the British Broadcasting Company would suffer through the abolition of the royalty payments, the Committee recommended that the share of the annual licence fee of 10s. to be paid to the Company should be increased from 5s. to 7s. 6d.[19] They also suggested that the licence period should be extended by two years, thus making it run until December 31st, 1926. But these concessions were made conditional upon the acceptance by the Company of the Committee's general scheme, the abolition of the £50 deposit, and a revision of the Company's Articles of Association. These were to be amended to provide :

" (i) that any dealer in or retailer of wireless apparatus in this country should have a right—such as is now possessed by manufacturers only—to obtain at least one £1 share ;

(ii) that if and when any fresh issue of capital is made, subscriptions may be invited from the public with a preference to the existing shareholders ; and

(iii) that adequate representation on the Board should be secured for the new membership."[20]

The Committee's recommendations would, of course, mean a very considerable change in the basis of the scheme. " Under our proposals the royalties would disappear, and the British Broadcasting Company would become an organiser and purveyor of broadcast programmes, the cost of which would be provided mainly, if not entirely, from licence fees to be collected by the Government." In these circumstances the Committee saw no reason why the management of the Company should be confined to radio manufacturers, although it was desirable that they should take a leading part in it.[21]

While the abandonment of the system of royalty payments may not have been wholly unwelcome to the manufacturers,* the

* The abolition of the royalty payments would reduce the revenue of the British Broadcasting Company. But it would also increase the profits of the members of the Company by the same amount. And they would be enabled to lower prices and thus raise their sales, and their profits would in fact increase by an amount greater than the loss of royalty payments to the Company. Of course, the directors of the British Broadcasting Company (if its affairs are considered separately from those of the constituent companies) would not like the change. But there is no reason to suppose that the manufacturers would want to resist the abolition of royalty payments.

recommendations of the Sykes Committee ignored one part of the agreement with the Post Office to which the manufacturers attached great importance, that is, it failed to give them protection against foreign competition. The Committee expressed agreement with the view that " it is wrong in principle to attempt to control the manufacture and importation of wireless apparatus—which is a function of the House of Commons—by means of licences issued by the Postmaster-General." [22] But, rightly or wrongly, an agreement had been made by which it had been intended to give the radio manufacturers protection against foreign competition for two years ; and the recommendations of the Sykes Committee did not provide for this. This was pointed out in a Reservation to the Report by Mr. J. C. W. Reith, then General Manager of the British Broadcasting Company, who was a member of the Committee. He said that the broadcasting service had been established " on condition that such measures would be taken by the Government Department concerned as would, for a limited period, conserve the business of making and selling receiving apparatus to British manufacturers." And he concluded his Reservation in the following words : " I submit that it is unreasonable to ask them (the manufacturers) to agree to radical alterations which do not include the safeguarding to British manufacturers in general of this fundamental issue, however willing they should be to adopt any or all of the other conclusions as may be found compatible with the technical and general efficiency of a broadcasting service to the people." [23]

3. THE FUTURE ORGANISATION OF BROADCASTING

The Sykes Committee considered that there must be public control of broadcasting. Their reasons were that the importance of broadcasting made it essential " that permission to transmit, and the matter to be transmitted, should be subject to public authority " ; that, if the recommendations of the Committee were adopted, the bulk of the funds for running broadcasting would be collected by the State ; and that regulation of the power and wavelengths of broadcasting stations was necessary if chaos was to be avoided. They concluded that the ultimate control of broadcasting should be exercised by a Minister responsible to Parliament. But to assist him the Committee suggested that a Broadcasting Board should be established—" it would advise on such questions as who should operate broadcasting, how many stations should be operated, how revenue should be raised and how allocated, what should be the general character of the matter to be broadcast and what regulations are necessary to prevent interference. It would become the authority to whom complaints and suggestions of all kinds concerning broadcasting would be sent. . . ." And they proposed that the Board should be composed of an independent Chairman and twelve members (in the main representative of various interests and bodies). But they added that " broadcasting may eventually become so great a national responsibility as to demand the creation of a small body of experts, to whom (always subject to the Postmaster-General) its control should be entrusted." [24]

The Committee then pointed out that while public control was essential, the problem of who should operate the broadcasting stations was one to which there were many solutions. Only one of these solutions was rejected by the Committee, and that was State operation of the stations. The arguments which led them to this decision were two. First, they considered " a Government Department would not be a suitable body to undertake the entertainment side ; and a Minister might well shrink from the prospect of having to defend in Parliament the various items in Government concerts." Second, they thought that a Government which had to select the news and talks to be broadcast " would be constantly open to suspicion that it was using its unique opportunities to advance the interests of the political party in power ; and, in the endeavour to avoid anything in the slightest degree controversial, it would probably succeed in making its service intolerably dull." [25]

The Committee considered it unnecessary for them to decide between the various methods of organising the broadcasting service ; that was a matter for the Broadcasting Board and the Postmaster-General. They did, however, set out the alternative methods which they considered to be available :

" (a) the operation of large stations by the British Broadcasting Company or other authorities ; or

(b) the operation of smaller stations in different centres by the British Broadcasting Company, local Companies, Municipalities, Wireless Societies, or other bodies that may wish to undertake the work ; or

(c) the operation by any of the foregoing bodies of smaller stations (i.e. relay stations) connected with the larger central stations.

D

The allocation of the available revenue would present difficulties, but this would be one of the problems which the Postmaster-General, with the assistance of the suggested Board, would have to solve." [26]

What the Sykes Committee recommended was that there should be Government regulation of broadcasting. But this does not imply that the State should operate the broadcasting stations. Indeed, the Sykes Committee came to the conclusion that the State should not do so. Apart from the objection to State operation, the question of the future organisation of broadcasting in Great Britain was, so far as it concerned the actual operation of the stations, an open one to the Sykes Committee. There is no suggestion in the report that it was desirable that there should be a monopoly of broadcasting. Indeed, they recommended that, " subject to existing rights, the Government should keep its hands free to grant additional licences, and should consider various alternatives for the operation in the future, either by the Company or by other authorities, of local or relay stations in addition to large stations." [27]

4. THE AMENDED SCHEME

The unwillingness of the Company to agree to the recommendations of the Sykes Committee, because they failed to afford protection against foreign competition, led to a compromise agreement being entered into between the Company and the Postmaster-General. [28] This agreement incorporated all the major recommendations of the Sykes Committee but in such a way as to maintain up to December 31st, 1924 (the date when the original licence expired), the legal protection against foreign competition.

First let us consider the position regarding licence fees in the period up to December 31st, 1924. The ordinary licence and the experimenter's licence were both to remain in existence, but the Company was to receive 7s. 6d. out of the 10s. annual licence fee, instead of 5s. In addition, there was to be a constructor's licence, a condition of which was that the parts used should be British made. The licence fee in this case was to be 15s. The extra 5s. was intended to compensate for the home constructor's avoidance of royalty payments, which, during this period, continued to be part of the broadcasting scheme. But what of those who had already constructed their sets, in many cases having used parts of foreign manufacture ? For them there was to be an interim licence, the annual licence fee being 15s., as in the case of the constructor's licence. This licence had to be applied for before October 15th, 1923. Those who applied would not be charged for the past use of the sets, nor would any proceedings be taken against them. The announcement of the plan led to a rapid increase in the number of licence holders. According to a report published in *The Times*, the number of licences issued increased in ten days from 180,000 to 414,000, of which about 200,000 represented the interim licence and about 27,000 the new constructor's licence.[29] But what I have described is that part of the agreement regarding licences which applied to the period up to December 31st, 1924. After that date, the uniform licence of 10s. recommended by the Sykes Committee was to come into force. In the event, the growth in the number of licences* enabled the constructor's licence to be dropped and a uniform 10s. licence to be introduced on July 1st, 1924, six months earlier than had been provided in the agreement. The prohibition against the employment of apparatus of foreign manufacture was, however, maintained until December 31st, 1924, when a single form of licence was introduced containing no restrictions concerning the apparatus which might be used.[30]

The terms of the new agreement did not provide for the immediate abolition of the royalty payments as had been recommended by the Sykes Committee. During the period up to December 31st, 1924, royalty payments were to continue, although they were to be on a reduced scale. But at that date royalty payments were to come to an end. In fact, they were abolished when the uniform licence was introduced on July 1st, 1924.[31]

In other respects, the recommendations of the Sykes Committee were accepted with very little modification. Membership of the Company was broadened so as to include dealers. The deposit of £50 was abolished. An Advisory Board was set up to assist the Postmaster-General.[32] The period of the licence (with the amended conditions) was extended for another two years, that is, until the end of 1926. But the conditions which are especially interesting in a study of the evolution of the monopoly in broadcasting are those concerning advertising and the power of the Postmaster-General to license competing broadcasting undertakings.

The obscurely worded clause in the original agreement which

* See Appendix I.

was intended to prohibit the broadcasting of advertisements was rewritten as follows :

" The Company shall not without the consent in writing of the Postmaster-General receive money or any valuable consideration from any person in respect of the transmission of messages by means of the licensed apparatus :

Provided that nothing in this Clause shall be construed as precluding the Company from—

(1) Broadcasting matter provided gratuitously by any person with or without an acknowledgment of such provision by means of the broadcasting service.

(2) Receiving a consideration for broadcasting names of publishers and prices of matter which is broadcast.

(3) Receiving a consideration for broadcasting commercial information approved for broadcasting by the Postmaster-General subject to such conditions as he may prescribe and

(4) (So far only as the licence of the Postmaster-General is required) from using for broadcast purposes, without payment, concerts, theatrical entertainment or other broadcast matter given in public in London or the Provinces." [33]

The purpose of this clause was to allow the Company to broadcast sponsored programmes and commercial information—the two methods of supplementing the income of the Company which were approved by the Sykes Committee. In fact, some sponsored programmes were broadcast in 1924 and 1925.[34] The broadcasting (in code so that others could not understand it) of commercial information to subscribers does not appear ever to have been begun by the Company.

Unlike the original agreement, the revised version was explicit about the question of the monopoly. During the period up to December 31st, 1924, the Postmaster-General agreed not to license " any other person to carry on broadcasting in Great Britain," although this was on condition " that the Company supply a satisfactory broadcast service and erect additional stations where the Postmaster-General may reasonably consider them to be necessary within a reasonable time after being required by the Postmaster-General to do so. . . ." During the two years up to December 31st, 1926 (the extended period of the licence), it was provided that " where . . . the Postmaster-General may reasonably consider additional stations necessary to serve particular towns or geographical areas not in his opinion adequately served by the Company's stations and where the Company fail to provide and operate such stations to his satisfaction within a reasonable time after being required by the Postmaster-General to do so the Post-master-General reserves the right to grant licences to any other person to carry on broadcasting services in such areas and in the event of his licensing such other person he shall be entitled to withhold from the Company the sums to which they would otherwise have been entitled under the provisions hereinbefore contained in respect of licences issued for the first time after the date of com-mencement of a regular service by the new undertaker to persons residing within the area served by such undertaker. The limits of such area shall be based on the receptive capacity of an ordinary crystal set." Furthermore, it was provided that the Postmaster-General " reserves the right during the extended period to grant licences to any person other than the Company to carry on services additional to those carried on by the Company whenever he may consider them desirable without withholding from the Company any part of the sums to which they may be entitled under the provisions hereinbefore contained." [35] The effect of these clauses was that the Company could count (except in most unlikely circum-stances) on having a monopoly up to December 31st, 1924. But during the rest of the licence period (in the two years up to December 31st, 1926), the Postmaster-General reserved the right to license additional broadcasting authorities. But these would be given a share of the licence revenue only if the Company itself had refused to provide the facilities. And it is interesting that the basis for the division of the licence revenue is given. After the end of 1926, the Postmaster-General was, of course, quite free both to license any authorities he pleased and to make any arrangements concerning the sharing of the licence revenue. These clauses carried out completely the recommendation of the Sykes Committee that the Government should " keep its hands free to grant additional licences. . . ."

If we take the long view and confine ourselves to the period after December 31st, 1924, it is clear that the amended agreement carried into effect the main recommendations of the Sykes Com-mittee. The Company was to have an extended membership, the royalty payments were to be abolished and its revenue was to come from a uniform licence fee supplemented by money earned from sponsored programmes and from the broadcasting of commercial information. As for the future organisation of broadcasting, the Government made it quite clear that it was free to license additional broadcasting authorities. That is, provision was made for a move away from the monopolistic form of organisation if this was desired. What the Sykes Committee recommended was that the various alternatives should be examined.

NOTES ON CHAPTER 2

[1] See the *Westminster Gazette* for July 20th, 27th and 29th. See also the speeches of Captain Wedgwood Benn, Parliamentary Debates, House of Commons, July 28th, 1922, and August 4th, 1922. It may have been these criticisms which led the Post Office to press for certain modifications in the draft agreement designed to protect the interests of the smaller firms.

[2] Parliamentary Debates, House of Commons, July 31st, 1922.

[3] See the *Evening Standard*, March 10th, 1923.

[4] See *The Times, Evening News*, the *Westminster Gazette* and the *Yorkshire Evening News* of March 20th, 1923.

[5] See the *Daily Express*, April 5th, 6th, 7th and 14th, 1923.

[6] This account of the events leading up to the appointment of the Sykes Committee is based on the evidence of Mr. F. J. Brown to that Committee on May 2nd, 1923.

[7] See *Nature*, May 5th, 1923.

[8] See the evidence given to the Sykes Committee by Sir William Noble and Mr. J. C. W. Reith, questions 297-300, May 8th, 1923.

[9] See the evidence given to the Sykes Committee by Sir William Noble and Mr. McKinstry, questions 342-343, May 8th, 1923.

[10] See the evidence of Sir William Noble to the Sykes Committee, questions 365-366, May 8th, 1923.

[11] See paragraph 20 of the Sykes Committee Report.

[12] See paragraph 62 of the Sykes Committee Report.

[13] See the evidence to the Sykes Committee of Mr. E. Merriman and Mr. C. (later Lord) Latham, representing the British Radio Manufacturers' and Traders' Association, on May 17th, 1923, and Mr. F. W. Challis and Mr. A. H. Rose, representing the Electrical Importers' and Traders' Association, on May 29th, 1923.

[14] See Mr. F. J. Brown's statement to the Sykes Committee, May 1st, 1923.

[15] See paragraph 20 of the Sykes Committee Report.

[16] In view of the importance of the proposal for a constructor's licence in the negotiations previous to the setting up of the Sykes Committee, it is surprising to find no mention of it in the report of that Committee. Whether this was deliberate or an oversight it is difficult to say. There was at one stage a proposal for the insertion of a paragraph on a " constructor's licence," but this was withdrawn. See the Minutes of the thirty-fourth meeting of the Sykes Committee, August 17th, 1923.

[17] This account of the views of the Sykes Committee on the methods of financing the broadcasting service is based on paragraphs 35-43 of the Report, from which all quotations are taken.

[18] See the Report of the Sykes Committee, paragraph 47.

[19] It was estimated that the costs of collection incurred by the Post Office amounted to 2s. 6d. per licence. See paragraph 44 of the Sykes Committee Report.

[20] See paragraph 62 of the Sykes Committee Report.

[21] See paragraph 63 of the Sykes Committee Report.

[22] See paragraphs 19 and 20 of the Sykes Committee Report.

[23] See Mr. J. C. W. Reith's Reservation, pages 38-39 of the Sykes Committee Report.

[24] See paragraphs 21-24 of the Sykes Committee Report.

[25] See paragraph 25 of the Sykes Committee Report. Mr. Charles Trevelyan, in his Reservation to the Report (pp. 39-41), expressed his regret that the Committee were opposed to the operation of the broadcasting service by the Post Office. In his opinion, " a situation may easily arise in which this may be the only satisfactory possibility." The Executive Committee of the London Labour Party had submitted a memorandum to the Committee in which they had advocated that " broadcasting should be publicly owned and controlled." See the *Wireless Weekly*, May 30th, 1923.

[26] See paragraph 32 of the Sykes Committee Report.

[27] See paragraph 76 of the Sykes Committee Report, Summary of Conclusions and Recommendations (9).

[28] See *The Times*, October 2nd, 1923, and *Copy of Supplementary Agreement between the Postmaster-General and the British Broadcasting Company, Ltd., providing for the modification of the Licence of the 18th of January published in Parliamentary Paper Command No. 1822 of 1923* (Cmd. 1976, 1923).

[29] See *The Times*, October 18th and 19th, 1923.

[30] See Appendix II to the Crawford Committee Report, p. 20.

[31] See the Memorandum submitted by Mr. J. C. W. Reith to the Crawford Committee, p. 12. It is interesting to note that it was on the initiative of the Company that the uniform licence was introduced and the royalties abolished six months earlier than had been provided in the agreement.

[32] See *The Times*, October 2nd, 1923. Its composition is given in the Appendix to Mr. Reith's *Broadcast over Britain*, p. 227. It does not seem to have played the prominent role set out for it in the Sykes Report. It was consulted on the subject of controversial broadcasting (see Mr. Reith's Memorandum to the Crawford Committee) ; on the question of setting up new relay stations (see House of Commons Debates, April 9th, 1924) ; on the alteration of the position of the London broadcasting station (see House of Commons Debates, June 24th, 1924). But it does not appear to have considered the general question of the future organisation of broadcasting in Great Britain.

[33] See Clause 2 of the *Supplementary Agreement*.

[34] See the *Radio Times*, January 9th, 1925.

[35] See Clause 8 of the *Supplementary Agreement*.

CHAPTER THREE

THE FORMATION OF THE CORPORATION

1. THE INFLUENCE OF MR. J. C. W. REITH

TO the Sykes Committee, the question of how broadcasting should be organised in Great Britain was an open one. It was something to be examined further. Yet only two and a half years later, in the report of the Crawford Committee on Broadcasting, we find that a monopolistic form of organisation is accepted as being the desirable one for broadcasting in Great Britain. There can be little doubt that this crystallisation of view was largely due to the influence of one man, Mr. J. C. W. Reith.*

Mr. Reith was appointed to be the General Manager of the British Broadcasting Company in December, 1922. He was then 33 years old. His unusual ability was quickly recognised by the Directors of the British Broadcasting Company and within a year of joining the Company he was made Managing Director. He had previously been General Manager of William Beardmore & Co., Ltd., Coatbridge. Before this he had held various Government appointments in the Admiralty and Ministry of Munitions (after having been wounded while serving in the Royal Engineers in 1915). He was an engineer by training, [1] the son of a clergyman, and a Scot.

In its Memorandum of Association, the Company is described as having as its first object the running of a " public utility service." But it was Mr. Reith who gave substance to this phrase.† Basic in his views was the conception of broadcasting as a public service. In the memorandum he presented to the Crawford Committee, he stated : " Broadcasting must be conducted, in the future as it has been in the past, as a Public Service with definite standards. The Service must not be used for entertainment purposes alone. In the narrow sense of the term this may once have been considered its only function, but to exploit so great and universal an agent in

---

* Mr. J. C. W. Reith became Sir John Reith in 1927 and Lord Reith in 1940. In this book I shall use the title appropriate to the period under discussion.

† This summary of Mr. Reith's views which follows is based on his book *Broadcast over Britain* (published in October 1924) and on his Memorandum and evidence to the Crawford Committee (December 1925).

the pursuit of entertainment alone would have been not only an abdication of responsibility and a prostitution of its power, but also an insult to the intelligence of the public it serves. The Broadcasting Service should bring into the greatest possible number of homes in the fullest degree all that is best in every department of human knowledge, endeavour and achievement." It was this " high conception of the possibilities of the service "[2] which dominated Mr. Reith's thinking on the problems of a broadcasting service. " The preservation of a high moral tone is obviously of paramount importance " (the Memorandum). This did not mean that " entertainment " was to be banished from the broadcasting service ; but it was to play its part in a larger scheme of things. " There is no harm in trivial things ; in themselves they may even be unquestionably beneficial, for they may assist the more serious work by providing the measure of salt which seasons."[3] " It is most important that light and ' entertaining ' items be sent out. The broadcaster puts as much energy and care into work of this nature, which shall constitute a pleasing relaxation after a hard day's work, as into items which tend to edification and wider knowledge."[4] Of course, the maintenance of standards demanded that certain things should not be broadcast. Jokes " on drunkenness, mothers-in-law, and so on can be dispensed with. . . ."[5] Furthermore, " There must be no support . . . for the school which interprets progress in terms of profit for the few and privation for the many, nor for those who countenance the doctrines of revolution " (the Memorandum). To those who criticised his policy on the ground that it did not give the listener what he wanted, Mr. Reith replied : " It is occasionally indicated to us that we are apparently setting out to give the public what we think they need—and not what they want, but few know what they want, and very few what they need. There is often no difference. One wonders to which section of the public such criticism refers. In any case, it is better to over-estimate the mentality of the public than to under-estimate it."[6]

The character of Mr. Reith's views and of his policy may best, I think, be illustrated with reference to the place which religion occupied in broadcasting and to the problem of the Sunday programme. Mr. Reith pointed out that in running the broadcasting service, " There has . . . been a definite, though restrained, association with religion in general, and with the Christian religion in particular."[7] And he went on to say : " It is, I think, one of the many questions on which it is often not only unprofitable, but also inadvisable to attempt to argue, or to justify and substantiate one's beliefs. So often arguments are feeble, easily refuted, even fallacious, though the conclusions may be incontrovertibly right." But although this was not the reason which prompted the decision, Mr. Reith indicated that there was a line of defence open. " . . . Christianity happens to be the stated and official religion of this country; it is recognised by the Crown. This is a fact which those who have criticised our right to broadcast the Christian religion would do well to bear in mind." [8]

Mr. Reith's views on Sunday broadcasting give a comprehensive illustration of his fundamental attitude towards broadcasting standards. " The surrender of the principles of Sunday observance is fraught with danger, even if the Sabbath were made for man. The secularising of the day is one of the most significant and unfortunate trends of modern life of which there is evidence. . . . One can often well understand why people do not go to church, but if they cannot there are other ways of observing the day. Apart from any puritanical nonsense, I believe that Sabbaths should be one of the invaluable assets of our existence—' quiet islands on the tossing sea of life.' It only requires a little thought to determine how best they may be employed, and how turned to greatest advantage. This is not to be achieved by sport or motoring or parading about the streets. It is a sad reflection on human intelligence if recreation is only to be found in the distractions of excitement—if no provisions are to be made for the re-creation of the mind and refreshment of the spirit ; the spirit is surely of at least as much moment as the body, and many of the ills of the latter are attributable to the neglect of the former. . . . The programmes which are broadcast on Sunday are therefore framed with the day itself in mind. There need be nothing dull in them. If they are dull or if they be thought so, then something is wrong somewhere. It may simply amount to this, that certain things are not done on Sundays which are done during the week. There have never been transmissions in Church hours except when a service is being broadcast complete. There are two hours of music in the afternoon, and then, except in the case mentioned above, nothing till eight or half-past. At that time a short service is sent out from all the studios. Familiar hymns, or, in Scotland, metrical psalms are sung ; usually there is an anthem, and a ten or fifteen minutes' address is given." [9]

The fact that Mr. Reith was in favour of the continuance of the broadcasting monopoly followed directly from his broader views. Not that he was unaware of the criticisms which can be brought against monopolies. In his Memorandum to the Crawford Committee, Mr. Reith stated : " Objections to monopoly are often obvious ; absence of competition engenders slackness ; out of privilege comes abuse." But " It is submitted and apparently now generally held that conclusive proof has been given that under no other system than unity of control can Broadcasting be conducted. Where expansion is so rapid, where no precedent exists, where mistakes are fraught with such far-reaching consequences and are so easily made, no other method is tenable. Any development, where- ever or however originated, is immediately incorporated for the benefit of the whole service. For efficiency and economy in operation the advantages of central control are enormous. The use of land- lines and the development of simultaneous broadcasting whereby any event anywhere is linked up to the entire system, are an outcome of central control, as are also many outstanding developments otherwise impossible. Unity of control is highly desirable in another aspect technically, namely, in the avoidance of interference between stations and in the protection of the waveband generally." But Mr. Reith continued : " Above all perhaps, it is becoming obvious that, however desirable central control may be for the reasons indicated, it is essential ethically, in order that one general policy may be maintained throughout the country and definite standards promulgated." Thus, Mr. Reith's case for maintaining the monopoly of broadcasting rested on two grounds. First, there were the technical arguments—any improvement wherever made could be incorporated for the benefit of the whole system, it facilitated simultaneous broadcasting and helped in the avoidance of inter- ference. But there was the second reason—and Mr. Reith leaves one in no doubt that this was to him the main reason—that without a monopoly, it would not be possible to maintain those standards which he believed to be so important. His comment on the American system makes this clear : " There is no co-ordination, no standard, no guiding policy." [10] In short, Mr. Reith believed that it was impossible to conceive of broadcasting conducted as a public service without there being a broadcasting monopoly.

But Mr. Reith's views on the need for broadcasting to be run as a public service also led him to favour a change in the constitution of the service. In his book *Broadcast over Britain* this view is implied rather than stated. " It has frequently been urged that a service fraught with such potentialities should be under the State, or a Board composed of representatives of the public with no other interests at stake. It would be fatuous to deny a strong element of rationality in this contention."[11] But Mr. Reith's approval of such a change comes out very clearly in his Memorandum to the Crawford Committee. In his evidence Mr. Reith stated that " We feel it is essential that broadcasting should be conducted for the benefit of the listener and not for the benefit of the broadcaster." And in the memorandum he wrote : " The sincerity of the Public Service policy of the present organisation has been recognised, but affairs might have been conducted differently." There had indeed been some trade opposition to the development of high-power stations and relay stations which made it possible for the programmes to be received on relatively cheap sets. This policy " was not altogether appreciated by certain sections of the trade, their manufacturing and selling programmes having already been planned on the old basis, involving high-powered apparatus."[12] The Company's policy was not formulated simply with reference to its effect on the profits of the manufacturers. It was also based, and probably mainly based, on what was considered best for the listener. But Mr. Reith pointed out that " Even those who are most definite in their appreciation of the Company's attitude, recognise the desirability of its being a Public Service not only in deed but in constitution. . . . No one denies the anomaly of the existing constitution, and the effect of it has been manifested in various directions" (the Memorandum).

These views Mr. Reith held from the very early days of his association with broadcasting. This is clear from the evidence which he gave to the Sykes Committee on June 14th, 1923, about six months after he had joined the British Broadcasting Company. Dr. W. H. Eccles asked whether there might not be economies in having all the broadcasting stations in one pair of hands instead of having the stations in separate hands. Mr. Reith replied : " I should say there was a very great economy in having one Broadcasting authority." The examination then continued as follows :

" *Dr. Eccles :* In what respect ?

Mr. Reith : It very much simplifies policy.

Dr. Eccles : Policy, yes ; but as regards economy, can you obtain, because you are one Company, better terms from programme providers ?

Mr. Reith : I think so, and in other respects also.

Dr. Eccles : And you find you can run the stations, so far as engineering cost is concerned, more efficiently if you have one central engineering staff.

Mr. Reith : One centralised control.

Dr. Eccles : Are there any other economical advantages concerned with a single control ?

Mr. Reith : Yes. I should think there is a very great advantage in having a uniform policy of what can or cannot be done on the broadcast. Practically nothing at the present moment is done on the broadcast without the Head Office knowing about it, that is to say, very clearly defined lines of activity are laid down. Station directors are allowed scope up to a point ; where anything that they may do verges on policy that has to be referred to, and decided on by, the Head Office, so that there is a unity of control and one could say even at present, and certainly much more definitely when the Company has been in existence a month or two longer and organisation has taken more effect (although there is already a very considerable degree of organisation), that we know in the Head Office just exactly what all the stations are doing ; they are under very definite continuous control. Their programmes are submitted ahead ; there are periodic conferences at which all sorts of matters are discussed ; people know what they may or what they may not do ; they know what is expected of them ; there is unified control which does, I think, present very great advantages.

Dr. Eccles : I was thinking just for the moment of economical advantages, but you have pointed out all sorts of administrative and censorship advantages.

Mr. Reith : Yes.

Dr. Eccles : You might or might not agree if I point out the lack of advantages such as censorship could be obtained by a single central body at the Post Office, for instance, even though separate stations such as Birmingham, Glasgow, London were operated by different Companies ; do you not agree ?

Mr. Reith : To a limited extent only.

Dr. Eccles : Or it might be that an Advisory Committee assisting the Post Office could have a central authority for deciding what type of news may not be published by a number of independent persons running broadcasting stations. There is nothing impossible in that suggestion, is there ?

Mr. Reith : Not that phase of it, perhaps, but in practical working I should think it would be found rather difficult. What seems to be an advantage at the present moment is that there is an executive officer in charge of the broadcasting all over the country, and the various stations conform to general instructions, and do so without limiting the individual initiative of the Station Directors. That one executive officer naturally reports to a higher authority in the nature of a Board. If the stations were controlled by different Companies, there would never be the unity of control. I should think the gentleman in the Post Office, whoever he might be, would find it difficult to have all his instructions carried out, and it would involve much more work, with loss of economy and efficiency." [13]

From this evidence I draw the conclusions that Mr. Reith considered that the main advantage of a monopoly of broadcasting was that it made possible a unified policy ; a view which he was later to develop and sharpen. It is also of interest that Mr. Reith considered at this early date that the broadcasting service should be run by a public corporation. He has told us that he suggested to the Sykes Committee that this was the proper way of organising broadcasting in Great Britain. " It was an instinctive, uninstructed and impulsive upthrust. It surprised the committee. They had expected me to defend the existing régime, this idea was revolutionary and probably unworkable." [14]

There can be little doubt of Mr. Reith's influence on his immediate circle in the British Broadcasting Company. And in 1924 we find Mr. C. A. Lewis, Deputy Director of Programmes in the Company, writing : " It must establish itself as an independent public body, willing to receive any point of view in debate against its adversary." [15] And again, " the B.B.C. intends to prove to the world that unified control in broadcasting is not only the most desirable thing from the technical point of view but that it is the cheapest and most efficient way to give the country a broad service of wide public utility." [16] And Mr. Reith's ideas were taken up outside his immediate circle. In *The Times Literary Supplement*, the reviewer of Mr. Reith's book wrote : " In a sense his book, which consists of a series of very friendly talks, is an apologia for a monopoly ; but the more one reads it the more one is impressed by the necessity of preserving the monopoly. . . . If Mr. Reith and his friends have their way there should be little to fear. . . . There are not many public services where the case for monopoly is so convincing, and broadcasting is in a peculiar position in that it is not only a highly complex piece of mechanism but it is also in a higher grade of reality a purely spiritual affair. . . . To apply it unworthily to the dissemination of the shoddy, the vulgar and the sensational would be a blasphemy against human nature." [17] In March, 1925, an article appeared in *The Times* suggesting that the monopoly should be retained (although with some modification in the constitution of the Company) ; and the leading article on broadcasting which appeared on the same day expressed cautiously worded approval. [18] And in the House of Commons, Captain (later Sir) Ian Fraser, who was later to be a member of the Crawford Committee, said : " I only hope the maintenance of unified control . . . may be brought about and may be continued, for I believe the success is largely due to that point, in which we differ from other great countries which have preceded us. . . ." [19]

It must not be supposed that during this period there was great public interest in the question of the future organisation of broadcasting in Great Britain. After the Sykes Committee report and the decision of the Postmaster-General following that report, interest seems to have subsided and did not revive until the appointment of the Crawford Committee. But whereas, after the Sykes Committee report, there was no clear opinion on how the broadcasting service ought to be organised in Great Britain, by the time the Crawford Committee started its investigations, Mr. Reith's views had filled the vacuum. [20]

Of course, it was not simply Mr. Reith's influence that caused people to think that the constitution of the British Broadcasting Company was too narrow. It had indeed been the view of the Sykes Committee that this was so. They had suggested an immediate widening of the membership of the Company by the inclusion of dealers in radio equipment and also that when a fresh issue of capital was made, the public should be invited to subscribe (which would have brought with it some representation on the Board of Directors). The fact that from December 31st, 1924, nearly all the income was derived from licence fees was bound to make exclusive control of the management by radio manufacturers and dealers appear rather anomalous ; some seem to have thought that the saturation point might have been reached in the sales of radio receiving sets and that the interest of the radio manufacturers in ensuring an efficient service might be lessened [21]; and the objection of some of the radio manufacturers to the setting up of the high power and relay stations, though it was in fact ineffective, had shown some of the dangers of control by the radio trade. In May, 1925, there appeared in the *Radio Times* (which was, of course, published by the British Broadcasting Company) an article by the Duke of Sutherland, President of the Radio Association. This Association had been formed at the end of 1922 in view of the dissatisfaction then felt about the broadcasting scheme. In an editorial comment on the Duke of Sutherland's article it was stated : " We are glad to note that the Radio Association had abandoned ' the bogeys ' of three years ago and that fear of ' the alleged monopolies and privileges ' has now given way to appreciation of the B.B.C., which, in the Duke's words ' stands as the finest broadcasting service in the world.' " But even in this article it was suggested that the constitution of the Company should be altered : " the basis of the Directorate of the British Broadcasting Company should be widened by the inclusion of representatives of, say, the Listeners, the Press, the F.B.I., the Trade Unions and the Arts, instead of, as at present, purely representing the manufacturers." [22]

By the time the Crawford Committee started to consider the problem, there appears to have been general support among those who wrote or spoke about broadcasting both that broadcasting should in Great Britain remain a monopoly and that it should in future be directed by a Board representing interests wider than those of the radio trade. At a meeting arranged by the Radio Society of Great Britain in conjunction with the Selfridge Radio Society, in November, 1923, the motion was debated " That the present system of Broadcasting, as represented by a single monopoly, is the best for this country." The motion was carried by an " overwhelming majority." [23]

It may be asked why I ascribe such a dominant influence to Mr. Reith in forming opinion on this question. My reason is simple. I can see no other explanation. Nor, to my knowledge, has anyone else who has made a serious study of the question. Of course, Mr. Reith, who was an extremely able administrator, knew that it was necessary that he and those associated with him should do more than write books and articles in order to spread their ideas. The British

Broadcasting Company had from the beginning a public relations department.[24] And no doubt it saw that Mr. Reith's views were brought to the attention of those who were interested in the problems of broadcasting. This would not be a large group at that period ; but it would be all-important when broadcasting policy came to be considered.

I cannot do better in ending this section than to give Mr. P. P. Eckersley's view on Mr. Reith's influence.* I quote from page 55 of his book *The Power Behind the Microphone*, published in 1941 : " The form, content and influence of the broadcasting service as we know it to-day is the product of one dominant mind : it represents one man's conception of the rôle of broadcasting in a modern democracy. No one who is serving or who has served the B.B.C. has had an influence in any way comparable with that exercised by its first chief executive. . . . He was the only man who made up his mind about policy, who knew what he wanted and who had the power and will to carry his ideas into practice."

2. THE CRAWFORD COMMITTEE

A Committee of Inquiry under the Chairmanship of the Earl of Crawford and Balcarres was appointed in the summer of 1925. Its terms of reference were : " To advise as to the proper scope of the Broadcasting service and as to the management, control and finance thereof after the expiry of the existing licence on December 31st, 1926. The Committee will indicate what changes in the law, if any, are desirable in the interests of the Broadcasting service."

At the start of their investigations the Committee were presented with a memorandum on broadcasting by Sir Evelyn Murray, Secretary of the Post Office. This memorandum, according to Dr. Lincoln Gordon, " had not lacked the previous scrutiny of B.B.C. officials." [25] Section IV, *The Broadcasting Authority*, was concerned with the problem of how broadcasting in Great Britain should be organised. The first question considered in this section was whether there should be one or several broadcasting authorities. It was pointed out that the British Broadcasting Company had in practice been a monopoly. Although the *Supplementary Agreement*

---

* Mr. P. P. Eckersley was the first Chief Engineer of the British Broadcasting Company and continued with the Corporation until 1929, when he resigned.

E

explicitly reserved the right of the Postmaster-General to grant additional licences for broadcasting, the memorandum stated that " no demand has been forthcoming and no occasion for granting an additional licence has arisen." [26] At the time the memorandum was prepared (November, 1925,) the right of the Postmaster-General to grant additional licences had, of course, existed for only ten months.

Paragraph 17, which dealt with the question of whether there should be one or several broadcasting authorities, opened in the following way : " In the opinion of the Post Office, the experience of the past three years, and in particular the lines on which the technical development of Broadcasting has proceeded, tend to confirm the original decision in favour of a monopoly. The case for a single controlling authority may be summarised as follows." And six reasons were then given for thinking that it was preferable to have a single broadcasting authority. These were :

(1) The locating of broadcasting stations so as " to reach the maximum population (most of whom use crystal sets) with the minimum number of wavelengths . . . can be done most effectively by a single authority." If the policy in the future should be to erect " a few relatively high-powered stations, instead of a multiplication of small stations, a single authority would seem inevitable."

(2) A single broadcasting authority " would consider itself bound to cover the widest possible area ; a number of separate authorities would tend to concentrate upon the populous centres, yielding the largest revenue, and none of them would be under an obligation to cater for the less remunerative districts."

(3) " If separate authorities, and in particular municipalities, were licensed, it would be difficult to prevent the establishment of numerous separate stations in adjacent towns with the consequent overlapping of services and risk of interference."

(4) By means of simultaneous broadcasting " the London programme can be distributed over the whole country and London can get the advantage of any item of special interest transmitted from a Provincial station. To carry this out effectively and systematically all stations need to be under a single control."

(5) The division of the licence fee (if this remained the principal source of revenue) would present great difficulties if there were separate broadcasting authorities. It would not be fair to the authority providing the most expensive programme, which would

be listened to by those in other regions, if all the licence revenue from those regions went to the local station.

(6) A single broadcasting authority could probably employ a better technical staff and provide better programmes than could separate authorities spending the same amount of money. "There would be a saving in administrative and overhead charges and the multiplication of fees for news, copyright royalties, etc., would be avoided. The difficulty of providing facilities for several organisations to broadcast important functions, speeches, etc., would not arise."

The memorandum then continued : "If a single authority is decided upon, should the B.B.C. be continued, with or without changes in its constitution ? " [27] The answer given to this question was that the Company had been very successful but that it " would probably not be acceptable as a permanent solution, either to Parliament or to the public " for the management of the broadcasting service to remain in the hands of a body representative of radio manufacturers. A broader-based authority would appear desirable. " Moreover, as the sale of apparatus approaches the point of saturation, the interest of manufacturers, as such, in the conduct of the service tends to disappear, and there is reason to think that the manufacturers themselves would not be averse to the Company being replaced by a new authority." [28]

The memorandum then considered what alternatives there were. It rejected the suggestion that broadcasting should be run by the Post Office or some other Government Department for similar reasons to those which led the Sykes Committee to the same conclusion. It would be difficult for a Government Department " to administer an organisation for providing daily public entertainment throughout the country, and it would probably be quite impracticable unless the detailed financial control and Parliamentary criticism which is ordinarily applied to the operations of a Department of State were abolished." [29] A possible alternative to State operation was to set up a Corporation with a widely representative Governing Body.[30] Such an authority could be incorporated by Charter, under the Companies Act or by Statute. [31]

Some powers would, of course, have to remain with the Postmaster-General. He should control the location (allocation is the word used in the memorandum), power, wavelength and hours of working of the broadcasting stations ; he should have power to order a temporary closure of the stations or to take them over in a time of national emergency ; " possibly " he should " exercise some censorship over the broadcasting of controversial matter."

But, " Generally speaking, it seems desirable that the Corporation should enjoy a large measure of independence and should not be subject either in its general policy or its choice of programmes to the detailed control and supervision of the Postmaster-General, from which would flow the corollary that the Postmaster-General would not be expected to accept responsibility or to defend the proceedings of the Corporation in Parliament." [32]

After the evidence of Sir Evelyn Murray, which was largely explanatory of his memorandum, Mr. J. C. W. Reith was examined by the Committee. He, too, presented a memorandum, but it was " on behalf of broadcasting," not on behalf of the British Broadcasting Company. [33] We have already seen what his approach to the problem of the organisation of broadcasting was. Mr. Reith advocated the continuance of the monopoly, but he relied less on the technical arguments used in the Post Office memorandum (although some of these were mentioned) and more on the need for a monopoly in order to maintain standards. On the question of the constitution of the body which was to operate broadcasting in future, Mr. Reith was suitably cautious, in view of his position as the head of a Board largely representative of the radio trade, but he indicated that in his view the broadcasting service should be run by a public authority and he hoped it would not be a Government Department. [34]

The evidence which followed was remarkable for its unanimity. The representatives of the Radio Society of Great Britain, the Newspaper Proprietors' Association, the Newspaper Society, the Scottish Newspaper Society, the Wireless Press, the National Association of Radio Manufacturers and Traders, the Wireless League, the Radio Association, the Wireless Association of Great Britain, the British Institute of Adult Education and the South London Philharmonic Society were all agreed that there should be a single broadcasting authority and that the body which controlled it should be more broadly based than the British Broadcasting Company. The respects in which they differed concerned who should be represented on the new board and the degree of Government control.

In the circumstances it is not surprising that the Crawford Committee in their report were able to open—and close—their discussion of the question of the monopoly with the following sentence : " It is agreed that the United States system of un-controlled transmission and reception is unsuited to this country, and that Broadcasting must accordingly remain a monopoly—in other words that the whole organisation must be controlled by a single authority." [35]

The Committee stated they did not recommend a renewal of the licence of the British Broadcasting Company or the setting up of some similar body and the report continued : " We think a public corporation the most appropriate organisation. Such an authority would enjoy a freedom and flexibility which a Minister of State could scarcely exercise in arranging for performers and programmes, and in studying the variable demands of public taste and necessity." The Committee pointed out that it could be set up by Statute or under the Companies Acts—curiously enough, no mention was made of the possibility of the new authority being incorporated by means of a Royal Charter. The title they suggested for the new authority was the " British Broadcasting Commission." [36]

The Committee recommended that the Governing Body should not be made up of " persons representing various interests such as music, science, drama, education, finance, manufacturing and so forth," but should consist of " persons of judgment and inde-pendence, free of commitments, and that they will inspire confidence by having no other interests to promote than those of the public service. We hope they will be men and women of business acumen and experienced in affairs." The Committee recommended that the Governing Body should not have less than five members or more than seven. [37]

This proposal for the establishment of a British Broadcasting Commission shows very clearly the influence of Mr. Reith. This is evident in the passage in the report which describes the status of the Commission : " We feel that the prestige and status of the Commission should be freely acknowledged and their sense of responsibility emphasised. We have framed our report with this object constantly in our minds, and we have done so with the knowledge that the State, through Parliament, must retain the right of ultimate control. We assume that the Postmaster-General would be the Parliamentary spokesman on broad questions of policy, though we think it essential that the Commission should not be subject to the continuing Ministerial guidance and direction which apply to Government Offices. The progress of science and the harmonies of art will be hampered by too rigid rules and too constant a supervision by the State. Within well-defined limits the Commission should enjoy the fullest liberty, wide enough to mark the serious duties laid upon it, and elastic enough to permit variation according to technical developments and changes in public taste. It would discourage enterprise and initiative, both as regards experiments and the intricate problem of programmes, were the authority subjected to too much control. The aspirations and the public obligations of Broadcasting can best be studied by a body appointed *ad hoc*, endowed with adequate tenure, and concentrating on this particular duty. The Commissioners should therefore be invested with the maximum of freedom which Parliament is prepared to concede." [38] Mr. Reith's influence also shows in a paragraph on the need for maintaining high standards. There is one characteristic passage. " Special wavelengths or alternative services may provide an escape from the programme dilemma, but we trust they will never be used to cater for groups of listeners, however large, who press for trite and commonplace performances." [39]

The Committee noted that experience might show that the arrangements they were proposing would need to be modified. " On the one hand it is conceivable that Broadcasting might have to become a department of State like the telephone service : on the other it is possible that its character as a monopoly might have to disappear, and that the rights of transmitting should be distributed." They therefore recommended that the Government should retain the power " to supersede or modify the Commission." They suggested this should be done by embodying the terms on which the Commission operated in a Licence similar in character to the one granted to the Company. This they recommended should be for a period of not less than ten years and should be renewable. [40]

3. THE BRITISH BROADCASTING CORPORATION

The recommendations of the Crawford Committee that broadcasting should be organised as a monopoly and should be in the hands of a public corporation were accepted by the Government. The Postmaster-General, Sir William Mitchell-Thomson (later Lord Selsdon), announced the Government's decision in the House of Commons on July 14th, 1926. [41] A public corporation, the British

Broadcasting Corporation, was to be set up by means of a Royal Charter, a method of incorporation which had been included in the Post Office memorandum but was not mentioned in the report of the Crawford Committee. The Postmaster-General stated that the reason for using this method rather than incorporation under the Companies Acts or by a special Statute was to emphasise the independence of the new corporation.

By an agreement made between the British Broadcasting Company and the Postmaster-General, the Company agreed to transfer its assets to the new authority in return for repayment at par of the share capital of the Company.[42] The details of the new broadcasting scheme are to be found in the Royal Charter and in the Licence which the Postmaster-General granted to the Corporation.[43]

In the Charter is contained the constitution of the Corporation. There were to be five Governors, all of whom were named. Of these, Lord Clarendon was to be Chairman and Lord Gainford (the Chairman of the Company) was to be Vice-Chairman. Their term of office was to be five years, but they were all eligible for re-appointment. The Director-General was also named—he was to be Mr. Reith. In the Charter were set out the powers and duties of the Corporation. The Charter was granted for a ten year period from January 1st, 1927 ; but it was renewable at the end of the ten years.

The rest of the scheme was embodied in a Licence granted to the Corporation by the Postmaster-General. According to the terms of the Licence, the Postmaster-General had to approve the location, wavelength and power of the broadcasting stations. He had also to approve the hours of broadcasting. He had also power to take over the stations in the case of emergency. And there were many other provisions of a technical character. As regards programmes, the Corporation had to " send efficiently . . . programmes of broadcast matter." [44] The Postmaster-General could exercise control over the programmes in two ways. First, if a Government Department requested the Corporation to transmit any matter, it was obliged to comply. Second, the Postmaster-General could by means of a notice in writing " require the Corporation to refrain from sending any broadcast matter (either particular or general). . . ." [45] The Postmaster-General explained in the House of Commons that he had instructed the Corporation that, when it began operations, it was not to broadcast its own opinions on matters of public policy nor was it to broadcast on matters of political, industrial or religious controversy. A little more than a year after the formation of the Corporation, the prohibition on controversial broadcasting was withdrawn "experimentally," and it has never been re-imposed. [46]

The broadcasting service was to continue to be financed by means of licence fees on receiving sets but the determination of the amount of the annual licence fee which was to be paid to the Corporation was somewhat complicated. From the gross amount received the Post Office was to deduct $12\frac{1}{2}$ per cent. to pay for the cost of collection and administration. Of the sum which remained after the $12\frac{1}{2}$ per cent. had been deducted, the amount going to the Corporation was determined by a scale : from the first million licences issued in any year, the Corporation was to receive 90 per cent. ; from the second million, 80 per cent. ; from the third million, 70 per cent. ; and from all additional licences, 60 per cent. [47] The licence fee is not mentioned in the Licence but in fact it remained at 10s.

There are two other features of the scheme which are of interest. First of all, the restrictions on the news which could be broadcast were removed. One of the objects of the Corporation as stated in the Royal Charter was : " To collect news of and information relating to current events in any part of the world and in any manner that may be thought fit and to establish and subscribe to news-agencies." [48] Secondly, the ban on advertisements was continued but the use of sponsored programmes was still to be allowed. [49]

But one of the most important features of the scheme is not to be found in either the Charter or the Licence and Agreement. The Corporation was to be a monopoly. Legally, this was not so. But there was no mention, as there was in the revised Licence issued after the Sykes Committee report, of the Postmaster-General's reserving the right to license new broadcasting authorities. There can be no doubt that the intention was that there should be a monopoly. This was made clear in the speeches of the Postmaster-General, Sir William Mitchell-Thomson, and the Assistant Postmaster-General, Lord Wolmer, in the debate in the House of Commons on the proposed scheme. [50]

One feature of the scheme was that broadcasting was to be run by a public corporation. To the historian of the public corporation, the fact that this form of organisation was adopted in 1926 in the case of broadcasting is of the greatest importance. For experience of the public corporation in the case of broadcasting was a major factor leading to its general acceptance as the proper method of organising public enterprises. But, as regards broadcasting itself in Great Britain, the replacement of the Company by the Corporation made very little difference. In a memorandum which the Company issued to Members of Parliament before the debate on the transfer of broadcasting from the Company to the Corporation, it was stated : " The policy of the B.B.C. during its stewardship of the Service has led logically and indeed inevitably to the creation of a Public Corporation as the permanent Broadcasting authority."[51] The Company had gradually reduced " its commercial scaffolding " [52] and when the actual transfer of broadcasting to the Corporation occurred, the change was really one of form rather than of substance. It did not imply any alteration in the policies of those directing the broadcasting service.

In later chapters I shall be concerned with the results of the fact (whatever the legal position may have been) that the British Broadcasting Corporation possessed a monopoly of broadcasting in Great Britain. With the discussions which arose because a broadcasting authority was a particular kind of organisation, the public corporation, I shall be concerned only in so far as it is relevant to my main theme.[53] My interest is in the monopoly.

Notes on Chapter 3

[1] He had served a five years' engineering apprenticeship in Glasgow. These biographical details are taken from *Who's Who*, 1947.

[2] *Broadcast over Britain*, p. 26.

[3] *Op. cit.*, pp. 212-213.

[4] *Op. cit.*, p. 123.

[5] *Op. cit.*, p. 213.

[6] *Op. cit.*, p. 34.

[7] *Op. cit.*, p. 191.

[8] *Op. cit.*, p. 192.

[9] *Op. cit.*, pp. 195-197.

[10] *Op. cit.*, p. 81.

[11] *Op. cit.*, pp., 59-60

[12] *Op. cit.*, p. 62.

[13] See the evidence of Mr. J. C. W. Reith to the Sykes Committee on July 14th, 1923, questions 3310-3317.

[14] See Lord Reith : " The B.B.C. Shows a Middle Road," *Picture Post*, July 25th, 1942. This suggestion was not recorded in the minutes.

[15] *Broadcasting from Within*, p. 50.

[16] *Op cit.*, p. 45.

[17] *The Times Literary Supplement*, January 15th, 1925.

[18] See *The Times*, March 7th, 1925.

[19] See Parliamentary Debates, House of Commons, July 20th, 1925.

[20] For example, newspaper comment when the Crawford Committee was set up and also when it started its investigations was, on the whole, very favourable to the continuance of an organisation like the British Broadcasting Company and opposed to competition in broadcasting. See, for instance, *The Daily Telegraph*, July 18th, 1925, *Evening Standard*, August 8th, 1925, the *Sunday Times*, August 9th, 1925, the *Manchester Guardian*, November 28th, 1925. Compare also the *Wireless World*, August 12th, 1925. I have come across only one article which was hostile to the monopoly of broadcasting. This was in the *Daily Express*, November 28th, 1925.

[21] This was mentioned in Sir Evelyn Murray's memorandum to the Crawford Committee.

[22] See the *Radio Times*, May 29th, 1925.

[23] See the *Wireless World*, December 9th, 1925.

[24] See T. O'Brien, *British Experiments in Public Ownership and Control*, p. 195.

[25] See Lincoln Gordon, *The Public Corporation in Great Britain*, p. 164.

[26] See paragraph 16 of the memorandum.

[27] See paragraph 18 of the memorandum.

[28] See paragraph 19 of the memorandum.

[29] See paragraph 20 of the memorandum.

[30] See paragraph 21 of the memorandum.

[31] See paragraph 22 of the memorandum.

[32] See paragraph 27 of the memorandum.

[33] See the evidence of Mr. J. C. W. Reith to the Crawford Committee on December 3rd, 1925, question 4. The Board of Directors of the British Broadcasting Company had decided to make no representations to the Committee with a view to securing continuance of control by the radio trade. See the *Radio Times* for March 12th, 1926. Apart from Mr. Reith, evidence was given by two other members of the Board : Lord Gainford, the independent Chairman, and Mr. W. W. Burnham. But Mr. Burnham appeared not as a director of the British Broadcasting Company, but as Chairman of the National Association of Radio Manufacturers and Traders.

[34] See, for example, Mr. Reith's answers to questions 130, 144 and 145 in his evidence to the Crawford Committee on December 3rd, 1925. See also the references given in section 1 of this chapter.

[35] See the report of the Crawford Committee, paragraph 4.

[36] See the report of the Crawford Committee, paragraph 5.

[37] See the report of the Crawford Committee, paragraph 8.

[38] See the report of the Crawford Committee, paragraph 16.

[39] See the report of the Crawford Committee, paragraph 14.

[40] See the report of the Crawford Committee, paragraph 10.

[41] See Parliamentary Debates, House of Commons, July 14th, 1926.

[42] See Cmd. 2755 (1926).

[43] See *Wireless Broadcasting, Drafts of (1) Royal Charter for which the Postmaster-General proposes to apply for the incorporation of the British Broadcasting Corporation ; and (2) Licence and Agreement, the terms of which have been mutually agreed upon, between His Majesty's Postmaster-General and the Governors-designate of the British Broadcasting Corporation.* (Cmd. 2756, 1926.) These documents were reproduced as appendices to the report of the Ullswater Committee. (Cmd. 5091, 1936.)

[44] Clause 4 (1) of the Licence and Agreement.

[45] These provisions were contained in Clause 4 (2) and (3) of the Licence and Agreement.

[46] For the Postmaster-General's announcement of the restrictions on what the Corporation might broadcast, see Parliamentary Debates, House of Commons, November 15th, 1926. For the withdrawal of the prohibition, see Parliamentary Debates, House of Commons, March 5th, 1928. In the case of the Company, there had been no mention in the Licence of any prohibition of controversial broadcasts. Broadcasting had to be done " to the reasonable satisfaction of the Postmaster-General." But the Postmaster-General had early indicated that he thought controversial broadcasts should not be given and the Company had submitted a number of scripts to the Post Office for approval when it had been in doubt as to whether they were or were not controversial. For a discussion of this question, see Lincoln Gordon, *op. cit.*, pp. 173-176 and 214-229.

[47] See Clause 18 of the Licence and Agreement.

[48] See Clause 3 (*e*) of the Royal Charter. The Corporation began in 1930 to compile its own news bulletins. Previously they had been compiled in Reuters.

[49] See Clause 3 of the Licence and Agreement.

[50] See Parliamentary Debates, House of Commons, November 15th, 1926.

[51] *B.B.C. Archives.*

[52] See the *B.B.C. Yearbook* for 1928, p. 40.

[53] For an examination of this aspect of the work of the British Broadcasting Corporation, see Lincoln Gordon, *op. cit.*, pp. 156-244 ; W. A. Robson, " The British Broadcasting Corporation," in *Public Enterprise*, pp. 73-104 ; and T. O'Brien, *op. cit.*, pp. 96-201.

PART II

COMPETITIVE SERVICES

CHAPTER FOUR

WIRE BROADCASTING

1. The Origin of the Relay Exchange

THE story of wire broadcasting in Great Britain starts in about 1924 in Hythe, a village of about 6,000 inhabitants, near Southampton in Hampshire. Mr. A. W. Maton,[1] who owned an electrical shop at Hythe and ran the local cinema, was greatly interested in radio. He had built himself a radio receiving set. To enable his wife to hear the programmes when she was in another part of the house, Mr. Maton, as an experiment, connected the set by wire with a loudspeaker in another room. Finding that this was successful, Mr. Maton investigated the possibility of using wire for longer distances. In a field at the back of his house he ran out a length of wire to a distance of half a mile and, attaching a loudspeaker at the end, found that the broadcasts were reproduced with little, if any, loss of power. And he found that this was also the case if several loudspeakers were attached to the wire. These results caused him to carry his experiments farther. He arranged with friends in Hythe to allow him to install loudspeakers in their houses, which he connected with the receiving set in his own home. These friends were then able to hear the broadcasts without possessing a receiving set themselves. As no insurmountable difficulties were encountered, Mr. Maton decided that it would be possible to develop this system of distributing programmes on a commercial basis. He therefore began to charge 1s. 6d. per week for his service and extended his wire system in order to serve additional subscribers. In this way, the first relay exchange in Great Britain was started in January, 1925.[2] By August, 1926, Mr. Maton had twenty subscribers. This relay exchange continued in existence until 1941, when Mr. Maton decided to close it down owing to shortage of labour and materials. The relay exchange never had more than about 150 subscribers but it is remarkable, not only because it was the first, but also because it covered an area with a low population density. To secure his 150 subscribers Mr. Maton had to cover a wide area—the subscriber farthest from the exchange required ten miles of wire to reach him.

When Mr. Maton first started his system, he secured permission from the Southampton Post Office. This was granted on condition that each of the subscribers took out a receiving licence. This local decision was to have most important consequences, which were certainly not foreseen at the time this permission was granted. In August, 1926, Mr. Maton's relay exchange attracted some publicity in consequence of a letter written by a Hythe resident to a radio periodical. The General Post Office immediately became interested. They pointed out that Mr. Maton's action was clearly illegal. He was contravening the first condition of the receiving licence in which it was stated that the apparatus could only be used to receive messages in the premises occupied by the licensee. And it was also possible that Mr. Maton was infringing the Telegraph Acts.[3] But it could not be gainsaid that Mr. Maton had received local permission and the Post Office finally agreed to license him on terms which are described in the next section of this chapter.

Once it was clear that the Post Office was willing to license relay exchanges this new industry could develop. Additional relay exchanges began to be formed. Many came into being as a direct consequence of other people hearing about Mr. Maton's relay exchange. And in several cases Mr. Maton took an active part in equipping them, although these new exchanges were all run by others. By September, 1927, there were ten relay exchanges,[4] with 446 subscribers; by December, 1928, there were 23 relay exchanges,[5] with 2,430 subscribers; and by December, 1929, there were 34 relay exchanges, with 8,592 subscribers.[6] By the end of 1929 it was clear that a new industry had come into existence. It was as yet on a very small scale, run by small business men, but it had established itself.

2. OFFICIAL POLICY

At the time that Mr. Maton was setting up his relay exchange at Hythe (or perhaps a little earlier), the idea occurred to Mr. P. P. Eckersley, then Chief Engineer of the British Broadcasting Company, that one way of avoiding the difficulties caused by the limitation of wavelengths would be to distribute programmes by wire.[7] This would have the primary advantage that it would enable more programmes to be broadcast ; but it would also improve the quality of reception. Mr. Eckersley therefore tried to induce the Company to agree to the principle of wire broadcasting. But, according to Mr. Eckersley's own account, " the B.B.C. turned down any idea of substituting wire for wireless whether it was practical technically to do so or not. It had to. The B.B.C. was after all constituted, capitalised and controlled at that time by the wireless trade. It existed to create a market for wireless receivers. This revolutionary idea would upset the market. The B.B.C. would seem an ungracious child if, after all the money that had been spent on its upbringing, it turned on its parents and took away their livelihood." [8] The result was that the development of this new method of distributing programmes was left in the hands of Mr. Maton and the others whose activities I have described in the preceding section.

But this development created a problem for the Post Office. It had to determine the conditions upon which it would license the relay exchanges. Licences had to be granted by the Post Office for two reasons. First, a licence was required for receiving broadcasts. And secondly, a licence was required under the Telegraph Acts to pass messages over wires. The Post Office therefore raised with the British Broadcasting Corporation the question of the policy to be followed. The Corporation then proposed that it should itself operate the relay exchanges. " The B.B.C. argued that if there were no State control over rediffusion then it would be within the power of private companies and individuals to arrange what the listeners should, or perhaps more important, should not hear. . . . The Corporation pointed out that it had been given a programme monopoly, but this would cease to have any value if other organisations were given the unhindered power to dictate what large groups of listeners should or should not hear." [9] But the Post Office was not willing to agree to the operation of relay exchanges by the Corporation. The reason for this refusal on the part of the Post Office had little to do with the merits or demerits of the Corporation's arguments. The Post Office objected because it would mean that the Corporation would be competing directly with the radio trade. Listeners who used the relay exchanges would not need to buy a receiving set. "It would," argued the Post Office, " be against all precedent for a Government-appointed organisation such as the B.B.C. to compete with private enterprise." But the

F

Post Office added that it did not consider that the system was in fact likely to develop. [10]

When the Post Office first discovered the existence of the relay exchange they decided that its operators should take out a special licence. This was essentially a modified version of the ordinary receiving licence. The relay exchange was regarded by the Post Office as consisting of a master set which received the programmes, which were then amplified and distributed by wires to subscribers. The Post Office required the operators of relay exchanges to make a return of subscribers, but the main—and the only important provision—was that which required that the operator of the relay exchange and each of the subscribers should take out a receiving licence.

But, following the discussions between the Post Office and the British Broadcasting Corporation, a completely new form of licence was evolved. It was introduced in April, 1930. [11] In the main it reproduced the conditions of the old licence. But it made three important new conditions. The first (in Clause 4 (2)) ran as follows : " The Licensee shall not use or allow to be used the wires connecting the Stations with the premises of subscribers for any other purpose than the sending to Subscribers of messages received by the Stations in pursuance of the provisions hereinbefore contained "—these limited the stations to the receipt of broadcast programmes—" and in particular without prejudice to the generality of this provision the Licensee shall not himself originate at the Stations or collect by wire any programme or item whether musical or otherwise or information of any kind for distribution to subscribers." The Post Office had been unable to agree to allow the British Broadcasting Corporation to operate relay exchanges. But it did take steps to prevent competition between the Corporation and the relay exchanges. If an operator of a relay exchange thought that he could provide a programme of more interest to his subscribers than that transmitted by the British Broadcasting Corporation, he was not to be allowed to do so. If a concert was given in the same or a neighbouring town or village which he thought would interest his subscribers, he could not arrange to have his relay exchange connected with the concert hall—that, too, was forbidden. This clause was later to be interpreted so strictly as to preclude even the announcement of programme summaries. [12]

Whether this condition in the licence was aimed at an actual or a potential danger is not clear. But I have not heard of any operator originating programmes in this early period.

It will be noted that support for the monopoly by the Post Office in this case could not have been based upon the original arguments which led to the monopoly of broadcasting. The question of the limitation of wavelengths did not arise. This policy was based on the later arguments developed by Mr. Reith. What was being protected was the " programme monopoly " of the British Broadcasting Corporation—the right which was assumed to be vested in the Corporation of determining what people should be allowed to listen to, at any rate in their own homes. Of course, this " programme monopoly " was not complete. It was still possible to listen to programmes broadcast from abroad ; the limitation on this freedom, at least so far as operators of relay exchanges were concerned, was to come later.

The second of the new conditions was one which set a term to the licence. This was contained in Clause 12. The licence was to continue in existence until December 31st, 1932, and unless terminated by six months' notice on either side was thereafter to continue on an annual basis.

The third new condition was of a different character from the others. This provided for compulsory purchase of the plant by the Post Office. It was contained in Clause 11 of the Licence and the relevant portions ran as follows :

" (1) The Postmaster-General may by not less than three calendar months previous notice in writing to the Licensee require him to sell to him on the date of determination . . . such portions of the plant and apparatus forming the Stations and wires and other plant used by the Licensee for the purpose of connecting the premises of Subscribers with the Stations or installed by him at the premises as the Postmaster-General shall specify. . . .

(2) The consideration to be paid by the Postmaster-General to the Licensee for the purchase of the plant and apparatus referred to in Sub-Clause 1 hereof shall be a sum equal to the value thereof at the date of purchase as plant and apparatus *in situ* exclusive of any allowance or compensation for loss of profit compulsory sale goodwill the cost of raising capital or any other consideration.

(3) The Postmaster-General may remove the plant and apparatus purchased by him at his own expense in all respects and

the Licensee shall obtain for him all such facilities as may be necessary for that purpose. The Postmaster-General shall not be under any liability for any unavoidable damage which may be caused in or by such removal."

The effect of the first new condition was to restrict the scope of the service which a relay exchange operator might give. The effect of the second and third of the new conditions was to make the business of the relay exchange operator subject to compulsory purchase by the Post Office within a short period and upon terms which would discourage any investment which would not pay for itself within a short period of time. To install equipment in the relay exchanges or in the distribution system, the costs of which could be recouped only over a number of years became a risky undertaking.[13] Of course, some long-term investment would take place if the operators of relay exchanges believed that the Post Office would be unlikely to exercise its rights. And no doubt some operators did take this view. But the risk was there—and some discouragement to investment in relay exchanges must have resulted from these new conditions imposed by the Post Office.

Why did the Post Office take this action which it must have realised would result in restricting the growth of the relay exchanges? It is not possible to give a definite answer, since no official statement of the reasons was ever issued. Nor have I been able to discover any protest in the Press or question in Parliament which might have had the effect of provoking such a statement. The industry was, of course, in its early stages, small and uninfluential, and it was possible to carry out measures which would hinder its growth without any public justification being required. Mr. P. P. Eckersley has suggested that the object of the policy was to meet the British Broadcasting Corporation's objection to the development of independent relay exchanges without giving the control of the exchanges to the Corporation, which step the Post Office was unwilling to agree to. As Mr. Eckersley has said : " . . . the Post Office protected B.B.C. interests only by thwarting and hampering rediffusion." [14] Whether this was the only reason for the policy, it is impossible to say. But there can be no doubt that the desire of the British Broadcasting Corporation to protect their " programme monopoly " would have facilitated the acceptance by the Post Office of any policy which restricted the growth of independent relay exchanges.

3. THE DEVELOPMENT OF WIRE BROADCASTING 1930 TO 1935

There were four main reasons why those wishing to hear broadcast programmes might prefer to become subscribers to a relay exchange rather than buy a receiving set. These were :

(1) The loudspeaker which was installed in a subscriber's home was simpler to operate than a receiving set. Furthermore, it was less likely to develop faults ; or if it did there was the maintenance staff of the relay exchange to set it right.

(2) The substitution of a small weekly payment for the larger sum required to pay for a receiving set was a convenience to some subscribers. None the less, the advantage which the relay exchange subscriber would have over the purchaser of a set on hire purchase terms would be small.

(3) In areas such as ports in which there was considerable interference or in which, owing to natural features or the location of the transmitting station, reception was difficult on an ordinary receiving set, the subscriber to the relay exchange was able to hear the programmes very much more clearly. This was due both to the superior efficiency of the master set and to the special aerials which the relay exchange could erect. [15]

(4) The master set of the relay exchange was able to pick up programmes from foreign stations which it would be difficult, or impossible, to receive on an ordinary set.

Of course subscribers to the relay exchanges suffered the disadvantage that the exchanges distributed, in most cases, only two alternative programmes. But since most ordinary receiving sets were not able to receive more than this number with any clarity, this disadvantage was not, for most people, very serious.

At all events the service which the relay exchanges offered was preferred by a sufficient number of listeners for it to appear profitable for new exchanges to be started and for old ones to expand despite the discouragement to investment of the new conditions which the Post Office had inserted in the licence. Indeed, new companies were formed such as Rediffusion Ltd. and Radio Central Exchanges Ltd. (both in 1931) with a view to setting up relay exchanges in places not already served. The result of the activities of such companies and of others was a steady expansion both in the number of exchanges and in the number of subscribers.

	Number of exchanges	Number of subscribers
December 31st, 1929 ..	34	8,592
December 31st, 1930 ..	86	21,677
December 31st, 1931 ..	132	43,889
December 31st, 1932 ..	194	82,690
December 31st, 1933 ..	265	130,998
December 31st, 1934 ..	318	192,707
December 31st, 1935 ..	343	233,554

But there were three interests which did not regard the development of the relay exchanges with any favour. These were the radio trade, the Press and the British Broadcasting Corporation. The radio trade, of course, saw in the relay exchange a competitor which eliminated the need for a radio receiving set. And they organised opposition to the grant by local councils of concessions to relay exchange companies.[16] The Press (and the newsagents) objected because the relay exchanges could (and did) distribute commercial programmes broadcast from abroad. For example, Lord Iliffe (President of the Periodical Trade Press and Weekly Newspaper Proprietors' Association) said at the Annual Dinner of the Association in 1935 : " We view with the gravest concern the growth of the relay exchange system of broadcasting—a system which depends for its working on a licence of the Postmaster-General —which threatens, in our opinion, by the relaying of sponsored programmes from abroad to undermine the prohibition on microphone advertising enforced by the B.B.C. to-day. In our view, too, it constitutes a general menace by placing in uncontrolled hands the power to upset the balance of broadcasting opinion on controversial matter which is so carefully held by the B.B.C. to-day." [17]

The British Broadcasting Corporation disapproved of relay exchanges because they threatened the Corporation's " programme monopoly." The Corporation expressed its point of view as follows : " The system . . . contains within it forces which uncontrolled might be disruptive of the spirit and intention of the B.B.C. charter. The persons in charge of wireless exchanges have power, by replacing selected items of the Corporation's programmes with transmissions from abroad, to alter entirely the general drift of the B.B.C.'s programme policy. . . . With the small exchanges of the past no great danger could be foreseen. The matter assumes a different complexion, however, when exchanges controlled by large companies with heavy capital are already allowed ' for the present ' 100,000 subscribers each. Each exchange may increase to the stature of a B.B.C. in miniature, and furthermore the possibility must be visualised of several enlarged exchanges being merged under a single financial control. Concerns with sufficient capital would be in a position to buy time on the several Continental stations which will sell it, and produce their own programmes abroad on the existing American system." [18]

An example of the attitude of the British Broadcasting Corporation is furnished by a correspondence between the Corporation and the Relay Services Association concerning the publication of programmes by operators of relay exchanges. The Corporation indicated that it would be willing that operators should publish these programmes in full provided that the choice of the programmes distributed was made by the Corporation. This condition the Relay Services Association was unable to accept. In its reply, the Corporation stated : " We cannot . . . concede the deciding voice in programmes to individual operators. . . . We feel . . . that in present circumstances it would be a great mistake to part with any of our rights, particularly when so little is offered in exchange. We shall, therefore, expect wireless exchanges to adhere strictly to the abbreviated style of programme approved by us." [19]

This opposition did not result in this period in any change in the licence conditions sufficiently onerous to prevent the expansion of the relay exchanges. None the less, some new restrictive conditions were introduced (probably towards the end of 1932 or early in 1933). [20] These were :

(1) The Postmaster-General reserved the right to prohibit the relaying of programmes transmitted by any specific station. [21] This was, no doubt, the origin of Clause 11 in the present licence (itself introduced about 1937) which runs as follows : " The Licensee shall if and whenever he shall be required so to do by notice in writing from the Postmaster-General prevent Subscribers from receiving in their respective premises by means of the Stations such messages or classes of messages as may be directed by such notice as aforesaid."

(2) The relay exchanges were prohibited from distributing to subscribers, according to the British Broadcasting Corporation's interpretation, " any speech of political or controversial character broadcast in English from a foreign station." [22] Clause 4 (3) in the

existing licence runs as follows : " The Licensee shall not distribute to or allow Subscribers to receive in their respective premises by means of the Stations any Programme or message containing political social or religious propaganda received at the Stations in the English language from any Station outside Great Britain and Northern Ireland or any message received from any Station announcing the result of any sweepstake in connection with a horse race." The provision prohibiting the broadcasting of a sweepstake result may not have been introduced until 1935. [23]

(3) The relay exchanges were prohibited from receiving payment or other consideration for distributing any programmes transmitted by a foreign broadcasting station. This condition, which prevented the relay exchanges from financing their service by means of revenue from advertisements, may well have had a considerable effect in restricting the expansion of the relay exchanges. This provision appears in the following form in Clause 4 (5) of the existing licence : " The Licensee shall not receive any money or other consideration from any person (other than payment from a subscriber of the Licensee's usual rate of charge to Subscribers) for the distribution to Subscribers of any Programme or message received by the Stations."

(4) According to the *B.B.C. Year Book* for 1933, each separate relay exchange company was to be limited " to a maximum of 100,000 subscribers drawn from areas with an aggregate population of not more than 2,000,000." [24] This provision does not appear in any licence form nor does there ever appear to have been a Government statement that this was the policy of the Post Office.

In one important respect, however, the licence was amended to make the conditions less restrictive. The licence period was extended to December 31st, 1936. Although the conditions according to which the equipment of the relay exchanges could be taken over by the Post Office remained unaltered, the period of time the operators had in which to recoup themselves for their investment was lengthened. It still remained, of course, a very short period ; three years if the investment were made at the beginning of 1933 and less if it were made subsequently.

4. THE USE OF ELECTRICITY MAINS

Mr. P. P. Eckersley had been anxious while he was Chief Engineer of the British Broadcasting Corporation that it should enter the field of the relay exchanges. It was therefore natural that Mr. Eckersley, after leaving the Corporation in 1929, should take an interest in wire broadcasting. He became associated in 1931 with Rediffusion Ltd., one of the companies engaged in the relay exchange business. But shortly afterwards Mr. Eckersley became interested in the possibility of distributing programmes through the electricity mains, and he engaged on developmental work in connection with this project, first with the Dubilier Condenser Company and later with British Insulated Cables Ltd. By 1934, although there was more developmental work to be done, he was " sure that there were no real snags to prevent a practical system being devised." [25] Such a system would have advantages over the method of distribution by specially erected wires. First, there would be no need to erect a new overhead wiring system. Second, every additional programme requires two additional wires (with the methods commonly used) and the objection which local authorities feel to increased complexity in the wiring system as well as the additional expense has limited the number of alternative programmes distributed by the relay exchanges—in general the number of alternative programmes has been two. If the electricity mains were used, it would be possible to distribute a large number of programmes through the same mains. [26] These are solid advantages. Of course, there are disadvantages. It requires a more elaborate receiving unit than is needed with wire distribution. And not everyone is connected with the electricity mains. But there seemed no reason to suppose that the balance of advantage was definitely against distribution by the electricity mains; the company anxious to promote its use had the necessary capital and a skilled technical staff; and certain local authorities wished to give the system a trial. Yet no system for the distribution of programmes by the electricity mains has ever been established in Great Britain.

To explain why this has been so, it is necessary to go back to the Electric Lighting Act of 1882, the first of the electricity supply Acts. By Section 3 of this Act the Board of Trade is empowered to license undertakings to supply electricity for public and private purposes except the " transmission of any telegram." The aim of this provision was, of course, to protect the Post Office's monopoly of the telegraph. In the Telegraph Act of 1869, a telegram is defined as " any message or other communication transmitted or intended for transmission by a telegraph " ; and a telegraph is said to include "any apparatus for transmitting messages or other communication by means of electric signals." These provisions in the Telegraph Acts were to have far-reaching consequences. It was later held that a telephone was a "telegraph" and a telephone conversation was a "telegram" within the meaning of the Acts. In another decision it was held that any signal transmitted by electricity is a "telegram." The implications of this are clear, if unexpected. The distribution of programmes by the electricity mains is the transmission of a telegram and therefore an activity which no electricity supply authority was allowed to undertake. Consequently, if any electricity supply authority was to be able to distribute programmes through the electricity mains, new powers were required from Parliament. [27]

The Electricity Commission decided to sponsor a Bill giving electricity supply authorities the necessary powers. But in the meantime the Middlesbrough Corporation promoted a Bill in which, among other things, they asked for powers to distribute broadcast programmes through the electricity mains and the Electricity Commission decided not to proceed with their more general measure. [28]

The Middlesbrough Corporation's Bill came up for consideration in 1933. Its object was to give the Corporation power to carry out various municipal enterprises. But it included some clauses which would have empowered the Corporation to run a relay exchange— and to use the electricity mains for the distribution of the programmes. Opposition to the Bill was confined almost entirely to these clauses and although in the House of Lords the Bill was, after criticism, approved, in the House of Commons these clauses were rejected. [29] The main factor bringing about this result seems to have been the opposition by members of the Conservative Party to municipal trading and to its extension to new fields ; but many of the arguments used would have applied to any extension of the relay exchange system whether by public or private enterprise.

Lord Mount Temple, in moving in the House of Lords that the clauses which gave the Middlesbrough Corporation powers to establish a relay exchange should be specially considered by the Committee to which the Bill would be referred (a motion that was agreed to), while indicating his dislike of any extension of municipal enterprise, based his disquiet about the proposal mainly on the argument which had just appeared in the *B.B.C. Year Book* for 1933. He was concerned about the programmes which an independent relay exchange might distribute. " It was thought desirable and still presumably is thought desirable, that, however controversial the matter broadcast, in whatever realm of thought, a fair and independent neutral balance should be struck between opposing lines of thought. It was also thought desirable, and still presumably is, that programmes should be balanced in so far as the amount of each ingredient is concerned, that is, there should be something for everybody's taste together with something (to which nobody need listen if they do not wish) of an instructive and educational nature. My point is this : The wireless exchange may, and probably will, completely upset this balance. Either the exchange may broadcast an excessive amount of entertainment, to the detriment of the entertainment industry, or it may broadcast an excessive amount of one-sided controversial matter. The capitalist companies may select only items which express their economic views, and the Socialist municipalities those items which further Collectivism."

Mr. A. M. Lyons, who moved the deletion of these clauses in the House of Commons, argued that the relay exchange system would lead to unbalanced programmes, " it might very well be, according to the fancy or colour of the corporation then in existence." Furthermore, the relay exchange might distribute programmes from abroad which contained advertisements, " I will not say offensive matter, but matter which is not permitted over a British broadcasting station." These arguments were repeated by other speakers, but considerable stress was laid on the unfair competition with private enterprise which the granting of these powers would entail. There was first of all the competition with the entertainments industry. Mr. Louis Smith pointed out that " in this Bill the Middlesbrough Corporation seek to collect the most perfect programmes from all over the world and to relay them at about $2\frac{1}{2}$d. per night to their subscribers. What chance has a poor cinema or an old theatre in the various towns of the country to compete successfully against operas and dramatic entertainments if such relays come from over the world ? " * And Mr. A. Denville

* In a later speech, Mr. Denville said that a statement objecting to the proposal had been issued by the Entertainments Protection Association and the Society of West End Managers, and had been sent to all Members of Parliament. In this statement it was said that " the programmes broadcast by the British Broadcasting Corporation contain a certain proportion of light entertainment matter, and, therefore, do not constitute so serious a form of competition with the theatrical industry, but such competition from wireless exchanges concentrated solely on entertainment matter would be serious indeed."

asked " What is going to happen to the 4,721 shops which are selling radio sets ? . . . . If the relay system comes into force in this country it will mean that instead of a wireless set being in each house there will be only a loudspeaker and a switch. This will be installed by the corporation and the working man will pay 1s. 6d. per week for the use of it. What is going to happen to the makers of valves and wireless sets and all their component parts ? " The character of the opposition to the Middlesbrough Corporation's proposal may be summed up in a sentence of Mr. Lyons : " . . . Nobody lacks anything in the radio programmes that are distributed to this country, and there is no reason for municipal broadcasting in order to put private enterprise out of business." The Labour Party opposed the deletion of these clauses. The Postmaster-General, Sir Kingsley Wood, gave no lead to members in his speech and in the division the motion to delete the clauses was carried by 144 votes to 48.

Other municipalities tried to obtain powers to distribute programmes through the electricity mains, but they were also unsuccessful. The Cardiff Corporation decided to withdraw their proposal rather than jeopardise a Bill they were promoting. A similar proposal by the Tynemouth Corporation was withdrawn at the third reading, although it had previously been approved by a Select Committee. Attempts were also made to bring about an alteration in the general legal position. When the Electricity (Supply) Bill was being considered in April, 1934, Mr. W. S. Liddall moved an amendment which would have allowed electricity undertakings to use the electricity mains for distributing programmes. This was opposed by members of the Standing Committee and the amendment was withdrawn. Mr. Liddall later introduced a private members' Bill to give electricity undertakings these powers—the Electricity Supply (Wireless) Bill, July, 1934. But this was also unsuccessful. [30]

We have seen that the entertainments industry took steps to oppose the granting of these powers to electricity supply undertakings. Opposition also came from the radio trade. But what is interesting is that these moves were also opposed by the existing relay companies. It was claimed in their journal that the withdrawal of the Tynemouth Corporation Bill was " largely due to the vigilance and activity " of their Association. And it was observed : " . . . the attempt of the electrical industries to cash in on an enterprise and industry to which they have contributed nothing has been an additional trial which cannot be borne with equanimity nor regarded otherwise than as a predatory attack. . . . The lesson of the Tynemouth Corporation Bill is not likely to be lost on anybody concerned. It is to be hoped that no similar attack on the relay industry will be attempted again. There are other matters of more intimate concern to which we desire to be free to devote our attention." [31]

5. THE ULLSWATER COMMITTEE

The licence period for the relay exchanges had been extended to December 31st, 1936, the same date as that on which the Charter of the British Broadcasting Corporation ended. It was therefore natural that when the Ullswater Committee was appointed in 1935 to consider what changes, if any, should be made in the organisation of broadcasting in Great Britain after the Charter expired, it should also have included in its terms of reference " the system of wireless exchanges." The evidence before this Committee was not given in public, the minutes of evidence were not published, and they are still regarded as confidential. It is, therefore, impossible to review the evidence which was presented to the Committee. There is no alternative but to start with the report.

The section of the report[32] which dealt with the relay exchanges had an historical introduction, mentioned some of the advantages of the system and continued : " We recognise a considerable public value in the system provided that it is conducted under conditions which will ensure its development in the public interest, good technical equipment, and a programme policy in accordance with B.B.C. standards. Present conditions have a contrary effect. A system of separate privately owned exchanges naturally results in the provision of service only to those centres of population where conditions are most favourable for making a profit, whereas the endeavour of a national service would be to meet public needs with as wide a measure of equality as possible. It is claimed that the apparatus and wiring of the larger companies are equal to those of the public telephone service, but many of the undertakings are small and less efficient. We have had evidence from many quarters that the proprietors of relay exchanges are in a position materially to damage the Corporation's programme policy by taking a large proportion of material from foreign sources, selecting some parts of the Corporation's programmes and omitting others, and upsetting the balance upon which those programmes are constructed. Anxiety has been expressed lest the system should be used to disseminate advertisements or betting news from stations abroad, to colour the religious or political outlook of subscribers by a one-sided selection from home programmes, and to lower the level and lessen the impartiality of the broadcast service." That is, the Committee considered that the development of the relay exchanges had not been "in the public interest" because unprofitable areas had not been supplied, because some undertakings had not "good technical equipment" and because operators, by selecting the items which they relayed, could "damage the Corporation's programme policy." There were, however, other factors to be taken into account. Private relay exchanges "would involve extensive wiring networks, duplicating the telephone network but uncoordinated with it. . . . There is also a prospect of the future local distribution of broadcast programmes over the telephone system itself by means of high-frequency carrier currents which could convey two or more alternative programmes without in any way interfering with the normal use of the telephone. We have heard evidence, too, as to possible distribution by similar means over electric light and power mains. We see no good purpose in the independent development of these various methods of broadcasting by wire, but consider that the time has come for unification and co-ordinated development in the hands of the Post Office." The report continued : " We recommend that the ownership and operation of Relay Exchanges should be undertaken by the Post Office and the control of their programmes by the Corporation." [33]

There was a reservation by Lord Selsdon to this section of the report.[34] He argued that it would be unwise for the Post Office to take over the existing plant and equipment of the relay exchanges since, in his view, distribution by the telephone lines was likely to prove a superior method. He therefore suggested that the licence period should be extended for another two years (to December 31st, 1938) and that at the end of this period the Post Office should have the right but not the obligation to acquire such plant as it wished " at its value as apparatus *in situ*, but without any other element of compensation whatsoever and especially without compensation for severance." Lord Selsdon suggested that, in the meantime, the Post Office should experiment with distribution by telephone lines and if the results justified it should " establish a service in suitable areas, even though this involves for the moment some duplication." This arrangement would have left the relay exchanges free to " damage the Corporation's programme policy " for another two years. Lord Selsdon answered this objection in the following words : " I am not much impressed by the contention that such maintenance of the existing arrangements impairs the ' programme balance ' of the B.B.C. The owner of an ordinary wireless set has— within the limits of the power and selectivity of his set—full freedom to receive B.B.C. or foreign programmes at will, and I do not see why, within reasonable limits, a similar freedom should not be vicariously enjoyed by subscribers to exchanges. There must, of course, be some limits set in the licence in order to prevent possible abuse ; e.g. it might be prescribed that if one of a set of talks or speeches be given, the whole series must be included. Further, it should be definitely laid down that, during British Broadcasting hours, all stations shall relay one of the B.B.C. programmes, whether they provide an alternative programme or not. I see no valid reason for ' censoring ' (except in regard to *propaganda*) the make-up of such alternative programmes or of material broadcast out of British hours. After all, the relay Companies, if they are to succeed, must give their public what that public wants and, in trying so to do, they have the advantage that, by measuring the relative loads, they can estimate with some approximation to accuracy how many of their subscribers are listening at any given moment to one or other of two alternative programmes." That is, it was Lord Selsdon's view that the relay exchanges should be allowed " within reasonable limits " (which might be rather narrow) to distribute what they wished. This would, of course, in general, be what their subscribers wanted to hear.

But this was a minority view. The majority of the Ullswater Committee was quite clear as to what should be done. The Post Office should take over the relay exchanges and the programmes they distributed should be determined by the British Broadcasting Corporation. The Committee did, however add : " We regard it as incumbent on the B.B.C. to take into consideration any desire of the subscribers for a selection from foreign programmes." [35]

The Ullswater Committee issued their report on March 16th, 1936. On the same day, the British Broadcasting Corporation issued a statement on the report. This expressed approval of the Committee's recommendations on the relay exchanges and stated : " The continuance and extension on its present basis of the system of relay exchanges would endanger the maintenance of the policy which Parliament has throughout approved, and the Committee has endorsed, for the control of the national broadcasting system. The progressive introduction into the country of programmes, which would be excluded from the national system on account of advertising and other undesirable qualities would thus be made possible." [36] On April 29th, there was a general debate in the House of Commons on the report of the Ullswater Committee. No Government proposals were put forward ; these were to be considered in the light of the debate.[37] Although the debate covered the whole of the report, the topic to which most attention was given was the question of the relay exchanges. Members of the Labour Party supported the transfer of the relay exchanges to the Post Office. Mr. H. B. Lees-Smith, who opened the debate, argued that the Post Office would be able to give a better service because of its technical knowledge and because it could use the telephone wires. He also argued that the Post Office could operate the business as a public service. Private enterprise would only establish relay exchanges in the profitable areas ; it was " skimming off the cream of the business." The Post Office would aim " to give a good service on equal terms to as large a number of the population as possible." It will be seen that Mr. Lees-Smith used two of the three reasons given in the Ullswater Committee report for transferring the relay exchanges to the Post Office ; he made, however, no reference to the third, that private relay exchanges could " damage the Corporation's programme policy." This argument was, however, taken up by other speakers, in particular by those who had been members of the Ullswater Committee. For example, Major J. J. Astor stated : " I have been forced to the conclusion that, having set up the British Broadcasting Corporation, with a system of checks, safeguards and controls, it would be illogical and inconsistent to set up a rival authority which might have a different policy for broadcasting; an authority which might ignore and cut across the very principles and considerations upon which the present constitution of the B.B.C. is based." Several members of the Conservative Party were critical of the proposals. Mr. (later Sir Wavell) Wakefield, who was a Director of one of the largest relay exchange companies, disputed the technical arguments which Mr. Lees-Smith had used to support the transfer of the relay exchanges to the Post Office, but did not directly attack the view that the relay exchanges upset the balance of the Corporation's programmes. His main purpose appears to have been to justify continued operation of the relay exchanges by private enterprise. It is true that he pointed out that the criticism of the relay exchanges was " merely that they give what the public require." And he explained that the operators of relay exchanges had load meters which told them which programmes were popular and which were not. But Mr. Wakefield maintained that the argument that the relay exchanges were damaging the Corporation's programme policy could be met by stating in the licence that one of the programmes distributed was to be the national programme of the British Broadcasting Corporation.[38] He also suggested that a relay board might be set up and that there might be a grouping of exchanges to create larger companies in some districts.

It was Mr. Richard Law who called in question the " balance of programme " argument. He said : " The argument in the Ullswater Report that the relay companies were in the position to damage the B.B.C. programme policy was either meaningless or sinister. . . . Are we to understand from those sentences that the only way in which the Corporation can achieve a balanced and good programme is to have everybody in the country listening to the B.B.C.'s programme, and nothing else, all the time ? . . . There is another interpretation that may be put upon it, that is, that the Corporation has a duty to establish a kind of cultural dictatorship over the people of this country through broadcasting. . . . It is not a question of whether the programmes are good or bad, but it is undesirable that anybody should have the power, not only to say what should be broadcast in this country, but to say what should be listened to, not by the country as a whole, but merely by the poor and less fortunate listeners."* But this speech by Mr. Law appears to have cut no ice. It is not easy to obtain " the feeling of the House " from reading Hansard. But Mr. Eckersley was present and he has told us that the House of Commons " gave the clearest indication that could be shown without a division, that it fully supported the Ullswater Committee's recommendation that re-

---

* This was a reference to the fact that at that time subscribers to the relay exchanges consisted largely of poorer people.

G

diffusion should be taken out of private hands and put in charge of the Post Office." [39] And newspaper comment after the debate was also, on the whole, favourable to the Ullswater Committee's recommendations. [40]

But when the Government announced its policy in a White Paper issued in June, 1936,[41] it was found that it had been decided not to adopt the recommendation of the Ullswater Committee but (in a modified form) the suggestion which Lord Selsdon had put forward in his note of reservation. The Government's proposals may be summarised as follows :

(1) The licences of the relay exchanges were to be extended for three years, that is, until December 31st, 1939.

(2) The compulsory purchase terms were to remain unaltered. A warning was given to the operators of relay exchanges and to " those responsible for arrangements entered into with them such as local authorities " that they " have no guarantee or assurance in any form that any licences will be continued beyond the end of the year 1939, and that there can be no question of compensation for any commitment beyond that date."

(3) In the meantime the Post Office was to undertake experimental work on wire broadcasting.

(4) Two new conditions were to be added to the licence. Relay exchanges had to reach " a reasonable standard of efficiency in technical and other respects." And, for relay exchanges which distributed two programmes, one of these would be required to be a programme of the British Broadcasting Corporation—at least during the hours in which the Corporation broadcast. It would also be considered whether it was practicable to require relay exchanges which distributed one programme " to arrange to give their subscribers a choice between two programmes."

These proposals were justified by the Government on the ground that the negotiations with the proprietors of the 340 relay exchanges, the necessary staffing and administrative arrangements on the part of the Post Office and the investigation of the technical problems would in any case mean a delay of two or three years before the Ullswater Committee's recommendations could be carried out, even if they were accepted in principle. " But the same interval, while giving time for experience to be gained and experimental work undertaken, should enable a more correct estimate to be formed as to the probable and best lines of development . . . than can be formed at present." [42]

This decision of the Government was debated on July 6th, 1936.[43] Major G. C. (later Lord) Tryon, the Postmaster-General, opening the debate for the Government, did little more than restate the arguments which were in the White Paper. He underlined the warning to the operators of the relay exchanges. "The Government's explicit statement now should make it clear that any further capital investment which is unlikely to be recouped before the end of 1939 is made at a risk." On the question of the relaying of foreign broadcasts containing advertisements, Major Tryon said : " I think it will be agreed that it is undesirable to proceed to actual prohibition and that we rely on relay exchange owners to keep such advertisement to a minimum." Later in the debate he explained that he would not forbid the relaying of foreign broadcasts which contained advertisements because listeners who had their own sets could listen to them. In the speeches which followed, all the arguments which had been used in the previous debate were repeated. And considerable dissatisfaction with the Government's decision was expressed. Lord Wolmer pointed out that " the decision to come to no decision would mean that the whole service would be paralysed." And many speakers deplored the fact that the Ullswater Committee's recommendations had not been adopted. One of these was Sir Ian Fraser. He said that, quite apart from the question of who should own the relay exchanges, there was the question of the programmes to be relayed. He argued that the British Broadcasting Corporation should control what was distributed by the relay exchanges. " That is a much more important and much less controversial matter than the question of who should own the service." He said : " I cannot see any argument against the Corporation completely and absolutely controlling what shall be relayed . . . we take immense pains to set up a machine which will choose fairly, honestly, and beyond reproach what shall be broadcast and then we permit private persons to interfere, certainly in a very small way, because they happen to own a vehicle that takes the message to some of the listeners." The same point of view was forcibly expressed later in the debate by Mr. E. J. Williams : " For experts and specialists to be engaged by the B.B.C. in order to give this country what it requires, and then to find that it is possible for certain individuals to set up a system in contradistinction, and to supply the poor people . . . with some alternative programme to that which the B.B.C. has arranged, is something which ought never to be defended by hon. Members." Mr. C. R. Attlee introduced a new argument into the debate when he suggested that there was "nothing to stop an enterprising foreign power from putting a lot of money into these relay exchanges." Notwithstanding the general criticism, the Labour Party's motion condemning the decision was defeated.

6. The period after the Ullswater Committee

The Postmaster-General amended the licence granted to the operators of the relay exchanges so as to make it compulsory for them to distribute one of the Corporation's programmes during the time that the Corporation was broadcasting. And he also sent a letter to the operators warning them against distributing foreign programmes which contained advertisements. The letter from the Post Office included the following passage : " Whilst the Postmaster-General is anxious not to fetter the discretion of relay undertakings in regard to their choice of programmes . . . he sees very great objection to any growth in the relaying of advertisements included in certain programmes from abroad. In the circumstances he hopes that those responsible for relay undertakings will bear in mind this expression of opinion, as if the relaying of advertising programmes should grow to serious proportions, he might have to take drastic action in regard to it."[44] But the main effect of the new arrangement was to create a feeling of uncertainty among operators of relay exchanges about the future of the industry.[45] There ensued a period of stagnation. Few, if any, new relay exchanges were formed, and the industry, which had shown a steady growth up to 1935, ceased to expand. The statistics of the number of exchanges and the number of subscribers are given below :

	Number of exchanges	Number of subscribers
December 31st, 1935 ..	343	233,554
December 31st, 1936 ..	333	250,978
December 31st, 1937 ..	331	255,236
December 31st, 1938 ..	325	256,294

And in another respect development ceased. The British Insulated Cables Ltd., which had been financing Mr. Eckersley's work on the use of the electricity mains, decided, in view of the Government's decision, not to proceed any further. But some work was continued by Mr. Eckersley, in collaboration with certain other sponsors. [46]

In December, 1937, the Assistant Postmaster-General, Sir Walter Womersley, announced in the House of Commons that the Post Office had decided to set up an experimental relay exchange in Southampton. The service was to start in the late summer or autumn of 1938. The distribution of the programmes was not to be by overhead wires but by cables. Subscribers were to have the choice of several programmes and Sir Walter Womersley added : " I am in consultation with the British Broadcasting Corporation concerning the arrangements for their selection." The total cost of the Southampton scheme was estimated at £200,000. [47] The Southampton Works Committee had indicated to the Post Office that they would be willing to allow a relay exchange to be established. But when the matter came up before the main council (the permission of the council, as the highway authority, was required), permission was refused by 34 votes to 23. The defeat of the proposal was apparently due largely to the opposition of the radio trade. [48] One result of this check appears to have been to turn the attention of the Post Office to the possibilities of using the electricity mains or the telephone system.

In the meantime, opposition from the radio trade, no doubt encouraged by its success at Southampton, continued to be active. Towards the end of 1938 the Radio Manufacturers' Association issued a pamphlet, " The Case against a Post Office Radio Relay Exchange System." They argued that Government competition with the radio trade would be unfair and unwise. [49] In this campaign the radio trade was assisted by the existing relay exchanges. Mr. J. W. C. Robinson, a prominent relay exchange operator, stated that they had been able to bury their differences and " work together in close co-operation to oppose the nationalisation of Relay Services." [50]

On March 30th, 1939, in answer to a Parliamentary Question, the Postmaster-General, Major Tryon made an announcement of Government policy in relation to the relay exchanges. He said that, as a result of the Post Office's investigations, it had been decided that there was scope for the provision of services by two systems—the first by the relay exchange companies and the second by the Post Office. The Post Office service was to be over the telephone wires for use in connection with a radio receiving set. [51]

It would give a choice of three or four programmes and it would be possible to use the telephone at the same time that broadcast programmes were being received. The Government had decided that both these systems should be developed. The licences of the operators of relay exchanges were to be extended for an additional ten years, that is, to December 31st, 1949, subject to certain modifications of the licence terms. These related to programmes and to the control of the exchanges in time of emergency. It was hoped that the Post Office service would be started in a few districts in 1939 and that it would be extended later. At the outset, the service was to be restricted to telephone subscribers ; but later, if experience warranted it, it was hoped that it would be extended to non-telephone subscribers. It was made clear by the Postmaster-General that a dominant consideration leading to the decision was the value of the relay exchange for communication in time of war.

A debate on the decision, which was opposed by the Labour Party, followed.[52] In this debate the decision to extend the licences for another ten years was denounced. " It is a ramp. It is a surrender to the clamant voice of private enterprise " was the view of one Labour member. Mr. Lees-Smith repeated the arguments which he had used three years before in favour of the relay exchanges being transferred to the Post Office. But the main interest of the debate from the point of view of this study lies in the speeches of the Postmaster-General. He emphasised that it was desired to extend the wire broadcasting system " for defence purposes." They were therefore " proposing to call in both the resources of the relay companies and the Post Office." The Post Office alone could not do what was required, since, as Major Tryon explained, "the work of the Post Office is very heavy at the present time." The aim of the ten-year licence was " to encourage development." And after referring to the fact that local authorities had often refused to grant wayleaves, the Postmaster-General said : " I express the hope that these local authorities will bear the question of Defence in mind when they get applications from relay companies." The alterations in the provisions regarding the programmes which could be distributed were as follows :

(1) New services were to be required to distribute two programmes.

(2) Existing one-programme services would be required to distribute a B.B.C. programme for 90 per cent. of the total time.

(3) Two-programme services would be required to distribute one B.B.C. programme and 75 per cent. of the total time on the other programme was to consist of B.B.C. transmissions.

(4) In the case of services which distributed more than two programmes, two of these were to consist of B.B.C. transmissions. These new provisions did not encounter any criticism in the debate. They were, indeed, probably intended to forestall criticism.

The development of the relay exchanges which the Government's policy had been intended to promote was brought to an end by the war. The Post Office had been planning to introduce its relay system, using the telephone wires, in London, Birmingham, Manchester and Edinburgh[53] but these projects were abandoned.[54] Discussions took place just prior to and in the early part of the war between the Electricity Commission and associations representing the electricity supply industry with a view to preparing a clause which would remove the legal prohibition on the transmission of programmes through the electricity mains. But the matter was not brought to any conclusion and was left in abeyance.[55] Few new concessions had been granted by local authorities to relay exchange operators and in 1940, the Post Office forbade the setting up of new exchanges. But they were permitted, so far as the supply of materials and labour allowed, to extend in the areas in which they were already operating. In fact, a very considerable increase in the number of subscribers occurred during the war years, " largely because of the difficulties of direct wireless reception in many districts under war conditions ; the scarcity of domestic receiving sets, components and batteries ; and the shortage of servicing electricians." [56]

	Number of exchanges	Number of subscribers
December 31st, 1939	284	270,596
December 31st, 1940	284	297,691
December 31st, 1941	278	369,420
December 31st, 1942	277	435,073
December 31st, 1943	275	494,559
December 31st, 1944	274	551,703
December 31st, 1945	274	634,474
December 31st, 1946	283	714,505
December 31st, 1947	297	793,582
December 31st, 1948	314	865,539

Note.—The figures in this table for the number of relay exchanges exclude secondary or standby stations and are not comparable with those shown earlier in this chapter, which include these stations.

After the war, in October, 1945, permission was again given for new relay exchanges to be established and the number of exchanges began to grow.   In the *White Paper on Broadcasting Policy*, issued in July, 1946, it was stated that the Government had deferred a decision on the future of wire broadcasting " pending a further review nearer the date on which the licences held by the relay exchange proprietors are terminable." [57]

7. The consequences of the monopoly of broadcasting

What has been the effect on the development of wire broadcasting in Great Britain of the fact that broadcasting has been organised on a monopolistic basis ?   Such a question cannot, of course, be settled in a completely scientific manner.   The answer must to some extent be a matter of judgment since it involves a conjecture of what would have happened had matters been arranged differently.   None the less, I believe that there are certain conclusions which can be drawn from a study of the history of wire broadcasting in Great Britain.

There can be little doubt, in my view, that the development of wire broadcasting in Great Britain has been seriously restricted as a result of the existence of a monopoly of broadcasting.   This does not imply that, had there been a number of independent broadcasting systems in Great Britain, these would not have attempted to obstruct the development of a competitive system.   It is probable, if there had been independent broadcasting systems, that an Association of Broadcasting Systems would have been formed and that this would have exerted such political influence as it possessed to prevent any grant of powers which would have facilitated the growth of wire broadcasting.   There are enough examples of similar action in this chapter to create a presumption that this would have happened.   But it must also, I think, be admitted that no such Association could have had the influence in official circles or among the general public which was possessed by a public authority such as the British Broadcasting Corporation, the policy of which was designed to serve the national interest. But this is not all.   The Corporation, which used such influence as it had to prevent the development of independent wire broadcasting, had one powerful argument which could not have been used by any Association of independent broadcasting systems. This was the doctrine of the "programme monopoly."

This doctrine did not, of course, play any part in the events which led up to the establishment of broadcasting in Great Britain as a monopoly. It came later—and was evolved by Mr. Reith. As we have seen in chapter 3, he argued that, quite apart from technical considerations, broadcasting should be organised as a monopoly on ethical grounds. Only by means of a monopoly could the right standards be maintained in the programmes broadcast. This argument has been of the greatest importance in forming opinion on the monopoly. Indeed, it has come to be regarded by many as the main justification for the monopoly of broadcasting in Great Britain. The development of any independent system for distributing programmes, such as wire broadcasting, was bound to be considered as a threat to the "programme monopoly" of the British Broadcasting Corporation. The relay exchanges were in a position to spoil the balance of the Corporation's programmes. We have seen that the Corporation considered that there was a danger in the development of wire broadcasting that each exchange "might increase to the stature of a B.B.C. in miniature." The Post Office appears to have been sympathetic to this point of view. Certainly this argument convinced the Ullswater Committee (on which members of all political parties were represented) and it was repeated in Parliament and Press. Many examples were given in section 5 of this chapter. But perhaps the most concise expression of this point of view was that contained in a leading article in *The Times* with the contemptuous heading "The Middlemen," printed the day after the first debate in the House of Commons. This ran as follows : "What is certain about the relay system is that, under present conditions, it will spread both widely and rapidly among the poorer classes of the population ; and this country will not for long be able to congratulate itself on a broadcasting system under which, while broadcasting is controlled with enlightenment and impartiality by a responsible public corporation, the listening is controlled by Tom, Dick and Harry."

There certainly can be no dispute that a series of steps were taken which prevented the relay exchanges from injuring the "programme monopoly" of the British Broadcasting Corporation. The first was taken very early—in April, 1930. In the standard licence which was introduced by the Post Office at that date, the

relay exchanges were prohibited from originating their own programmes. This, of course, removed the major threat to the
" programme monopoly " of the Corporation.* Other steps which
were taken later were merely designed to restrict the choice of the
relay exchanges in deciding which broadcast programmes to distribute, in particular, by reducing the proportion of programmes
which could be distributed which did not originate with the British
Broadcasting Corporation. Finally, the desire of the Post Office
to meet the Corporation's objection to wire broadcasting was
probably one element in the decision to impose conditions, such
as the compulsory purchase terms, which would tend to discourage
the expansion of the relay exchanges.

It is my view that the fact that broadcasting was organised
in Great Britain as a monopoly and the arguments by which this
monopoly was supported resulted in restrictions being placed on
the development of a competitive system, wire broadcasting. This
in itself is of great interest to the student of social institutions.
But it may also be of more direct practical importance. It has
been suggested, notably by Mr. P. P. Eckersley, that the future of
broadcasting lies with the distribution of the programmes by wire
rather than by radio waves. The difficulty with radio is the limitation of wavelengths, which means that only a small number of
different programmes can be broadcast without causing interference.[58] With the use of wires this difficulty is overcome. It
would then be possible, so Mr. Eckersley has argued, to distribute
a large number of different programmes simultaneously. It would,
of course, have been possible to introduce wire broadcasting before
radio broadcasting (and on a small scale this had been done) [59] but
until radio broadcasting had shown what a large audience there was
for broadcast programmes, it is not surprising that its potentialities
were not realised. It is unnecessary to consider whether this picture
of the broadcasting system of the future is well-founded or
not. All that is relevant here is that the monopolistic organisation
of broadcasting in Great Britain has made it more difficult of
fulfilment.

* Compare the statement of Sir Allan Powell, Chairman of the Board of Governors
of the Corporation, at the Annual Luncheon of the Relay Services Association, that
" The B.B.C. supported the view, as they were bound to do by the Charter, that they
must retain the monopoly of originating programmes." See the *Relay Association Journal*,
October 1943, p. 1365. I have been unable to discover a provision either in the Charter
of 1926 or that of 1936 which would bear this interpretation.

NOTES ON CHAPTER 4

[1] I am greatly indebted to Mr. Maton for information on which the great part of this section is based.

[2] This was not, of course, the first occasion on which programmes were distributed by wire. This had been done, among others, by the Electrophone Company. See note [59] below.

[3] For contemporary accounts of Mr. Maton's relay exchange and the problems it raised, see the *Daily Mail* for August 4th and 5th, 1926, and the *Daily Mirror* for August 5th, 1926.

[4] These exchanges were situated in Brighton (Sussex), Chadwell Heath (Essex), Colchester (Essex), Conisborough (Yorkshire), Frinton-on-Sea (Essex), Hoddesdon (Hertfordshire), Hythe (Hampshire), Lytham St. Annes (Lancashire), Newport (Pembrokeshire) and Southsea (Hampshire).

[5] New exchanges were established in Barrowford (Lancashire), Blackpool (Lancashire), Braintree (Essex), Burnley (Lancashire), Clacton-on-Sea (Essex), Copnor (Hampshire), Eastleigh (Hampshire), Fawley (Hampshire), Leicester (Leicestershire), London, Padiham (Lancashire), Ramsgate (Kent), Smethwick (Staffordshire) and Thetford (Norfolk). The Colchester exchange was discontinued in December 1927.

[6] These statistics and details of the early relay exchanges were made available to me by the Post Office.

[7] See *The Power Behind the Microphone*, p. 207. Mr. Eckersley gives the date as " about 1925-1926." I myself think the date was probably earlier. First, 1925-1926 was the period in which it was fairly clear to those concerned with broadcasting that the constitution of the broadcasting authority was almost certain to change and that the important rôle of the radio trade in the control of the broadcasting service was about to end. It was a most unsuitable moment for considering such a fundamental change in policy—and it seems difficult to believe that Mr. Eckersley would have brought it forward at that time. But there is a second and more important reason for thinking that Mr. Eckersley's idea dates from an earlier period. Mr. C. A. Lewis, in his book *Broadcasting from Within*, published in 1924, refers to the possibility of wire broadcasting (p. 135), and he would almost certainly have taken this idea from (or discussed it with) Mr. Eckersley. At that time Mr. Lewis was Deputy Director of Programmes and Mr. Eckersley was Chief Engineer of the British Broadcasting Company.

[8] *Op. cit.*, p. 208.

[9] *Op. cit.*, p. 214.

[10] *Op. cit.*, p. 214.

[11] The Post Office kindly made an early licence form available to me.

[12] " Exceptionally applications have been granted in a number of cases to use a microphone for emergency purposes, such as to explain a dislocation of the service through technical fault, and very occasionally in connection with opening ceremonies, but in no other circumstances." See a letter from the Postmaster-General quoted in the *Relay Association Journal*, November 1937, p. 154. Compare also the statement of the Postmaster-General : " It has been the practice to refuse all requests for permission to distribute local announcements through the local relay exchanges in normal times." See Parliamentary Debates, House of Commons, June 16th, 1939. There was some relaxation of this rule during the war, for example, to allow A.R.P. announcements to be made. But permission to use a relay exchange for a Salvage Drive appeal was refused. See the *Relay Association Journal*, December 1941, p. 1029. In February 1948, however, the Post Office informed relay operators that there would be no objection to their making a daily announcement of the foreign programmes they were going to relay provided that they did not interrupt any of the programmes of the British Broadcasting Corporation in order to do so.

[13] Compare Eckersley, *op. cit.*, p. 216.

[14] *Op. cit.*, p. 215.

[15] See an example given by Eckersley, *op. cit.*, pp. 217-218.

[16] For examples, see the *Southern Daily Echo*, February 12th, 1931 ; the *Nottingham Evening Post*, September 8th, 1931 ; the *Northampton Chronicle and Echo*, August 1st, 1933. There are many instances to be found in the *Radio Relay Review* and the *Relay Association Journal*.

[17] See the *Daily Telegraph*, June 15th, 1935. For examples of the hostility of the Press to the relay exchanges, see the *Advertisers' Weekly*, December 22nd, 1932, and the *Newsagent and Booksellers Review and Stationers Gazette*, December 31st, 1932.

[18] See the *B.B.C. Yearbook* for 1933, p. 71.

[19] See the *Radio Relay Review*, April 1933, p. 3.

[20] These restrictions were reported in the *B.B.C. Yearbook* for 1933 and were referred to in a reply to a Parliamentary question by the Postmaster-General on March 20th, 1933.

[21] This is based on the *B.B.C. Yearbook* for 1933. But in view of the Postmaster-General's statement that " programmes are available to listeners without prohibition in respect of particular stations " (see Parliamentary Debates, House of Commons, March 20th, 1933), it is possible that the original prohibition was in the form of Clause 11 of the existing licence.

[22] *B.B.C. Yearbook* for 1933, p. 71.

[23] See the statement of Mr. (later Sir Wavell) Wakefield, Parliamentary Debates, House of Commons, April 29th, 1936. It is referred to in an answer to a Parliamentary question by the Postmaster-General on April 1st, 1935.

[24] *B.B.C. Yearbook* for 1933, p. 71.

[25] This account is based on Eckersley, *op. cit.*, pp. 218-223.

[26] It should be noted that it is not the use of the mains as such but the carrier system (which has to be employed to make it possible to use the mains) which enables several programmes to be distributed without a multiplicity of special pairs of wires. A relay service using the carrier system, which enables several programmes to be transmitted through one pair of wires, was started in Rugby in November 1946.

[27] This account of the legal position is based on Will's *Law Relating to Electricity Supply*, pp. 101-103.

[28] See Eckersley, *op. cit.*, p. 224.

[29] See Parliamentary Debates, House of Lords, March 30th, 1933, and House of Commons, July 3rd, 1933.

[30] See the *Radio Relay Review* for July 1934, p. 4, and Eckersley, *op. cit.*, p. 225.

[31] See the *Radio Relay Review* for August 1934, p. 4.

[32] Cmd. 5091 (1936). The section of the report dealing with the relay exchanges is contained in paragraphs 130 to 136.

[33] This was followed in the Report by the sentence : " The considerations on which we base these conclusions are, in brief, those which have led to the establishment of the postal, telegraph, and telephone services, and, indeed, the broadcasting service itself, as unified national undertakings in public ownership and control." It is not easy to interpret this sentence. The assumption that the same considerations led to the establishment of the State monopoly in the postal services in the beginning of the 17th century, in the telegraphs shortly after the middle of the 19th century, in the telephone at the beginning of the 20th century, in broadcasting later in the 20th century, and to the proposal to transfer the relay exchanges to the Post Office implies a simplified view of the character of these events the nature of which I am unable to infer. The reasons which led to the State monopoly of the postal services have been described by Mr. H. Joyce : " However it may have been in after years, the original object of the monopoly, the object avowed indeed and proclaimed, was that the State might possess the means of detecting and defeating conspiracies against itself. A system such as this object implies is absolutely abhorrent to our present notions " ;—Mr. Joyce was writing in 1893—" and yet it is a fact beyond all question that the posts in their infancy were regarded and largely employed as an instrument of policy. It was not until the reign of William the Third that they began to assume their present shape of a mere channel for the transmission of letters." See his *History of the Post Office to 1836*, p. 7. Compare

also Hemmeon, *History of the Post Office*, pp. 189-201. The main impetus to the State operation (and later monopoly) of the telegraphs was given by Mr. Scudamore's report, which enumerated many reasons for State operation, but included the arguments that private companies served only certain areas of the country and that their competition was wasteful, see Hemmeon, *op. cit.*, pp. 202-208. The events which led to State operation of the telephone are rather complicated and do not lend themselves to summary treatment, although the fact that the Post Office already operated the telegraphs played its part. See Hemmeon, *op. cit.*, pp. 219-236, and A. N. Holcombe, " The Telephone in Great Britain," *Quarterly Journal of Economics*, 1906-7. The events which led to the formation of the British Broadcasting Corporation have, of course, been set out in the first three chapters of this book.

[34] See pp. 52-53.

[35] See paragraph 136 of the Ullswater Committee Report.

[36] See *Observations by the Board of Governors of the B.B.C. on the Report of the Broadcasting Committee, 1936*. The fact that the Corporation were able to issue a statement on the report on the day it was issued was adversely commented on in Parliament. See Parliamentary Debates, House of Commons, April 29th, the speeches of Mr. Moore Brabazon (later Lord Brabazon) and Mr. Clement Davies.

[37] See Parliamentary Debates, House of Commons, April 29th, 1936.

[38] This proposal was included in a statement issued by the Relay Services Association of Great Britain, see *The Times*, April 29th, 1936. It had also appeared, as we have seen, in Lord Selsdon's note of reservation.

[39] *Op. cit.*, pp. 230-231.

[40] Support for the recommendations of the Ullswater Committee was expressed in *The Times*, the *Daily Telegraph*, the *Daily Mail*, the *Glasgow Herald* of April 30th, and the *Observer* of May 3rd, 1936. Qualified approval was expressed in the *Manchester Guardian*, the *Birmingham Post* and the *Scotsman* of April 30th, 1936.

[41] See the *Memorandum by the Postmaster-General on the Report of the Broadcasting Committee 1935* (Cmd. 5207, 1936), pp. 7-9.

[42] See p. 8 of the Memorandum.

[43] See Parliamentary Debates, House of Commons, July 6th, 1936.

[44] See the *Relay Association Journal*, May 1937, p. 1.

[45] For statements expressing the point of view of the relay exchange operators, see the *Relay Association Journal* for March 1937, p. 246, and November 1937, p. 154.

[46] See Eckersley, *op. cit.*, pp. 231-232.

[47] See Parliamentary Debates, House of Commons, December 23rd, 1937.

[48] See the *Hampshire Advertiser and Southampton Times*, February 19th, 1938, and *The Times* and the *Daily Telegraph* for February 17th, 1938.

[49] Other associations which opposed the Government's proposals were the Wireless Retailers' Association, the National Association of Radio Retailers and the Electrical Contractors' Association. See the *Relay Association Journal*, November 1938, p. 405.

[50] See the *Relay Association Journal*, May 1939, p. 512. None the less, the alliance must have been somewhat uneasy. The annual report of the Radio Manufacturers' Association, issued on January 12th, 1940, referred to a conference with the Relay Services Association to explore common action against Government competition. But it also referred to the formation of a sub-committee " to consider what steps should be taken to develop sales of radio as against relay, and to hinder the introduction of relay services into new areas."

[51] This feature appears to have given satisfaction to the radio trade. See the *Wireless World*, May 1939, p. 455.

[52] See Parliamentary Debates, House of Commons, June 16th, 1939.

[53] See the *Relay Association Journal* for November 1939, p. 642.

[54] See the *White Paper on Broadcasting Policy* (Cmd. 6852, 1946), p. 27.

[55] Information furnished by the Electricity Commission.

[56] *White Paper on Broadcasting Policy*, p. 27.

[57] P. 27.

[58] See Eckersley, *op. cit.*, pp. 195-208. Compare also Dr. T. Walmsley, " Wire broadcasting investigations at audio and carrier frequencies," *Journal of the Institution of Electrical Engineers*, September 1940.

[59] See Paul Adorian, " Wire Broadcasting," *Journal of the Royal Society of Arts*, May 23rd, 1945. Mr. Adorian gives a number of early examples. In Antwerp in 1880, by means of a wire connection, concerts given in one café were listened to in another café two miles away. A later example is furnished by the work in London of the Electrophone Company, the activities of which started about 1894. This Company connected telephone subscribers to some thirty theatres and churches, from which they could hear the performances or services. By 1906 the number of subscribers did not exceed 600. A similar service was started in Budapest. In this case " in addition to connections to various theatres, particularly the Opera House, a certain amount of special programme material was originated in the Company's studios and this was interspersed with frequent news bulletins." The number of subscribers reached between 4,000 and 5,000 in the first ten or twelve years.

CHAPTER FIVE

FOREIGN COMMERCIAL BROADCASTING

1. THE DEVELOPMENT OF FOREIGN COMMERCIAL BROADCASTING

ON the continent of Europe many broadcasting stations were financed by means of revenue obtained from advertisements. This made it possible for programmes to be transmitted from continental stations which were designed for British listeners and were sponsored by British firms. The first of such programmes appears to have been a fashion talk broadcast from the Eiffel Tower station in Paris in 1925 and sponsored by Selfridges. The response was small; only three listeners wrote to say that they had heard the programme. [1] The only programmes of a similar character during the next few years to which I have been able to discover a reference were broadcast from Hilversum in Holland and were sponsored by Kolster Brandes Ltd., a company manufacturing radio equipment. [2] It may be that there were others, but I have not been able to find any record of them, and if there were any the number must have been small.

It was in the 'thirties that foreign commercial broadcasting intended for listeners in Great Britain began to develop on a considerable scale. This movement was facilitated by the formation in March, 1930, of the International Broadcasting Company Ltd. This Company, which arranged for the broadcasting of programmes sponsored by British firms, was founded by Captain L. F. Plugge, who had earlier been responsible for arranging the Selfridges broadcast from the Eiffel Tower in 1925. In 1930, programmes sponsored by a gramophone record company were broadcast from Radio Toulouse. In 1931, most of the other gramophone record companies sponsored programmes which were broadcast from Radio Paris. [3] In 1932, the number of firms sponsoring foreign broadcasts, although still small, had grown considerably. The names of some 21 British firms which were stated to be sponsoring programmes from foreign stations were published at the end of 1932. [4] They included firms engaged in cigarette manufacture, food distribution, shipping, gramophone record manufacture, radio manufacture, the film industry, motor car distribution and retail distribution. From 1933, sponsored programmes began to increase rapidly in number. In 1934, the amount spent on radio advertising by British firms was probably in the neighbourhood of £200,000.[5] It has been estimated that in 1935 it was about £400,000. And in 1938, the total expenditure by British firms has been estimated to have been about £1,700,000.[6] Some 298 firms[7] were sponsoring programmes and the products advertised covered a very wide range.[8]

A large number of foreign broadcasting stations have at one time or another been used to broadcast sponsored programmes intended for listeners in Great Britain.[9] The International Broadcasting Company itself made experiments with broadcasts from over twenty different stations. But the most important of the stations broadcasting sponsored programmes to listeners in Great Britain from all points of view—the number of hours of sponsored programmes, the expenditure on radio advertising and the number of listeners—were undoubtedly Radio Normandy and Radio Luxembourg. Radio Normandy was originally called Radio Fécamp, the change of name taking place in 1929. Its history starts with the formation in 1923 of the Radio Club of Fécamp with some sixteen members. In the next year, 1924, to stimulate interest in the activities of the club, a small transmitter was built. Its transmissions, although on low power, caused interest locally, and also in England, where it could be heard. Then the International Broadcasting Company decided to organise the broadcasting from this station of programmes sponsored by British firms.[10] Later a new transmitter was built at Louvetot in Normandy with studios in Caudebec-en-Caux from which broadcasting started at the end of 1938.[11] Radio Luxembourg entered the field later than Radio Normandy, after the purchase of Radio Paris by the French Government. In 1930, a limited liability company, the Compagnie Luxembourgoise de Radiodiffusion, obtained from the Luxembourg Government a twenty-five years' concession for the running of a broadcasting station in Luxembourg.[12] This Luxembourg company was controlled by a French company, the Société Française Radio-Electrique.[13] Radio Luxembourg started broadcasting in the spring of 1933. It used a long wavelength, 1,191 metres, although the wavelength allocated to Luxembourg under the Prague Plan was in the medium waveband, and was one of the most powerful stations in Europe. It was run as a commercial broadcasting station and it broadcast programmes in French, English and German.[14] The first transmissions in English were on June 4th, 1933.

The heavy expenditure by British firms on radio advertising implied a belief that the programmes broadcast from foreign commercial stations for British listeners had a large audience. Surveys carried out in 1938 by a Joint Committee of the Incorporated Society of British Advertisers and the Institute of Incorporated Practitioners in Advertising, with Professor (later Sir) Arnold Plant as independent chairman, showed that this was the case. Listening was heaviest on Sunday ; one half, perhaps more, of the listening to foreign commercial programmes occurred on that day, the great bulk while stations of the British Broadcasting Corporation were transmitting. The audience to some of the programmes ran into millions ; and the total amount of listening to foreign commercial programmes on Sunday was of the same order of magnitude as that to the stations of the Corporation. In the rest of the week about half the listening was to programmes broadcast when none of the Corporation's stations were transmitting. When the Corporation's stations were broadcasting on weekdays, in general only a small proportion of listeners tuned in to the foreign commercial programmes ; but absolutely the number was not small and some of the weekday programmes had quite large audiences.[15]

2. THE ATTITUDE OF THE PRESS

The attitude of the Press to foreign commercial broadcasting cannot be understood unless we have regard to its attitude to broadcasting in general. The Press has always been conscious that broadcasting and the Press were, or might be, competitive. The broadcasting of news, commentaries and talks might reduce the sales of newspapers and periodicals ; if broadcasting were financed by advertisements, the advertisement revenue of the Press might suffer. The Press was aware of the danger in the earliest days of broadcasting and was able to protect its interests even before the broadcasting scheme of 1922 was brought into existence.

Meetings were held with representatives of the Press,[16] and in the Licence which the Postmaster-General granted to the British Broadcasting Company it was laid down that the Company should

H

not broadcast news or information in the nature of news except such as had been obtained from certain named news agencies. There was a supplementary argreement between the Company and the representatives of the Press (not incorporated in the Post-master-General's Licence) by which the Company agreed that no news should be broadcast before 7 p.m. The British Broadcasting Company was thus limited in the source of its news, and consequently also in its amount, since it could only broadcast what the news agencies supplied. It was also limited in the times at which news could be broadcast.[17] Some of the implications of this agreement are of considerable interest. The British Broadcasting Company was not able to give running commentaries. The transmission was limited to what the microphones themselves could pick up without any commentator being allowed to explain what was happening. Similarly, eye-witness accounts could not be given in the evening if the account could still be considered as news or " information in the nature of news."[18]

The character of the Press attitude to broadcasting can be discovered from the evidence which the representatives of the Press have given to the various Committees on broadcasting. Evidence was given to the Sykes Committee in 1923 by Lord Riddell on behalf of the Newspaper Proprietors' Association.[19] He described the system then employed for the collection and dis-tribution of news by the news agencies and explained that it would be impracticable for the British Broadcasting Company to organise such an efficient news collection.[20] But he went on to say that the newspapers were opposed to the Company's undertaking the collec-tion of news. They also objected to the Company broadcasting racing results and other items which can be easily collected, " thereby skimming the cream off the news."[21] And it was made clear that they did not agree with the argument that broadcasting would stimulate interest and encourage the purchase of news-papers.[22] Lord Riddell defended the agreement which had been made with the British Broadcasting Company. He even argued that the newspapers had been " unduly liberal " in making such an arrangement. He stated that the newspapers " recognise that it is very difficult having made a false step to retrace it. If they were considering this matter *de novo* they would probably object *in toto* to the circulation of news ; but having exhibited this generous attitude of mind . . . we do not want to go back on that, and therefore we should be prepared to acquiesce in what is really—I am speaking quite seriously—a very serious, I will not say infringement of newspaper rights, but a very serious experiment the effect of which on the Press remains to be seen." [23] The limitation of the hours during which news could be broadcast was essential ; the broadcasting of important news throughout the day would deprive the newspapers of the element of surprise. [24] They objected to the broadcasting of speeches in Parliament and elsewhere which were of the nature of news, although they had less objection after 7 p.m. [25] Furthermore, the Newspaper Proprietors' Association would not agree to the exceptional distribution of the results of a few special events such as the Boat Race and the Derby. This would introduce the thin edge of the wedge. [26]

Lord Riddell also gave the views of the newspapers on the financing of the broadcasting service by means of revenue from advertisements. The newspapers considered that " the prohibition of the use of broadcasting for advertising purposes should be continued and strengthened. . . . It is difficult to imagine anything more dreadful than that day and night . . . the atmosphere should be filled with announcements of the merits of Beecham's or some other Pills. Of course, a flagrant case of this sort can easily be dealt with, but there are other classes of advertisements which cannot be so easily defined or identified. The Company might be prohibited from accepting a payment for advertisements but this would not cover the cases we have in view, namely indirect payment by private concerns, etc. Supposing, for example, a firm gave a concert every night. This would be a valuable advertisement for them if their name were mentioned in connection with it. The Press thinks that means should be devised to prevent this sort of thing." [27] They also objected to any method of advertising which involved referring listeners to a particular page of a newspaper. " Our view is that that would be undesirable ; that if traders wish to advertise they should confine themselves to the existing methods." [28]

The case of the Newspaper Proprietors' Association can be summarised in a phrase from the memorandum which they submitted to the Committee : " It is in the national interest that newspapers should be safeguarded against unfair competition from a monopoly given by the State." [29] Some members of the Committee raised the question of whether the newspapers were not attempting to hold up progress. Lord Riddell agreed that " what is for the good of the race is not always for the good of the individual immediately concerned." But he continued : " It is very hard to convince a man who is going to lose his living that it is to the national advantage that he should be sacrificed. So far as the newspapers are concerned, they are not prepared to be sacrificed. That is why they send me here to-day. They are not at all illiberal about this . . . but what we do say is, that while the future is important the present is also important, and you have to recognise existing facts as well as future possibilities." [30] And later, Lord Riddell said : " The newspapers consider that they perform a public service and it is generally recognised that they do ; that they are an essential part of the social fabric." [31] Evidence was also given by Sir Roderick Jones, Chairman of Reuters Ltd., and Sir James Owen, representing the Newspaper Society. [32] Their evidence did not add very much on the questions considered in this section to that given by Lord Riddell, although more stress was laid on the fact that broadcasting was organised as a monopoly.

Evidence of a similar character was given to the Crawford Committee in 1925, although it concentrated on the news aspect, presumably because it was felt that there was then little danger of broadcasting being financed by means of advertisements. [33] What the evidence was that the Press gave to the Ullswater Committee it is impossible to discover, but there is no reason to suppose that the point of view of the Press had altered. In January, 1945, a policy statement issued by the Newspaper Proprietors' Association set out the views of the Association as follows : " The members of the N.P.A. are opposed in principle to the introduction of any system of sponsored radio broadcasting in this country. They consider that it would be detrimental to the interests of the public as listeners, and that it is unnecessary from the point of view of advertisers, whose requirements can in normal conditions be fully and adequately met by the Press and the other existing media of publicity. Further, the diversion of a large proportion of advertising expenditure to radio might seriously hamper the Press in discharging its responsibilities to the public and especially in reestablishing its services on the pre-war scale and thereby re-absorbing and expanding its highly skilled labour force." [34]

This being the attitude of the Press to broadcasting in general, it is not difficult to deduce what the attitude of the Press would be to the advent of foreign commercial broadcasting. These stations would be free to broadcast news at any time, at any length and in any form. They would also be financed by revenue obtained from advertisements. Furthermore, in their presentation of talks, they might not adopt the impartial and unsensational method used by the British Broadcasting Corporation. They might indeed adopt a technique similar to that used by some of the newspapers themselves.

By the early 'thirties, the potentialities of foreign commercial broadcasting intended for listeners in Great Britain had become clear. On December 21st, 1932, a deputation representing the newspaper interests waited on the Postmaster-General. The immediate occasion for the deputation appears to have been the broadcasts (early in the morning) of a running commentary from Paris of the Test Match in Australia. One trade periodical commented : " . . . the shock to the industry this week may serve to dispel the apathy and indifference with which the subtle intrusion of wireless into its domain has hitherto been regarded by all sections of the trade." [35] And in its issue a week later the same journal again commented : " Our reference last week to the Paris broadcast in connection with the Test Match at Sydney and to the growing interference of Radio with the function of newspapers, has evidently created widespread interest. Every section of the trade appears to have been deeply stirred by the startling demonstration of the fact that Wireless is a free, unfettered force, fraught with dangers for the newspaper industry such as it has never encountered before. . . ." [36] In another trade paper it was reported that " The recent running commentary on the first Test Match broadcast by Preservene Soap and Gillette from Paris is said to have had a serious effect on the sales of the late special editions of the morning newspapers and early editions of the evenings." [37] The deputation which was appointed to wait upon the Postmaster-General was reported to consist of the Newspaper Proprietors' Association, the Newspaper Society, the Periodical, Trade Press and Weekly Newspaper Proprietors' Association, the News Agencies, the Institute of Journalists, the National Union of Journalists and the Federation of Retail Newsagents. [38] This deputation put before the Postmaster-General a scheme which would prevent broadcasts similar to those on the Test Match. It was that the Government should make representations to all stations outside Great Britain to the effect that they should only broadcast such news in the language of their own country. The reply of the Postmaster-General, Sir Kingsley Wood, was described as " profoundly disappointing." He said that he personally was unable to deal with the matter and suggested that " some kind of international understanding would have to be arrived at." [39] According to another account, the Postmaster-General suggested that the newspapers should set their own house in order—although whether he meant that newspapers should not advertise themselves on foreign stations, or whether he meant that newspapers should not accept advertisements containing announcements of sponsored programmes, or whether he meant both of these, is not clear. [40]

The action which the British Broadcasting Corporation took to offset the broadcasts from Paris, which was itself to broadcast commentaries on the Test Match, was hardly such as to be welcomed by the newspapers. A good summary of the point of view of the Press was contained in an article written at the time by Sir Robert Donald. He considered that the Postmaster-General " should have shown an intelligent sympathy with the newspaper men in their troubles . . . an attempt should be made to allocate the respective spheres of radio and the Press. There should be international agreements to prohibit the distribution of propaganda either in the form of news, descriptions, comments or advertisements ; and the selling of time to advertisers in other than the language of the country in which the station is situated." [41]

The Press did, however, take such steps as lay within its power to obstruct the development of foreign commercial broadcasting. In January, 1933, members of the Newspaper Proprietors' Association agreed that they would not make use of foreign stations for advertising or publicity purposes, and the Newspaper Society, which represents the provincial papers, endorsed this resolution. [42] The *Sunday Referee* which had been sponsoring programmes from Normandy and Paris continued to do so and in consequence ceased to be a member of the Association. [43] The *Sunday Referee* rejoined the Association in November, 1934, on giving up this form of publicity. [44] The Newspaper Proprietors' Association also agreed that announcements of radio broadcasts for advertising purposes should not be embodied in newspaper advertisements. [45] This policy would, of course, very much hamper the development of foreign commercial broadcasting. [46] And in the international sphere, we find that in 1934 at the Antwerp Press Conference,

Mr. F. Peaker, a member of the British Delegation (from the Institute of Journalists) made an appeal to the foreign Press in the following terms : " If in your several countries you could use the influence of the Press to kill advertising by radio, especially in foreign languages, it would be to the advantage of newspapers and newspaper men all over the world. . . ."[47]

It is not possible to discover what proposals were made by the Press about foreign commercial broadcasting to the Ullswater Committee. But their attitude in January, 1945, can be found in the statement issued by the Newspaper Proprietors' Association : " It is understood that various commercial interests are already negotiating for concessions for sponsored broadcasting from Luxembourg, Normandy and other Continental stations, as well as from Eire and even Iceland. It is said that there is a plan for broadcasting from ships outside the three-mile limit. It is also said that developments in short-wave radio will very soon enable American stations to broadcast direct to this country. If the British market is to become an open target for bombardment of this kind it is certain that British advertisers will demand the right to defend themselves and the choice will be either to allow British money and British talent to flow abroad, or to provide facilities for sponsored broadcasting in this country.

" There seem to be two possible means by which this threat might be met. The first is by international agreements designed to limit and control radio broadcasts from one country directed at the people of another country. We are of the opinion that such agreements are very desirable in the interest of international friendship and understanding, and we hope that the Government will take every possible step to promote them. The second means, which requires no further emphasis, is by having programmes in this country so good, and offering so wide a choice to the listener, that sponsored programmes from outside will not pay."

There is one other question which must be considered. How far has this consciousness of trade interest affected the editorial policy of newspapers—the leaders and the other articles which were written on the subject of broadcasting ? On this, without an intimate knowledge of the newspaper world, it is impossible to come to any definite conclusion. Not all journalists would be as frank as one radio critic, Mr. G. Allighan : " Every newspaper man should put his paper first. I personally either make no reference to these sporting broadcasts or reiterate that 'the printed word is superior to the spoken.' If we let the B.B.C. usurp the functions of the Press we'll all soon be out of jobs ! " [48] But, of course, not all journalists would agree with Mr. Allighan's attitude. On this question it is not possible to go beyond the statement that this consciousness of trade interest must have exerted some influence in determining the views of those who wrote in the newspapers.

3. OFFICIAL POLICY

Foreign commercial broadcasting which was intended for listeners in Great Britain was regarded with disfavour by the British Broadcasting Corporation and the Post Office. [49] The only remedy, however, which was open to the Government if they were to prevent foreign commercial broadcasting lay in the international field. And it was here that action was taken.

The first British move against foreign commercial broadcasting arose out of a technicality. Luxembourg had been allocated a wavelength of 223 metres according to the plan drawn up at Prague in 1929 by the International Broadcasting Union. But it was learnt in 1932 that Radio Luxembourg intended to broadcast on a long wavelength of about 1,200 metres. In the Conference of the International Telecommunications Union at Madrid in 1932 and later at the conference at Lucerne in 1933, which met to consider the problem of European broadcasting and to complete the work of the Madrid conference, the British Government protested against the Luxembourg action. [50] According to Mr. Tomlinson, who has made a detailed study of the proceedings of these conferences, " the British Government has not been as deeply concerned with the failure of Luxembourg to abide by the technical regulations as it has been by the commercial advertising broadcast in English by Radio Luxembourg." [51] In June, 1932, the Council of the International Broadcasting Union adopted a resolution condemning Radio Luxembourg for its use of a long wavelength and declaring that it could not admit the Compagnie Luxembourgoise de Radiodiffusion to membership or authorise collaboration with it if it continued to claim (and use) this wavelength. [52]

But the protests by the British authorities against Radio Luxembourg, if not inspired by, were at least based on a technicality.

In December, 1932, as we have seen in the previous section, the representatives of the Press had suggested in an interview with the Postmaster-General that the Government should ask all foreign stations to broadcast news only in their own language. But when the British authorities took action it had a wider objective. In May, 1933, on the initiative of the representatives of the British Broadcasting Corporation, the Council of the International Broadcasting Union adopted the two following resolutions :

1. " The Council . . .

" Having regard to the principles adopted by the Madrid Convention concerning the national character of broadcasting,

" Holds that the systematic diffusion of programmes or messages, which are specially intended for listeners in another country and which have been the object of a protest by the broadcasting organisation of that country, constitutes an ' inadmissible ' act from the point of view of good international relations,

" Calls upon the members of the U.I.R. to avoid such transmissions . . .

" Requests administrations which control broadcasting organisations not belonging to the U.I.R. to do what they can to induce such organisations to observe these principles of good international understanding. . . ."

2. " The Council decides

" (*a*) That the Union can have nothing to do with any development in the technical field of broadcasting which does not pay the most scrupulous attention to the rules established by international conventions.

" (*b*) That the Union cannot sympathise with any type of programme which is essentially based on the idea of commercial advertising in the international field.

" (*c*) That the transmission of international programmes by a national organisation, which has not been internationally recognised, might give rise to such serious difficulties and disturb the good understanding among nations so profoundly that the transmission of such programmes despite the absence of international recognition must be considered by the Union as an ' inadmissible ' development in European broadcasting."[53]

The explanation given by the International Bureau of Telegraphic Union when drawing the attention of the various Governments to these resolutions is of interest. The Bureau pointed out that commercial broadcasting was forbidden in some countries. Nothing, of course, could be done about the fact that commercial programmes designed for the home listener could often be heard in foreign countries. But " it appears more difficult to admit, from the point of view of law, or even of simple international courtesy, the broadcasting of commercial programmes, when this was done principally or even often solely, for listeners in foreign countries, in their own language, in order by this indirect violation of national laws, to give large profits to the organisers." [54] To the International Bureau of the Telegraphic Union, foreign commercial broadcasting appeared to be a modern form of smuggling.

Representations were made to the French Government and later to the Luxembourg Government, calling their attention to these resolutions of the International Broadcasting Union. [55] But these representations did not result in the prohibition by these Governments of the broadcasting of sponsored programmes designed for British listeners. The only way in which the Post Office could hinder these broadcasts was to refuse telephone facilities for the relaying of programmes from Great Britain. And this it did. In consequence, many of the programmes were recorded on gramophone records in Great Britain and were then taken to the Continent for broadcasting. [56]

The next international conference at which the matter could be raised was that held by the International Telecommunications Union at Cairo in 1938. The British Government then submitted the following proposal : " Because of the difficulty of allocating to the broadcasting service between 150 and 1,500 kc/s a sufficient number of waves to allow each country in the European region to assure a satisfactory national service, no wave of this band must be used by a country in this region for transmissions in the nature of commercial publicity sent in any other language but the national language or languages of that country." The British representatives pointed out that sponsored programmes in English were broadcast from two continental countries ; and that the practice might well spread to other countries. " It is therefore necessary to decide whether or not this practice is legitimate. The British Parliament and Press already are roused over this question, and the Post Office has even been requested to interfere with the stations in question." The British proposal was approved by the First Sub-Committee of the Technical Commission after a brief discussion. But the French

Delegation, the only one which would be particularly affected by the proposal, had been absent at the time it was discussed. At the next meeting of the Sub-Committee, " the French challenged the jurisdiction of the Committee as well as the substance of the adopted proposal. After a few heated exchanges between the Chief of the French Delegation and the British Chairman of the Sub-Committee, the matter was referred to the Technical Committee." Notwithstanding the name of the Committee, Mr. Tomlinson tells us that the discussions " ignored the technical aspects of the question and emphasised the political character of the question." When a vote was taken, it resulted in a tie with fifteen votes for and fifteen votes against. There were twenty-three abstentions. Although the proposal related only to the European region, the majority of the countries voting were non-European.[57] Thus ended the last attempt before the war by the British authorities to end foreign commercial broadcasting.

What was the justification of this policy? The first—and still the most complete—statement of the case for the suppression of foreign commercial broadcasts in English was contained in the report of the Ullswater Committee in 1935. The argument ran as follows : " It has been widely recognised that the practice of excluding advertisements from broadcast programmes in this country is to the advantage of listeners. In recent years, however, this policy has been contravened, and the purposes sought by the unified control of broadcasting have been infringed, by the transmission of advertisements in English from certain stations abroad, which are not subject to the influence of the British authorities except by way of international agreement and negotiation." The report then referred to the resolution, of May, 1933, of the International Broadcasting Union and continued : " We understand that the Post Office and the Foreign Office take all steps which are within their power with a view to preventing the broadcasting from foreign countries in English of programmes which include advertisements and to which objection has been taken. We approve this policy, but it is obvious that co-operation with all foreign countries is necessary to make the policy internationally effective."[58] Some more light was thrown on the reasons which led to this policy by the Postmaster-General, Major Tryon, in the debates which followed the publication of the Ullswater Committee's report. In the final speech of the first debate, Major Tryon said : " I have spoken so often on tariff questions in the

old days that I am tempted to point out that the present arrangement is something like Protection reversed.   I can understand
people who think there ought to be free competition between two
nations, and there are some, of whom I am one, who think some
advantage should be given to producers in the home country. The
present arrangement is the exact opposite, because the British
Broadcasting Corporation are forbidden to broadcast advertisements
but foreign stations can broadcast them, and they get money out of
England for broadcasting to our people.   I do not think that is
fair to the British Broadcasting Corporation." [59] And in the second
debate after the Ullswater Committee report, Major Tryon was
able to give " an example of the dangers that exist when powerful
foreign stations are in a position to broadcast in this country not
only advertisements but propaganda of foreign Governments and
politics."   The example which he gave concerned the Brightside
Divisional Labour Party which was " dissatisfied with the facilities
they get from the B.B.C." and had passed a resolution recommending
" that steps should be taken to hire one or two foreign wireless
stations, possibly a French station now that there is a Socialist
Government in France, with a view to our policy being consistently
conveyed to a much larger number of electors than is possible
with existing arrangements." [60] In the first debate, Mr. Lees-Smith
spoke in opposition to the foreign commercial broadcasts. His
main argument was that Radio Luxembourg was using a wavelength that had not been allocated to it ; but this was an argument
which could not be applied to all the foreign stations broadcasting
programmes sponsored by British firms.

Representations to the foreign Governments concerned were
still being made in 1938, but I have not been able to discover
any further statement of the reasons for the official policy. After
the war, the Labour Government indicated that its policy would
not be different from that of the pre-war Governments.   In an
answer to a Parliamentary Question, Mr. Herbert Morrison, Lord
President of the Council, said that it was the policy of the Government " to do everything they could to prevent the direction of
commercial broadcasting to this country from abroad, and to this
end they would use their influence as necessary with the authorities
concerned." [61] What were the reasons for continuing this policy ?
This was the subject of a Parliamentary Question by Mr. Wilson
Harris. He asked : " What were the grounds for the Government's

announced policy of preventing British listeners from hearing commercial radio programmes from abroad ? " Mr. Herbert Morrison replied : " This is a free country—and anyone can listen to what he likes, but the Government consider that on general grounds it is undesirable that wavelengths in foreign hands should be used for advertising campaigns directed at the British public." [62] This reply does not greatly advance our knowledge of the subject ; it tells us that there were grounds for the policy—and that they were general. Later, Mr. Morrison explained that foreign commercial broadcasting designed for British listeners " is not in accordance with British broadcasting policy." And, in the same debate, Mr. Morrison, referring to the programmes of Radio Luxembourg, said : " Quite frankly, this particular type of sheer naked exploitation, not of the highest order, is one which we do not like. We feel that if we can discourage it we should discourage it." [63]

Government policy towards foreign commercial broadcasting did not give rise to much comment in the Press. It is not possible to say that (outside Parliament) this policy met with approval. What can be said is that it met with little disapproval. With one exception I have not been able to discover any criticism of this policy of excluding foreign commercial broadcasts, apart from that coming from the manufacturers of products advertised on these stations,[64] those connected with organising the programmes[65] and the Incorporated Society of British Advertisers. In 1938, the Society issued a statement criticising the official policy towards foreign commercial broadcasting. Two sentences from this statement form a good summary of the argument : " Any curtailment of the present facilities for sponsored programmes in English will bring ruin to many British firms and cause unemployment and misery among several thousand British workers. Millions of listeners in Great Britain will be deprived of a gratuitous enjoyment they now obtain by choice and be compelled to bow to the monopoly at present held by the British Authorities in this country."

The exception to which I referred is to be found in a leading article in *The Spectator*. In this article it was stated " The B.B.C. is a monopoly, and however a monopoly functions, it is wise to have an alternative to it. For many listeners the programmes of foreign stations and of relay services provide such an alternative, and ' sponsored ' programmes are sometimes better than those even of the B.B.C. There is no good reason why the Government should decide that all possible steps should be taken to prevent ' the broadcasting from foreign stations of advertisement programmes intended for this country.' Why should people who like Luxembourg advertisements not listen to them ? There are moments when even the most devoted admirer of the B.B.C. would prefer Luxembourg to Broadcasting House. The evils of broadcast advertisement are not in the programmes but in other dangers it involves ; if we can have the programmes without the dangers, so much the better. It is a defect and not a merit in the B.B.C. that it is a monopoly, though there are compensating advantages ; the programmes of foreign stations, even though dependent on advertisements, provide a useful element of competition that is otherwise lacking." [66] But this should not be taken as more than an expression of individual opinion on a matter which excited, judging from published material, little public interest.

4. THE CONSEQUENCES OF THE MONOPOLY OF BROADCASTING

The assessment of the part played by the monopoly of broadcasting in the development of foreign commercial broadcasting and in the formation of Government policy in this field is bound to be subject to a margin of doubt. But I believe that it is possible to arrive at conclusions on this question in the truth of which one can be reasonably sure, just as one could in the case of wire broadcasting. The first conclusion which I draw is that the development of foreign commercial broadcasting was to a very considerable extent due to the fact that broadcasting in Great Britain was organised on a monopolistic basis. The second conclusion is that the monopoly was an important factor, perhaps the main factor, leading to a Government policy which had as its aim the suppression of foreign commercial broadcasting designed for listeners in Great Britain.

The programme policy of the British Broadcasting Corporation did not necessarily involve broadcasting what listeners wanted to hear—or what a large number of listeners wanted to hear. This was above all true of the Sunday programmes. But another important factor was that the Corporation did not transmit programmes at certain times, for example, in the early morning. It was this unwillingness or inability to cater for the wants of a large number of listeners which gave the foreign commercial stations their opportunity. In 1938, probably more than half the total listening to foreign commercial stations occurred on Sunday and about half of the remainder at times when the Corporation's stations were not broadcasting. Of course, listening to foreign commercial stations at other times, although it constituted a small proportion of listening at those times and a relatively small proportion of total listening to foreign commercial stations at all times, was, in terms of the absolute amount of listening, substantial. But it may be doubted whether these broadcasts in English from the foreign commercial stations would have developed to any significant extent had it not been for the core of demand furnished by Sunday and early morning listening. Of course, it might be objected that it is unjustified to ascribe the programme policy to the monopoly. A number of independent broadcasting systems might have had a programme policy similar to that of the British Broadcasting Corporation. This is true. But though it is possible it is also improbable. If there were a number of competing broadcasting systems it seems likely that at least one of them would have attempted to secure a larger audience by broadcasting the kind of programme listeners liked to hear.

What was the basis for the Government policy which aimed at the suppression of foreign commercial broadcasting in English ? First of all, we know that the British Broadcasting Corporation viewed these foreign commercial broadcasts with disfavour. This was to be expected given Sir John Reith's policy ; and he was Director-General of the Corporation until 1938. His policy was based on the view that a monopoly of broadcasting was " essential ethically, in order that one general policy may be maintained throughout the country and definite standards promulgated." Without a monopoly, standards would decline. This was, of course, the basis of the doctrine of the " programme monopoly " which was discussed in chapter 4 in connection with wire broadcasting. The foreign commercial stations threatened the " programme monopoly " of the Corporation in much the same way as had the relay exchanges. Or, in the words of the Ullswater Committee, " the purposes sought by the unified control of broadcasting have been infringed " by these broadcasts.

It has been suggested that since all owners of radio receiving sets in Great Britain had to take out a licence, and since a proportion of the licence fee went to the Corporation, it would have no objection to people listening to sponsored programmes, since the revenue of the Corporation would not suffer.[67] But so far as the Corporation was concerned this argument would appear to be beside the point. Those directing the policy of the Corporation were not influenced by the profit motive. They were not interested in the material welfare of the Corporation ; their interest was in the intellectual and ethical welfare of the listeners. The nature of the danger presented by the foreign commercial stations was clearly indicated by a statement made in 1933 by Mr. Charles Siepmann, Director of Talks in the British Broadcasting Corporation. He said : " Even after ten years, it is almost certain that a popular vote on the apportionment of time to this or that item in broadcast programmes would sweep away much, if not most, of what is most significant in the achievement of the B.B.C." [68]

Of course, it must not be assumed that independent broadcasting systems, particularly if they were financed by means of advertisements, would have viewed with equanimity the rise of a foreign competitor or that they would not have attempted to use the political influence they possessed to induce the Government to take action to hinder these broadcasts. It is more realistic to assume the contrary. But I would argue, as in the discussion of Government policy in relation to wire broadcasting, that a public authority acting in the national interest would be likely to carry more weight with the Government and that, in any case, no body representing independent broadcasting systems could have used the powerful argument of the " programme monopoly."

But can it be said that the objections of the British Broadcasting Corporation were the only grounds for the policy which sought to prevent broadcasting by the foreign commercial stations for British listeners ? It cannot easily be maintained that this was so. Another factor determining official policy towards the foreign commercial stations arose from the fact that they were financed by means of revenue from advertisements. The programmes of the British Broadcasting Corporation did not contain advertisements and it seems to have been thought that these foreign broadcasts, by their existence, contravened a British Government policy.

But it is not a simple matter to say what the policy was that was being contravened. It is first necessary to distinguish between direct advertising and a sponsored programme, that is, the free provision (other than by the performer) of a programme which is the subject of a broadcast acknowledgment.[69] Although direct advertising had been frowned upon from the early days, this attitude did not apply to sponsored programmes as here defined. At the time the foreign commercial broadcasts started to develop on a considerable scale (in the early 1930's), no Committee had decided that sponsored programmes ought not to be broadcast from stations in Great Britain. The Sykes Committee in 1923 disapproved of direct advertising, but stated quite definitely that sponsored programmes were allowable, although the revenue was to be regarded as a means of supplementing the income of the Company.[70] And in the revised form of licence issued following this Committee's report, the Company was allowed to broadcast sponsored programmes. In fact, some were broadcast in 1923, 1924 and 1925.[71] The Crawford Committee in 1925 did not pronounce on this question ; this was something which the proposed British Broadcasting Commission would have to consider.[72] And the Licence and Agreement of 1926 (when the Corporation was established) allowed sponsored programmes, although none appear ever to have been broadcast.[73] No doubt this was due to the growth in the number of licences which made it unnecessary for the Corporation to seek supplementary sources of income, or, more exactly, means of reducing expenditure. Until the end of 1936, when the new Licence and Agreement prohibited the broadcasting of sponsored programmes,[74] the legal position was that direct advertising was prohibited (except with the permission of the Postmaster-General) but that sponsored programmes (as I have defined them above) were allowed. It is true that no sponsored programmes were broadcast—but this was because the British Broadcasting Corporation preferred not to have them.

But these niceties in the legal position would not have weighed very heavily with Ministers. To them it appeared that the policy of excluding advertising was being contravened. What was considered to be so wrong about this ? Unfortunately there has never been a Government statement explaining the reasons for this attitude, and it is not easy to follow the arguments which have been put forward by politicians in justification of this policy and which were quoted in section 3 of this chapter. There can be little question that some would have considered it unfair to those providing advertising facilities in other media in Great Britain ; and in this connection the attitude of the Press was no doubt of great importance.[75] It is certain that some considered that these broadcasts would be " unfair to the B.B.C." This attitude is summed up

I

in the phrase which characterised them as " protection in reverse."
I myself believe that a general dislike for advertising played its
part, although it is not easy to assess its importance.

The arguments used to support the suppression of foreign
commercial broadcasting certainly do not all depend on the
existence of a monopoly of broadcasting in Great Britain. None
the less, there can be little doubt that the move to suppress these
broadcasts gained greatly in strength from the fact that there was a
monopoly of broadcasting in Great Britain. Arguments which
could not otherwise have been used became available and a
powerful public body, the British Broadcasting Corporation,
existed which could see that their force was not overlooked. It is
difficult to escape the conclusion that the monopoly was an important
factor leading to a Government policy which had as its aim the
suppression of foreign commercial broadcasting designed for listeners
in Great Britain.

NOTES ON CHAPTER 5

[1] See *This is the I.B.C.* (a booklet issued by the International Broadcasting Company),
p. 3.

[2] See *John Bull*, April 13th, 1929.

[3] See *This is the I.B.C.*, p. 3.

[4] See *Everyman*, December 17th, 1932.

[5] See *Shelf Appeal*, October 1935, and the *Economist*, February 8th, 1936.

[6] See Nicholas Kaldor and Rodney Silverman, *A Statistical Analysis of Advertising
Expenditure and the Revenue of the Press*, pp. 103-104.

[7] Information supplied by the Legion Information Services Ltd.

[8] See Kaldor and Silverman, *op. cit.*, pp. 134-135.

[9] Among the stations stated to be broadcasting sponsored programmes intended for
British listeners at some time were :—in France : Paris (Eiffel Tower), Paris (Poste
Parisien), Normandy, Lyons, Mediterranean, Toulouse, Juan-les-Pins and Rennes ;
in Ireland : Dublin and Athlone ; in Spain : Madrid ; in Holland : Hilversum ;
in Luxembourg : Radio Luxembourg.

[10] This account is based on R. Chevenier, " La naissance et l'histoire de Radio
Normandie," *L'Illustration*, June 17th, 1939. See also A. Huth, *Radiodiffusion, puissance
mondiale*, p. 110.

[11] See *This is the I.B.C.*, pp. 36-40.

[12] See A. Huth, *op. cit.*, p. 193.

[13] See John D. Tomlinson, *The International Control of Radiocommunications*, p. 208.

[14] See John D. Tomlinson, *op. cit.*, p. 209.

[15] See the *Survey of Listening to Sponsored Radio Programmes* by a Joint Committee of
the Incorporated Society of British Advertisers and the Institute of Incorporated Practitioners in Advertising. (Report on the March 1938 survey and Supplementary
Report on the November 1938 survey.)

[16] See the evidence of Sir William Noble to the Sykes Committee on May 8th, 1923,
question 395.

[17] In this early period there were two news bulletins. " The first bulletin is chiefly of interest to dwellers beyond the reach of evening papers. The second bulletin gives a brief summary of the first, and news which ' breaks ' after the former one. . . ." The two bulletins amounted to some 3,000 words. See J. C. W. Reith, *Broadcast over Britain*, p. 137.

[18] Compare J. C. W. Reith, *op. cit.*, pp. 139-140. The restrictions were gradually relaxed by agreement between the Corporation and the Press. And in the Royal Charter of 1926 all legal restrictions were removed. But the British Broadcasting Corporation did not introduce a regular news bulletin earlier than 6 p.m. until September 4th, 1939 (the outbreak of the war).

[19] See the Minutes of Evidence of the Sykes Committee, May 29th, 1923.

[20] See questions 1474-1476.

[21] See question 1477.

[22] See question 1478.

[23] See questions 1491-1492.

[24] See question 1478.

[25] See questions 1541-1551.

[26] See questions 1585-1593.

[27] See question 1500.

[28] See question 1518.

[29] See question 1583.

[30] See question 1578.

[31] See question 1584.

[32] See the Minutes of Evidence to the Sykes Committee for June 5th, 1923.

[33] Evidence was given to the Crawford Committee on December 17th, 1925, by Lord Riddell, representing the Newspaper Proprietors' Association ; by Sir James Owen, representing the Newspaper Society ; and by Mr. H. D. Robertson, representing the Scottish Newspaper Society.

[34] This statement was referred to by Mr. Herbert Morrison in the House of Commons. See Parliamentary Debates, House of Commons, July 25th, 1946.

[35] See the *Newsagent and Booksellers' Review*, December 10th, 1932.

[36] See the *Newsagent and Booksellers' Review*, December 17th, 1932.

[37] See the *Advertisers' Weekly*, December 22nd, 1932.

[38] See the *Newsagent and Booksellers' Review*, December 17th, 1932.

[39] See the *World's Press News*, December 29th, 1932. At this meeting, the newspapers also drew the attention of the Postmaster-General to the " menace " of the relay exchanges. See the *Advertisers' Weekly*, December 22nd, 1932.

[40] See the *Advertisers' Weekly*, February 23rd, 1933.

[41] See Robert Donald, " The Radio Revolution. The B.B.C., the P.M.G. and the Press," *Everyman*, January 14th, 1933.

[42] Information supplied by the Newspaper Proprietors' Association.

[43] See the *Advertisers' Weekly* for February 23rd, 1933. See also the *Sunday Referee* for February 26th and March 12th, 1933.

[44] See the *Sunday Referee* for August 16th, 1934, and the *Advertisers' Weekly* for November 8th, 1934.

[45] See the *Advertisers' Weekly*, May 4th, 1933. This later gave an opportunity for the *Daily Worker* to provide a " unique radio feature." It decided to publish the week-end programme of Radio Luxembourg. " No other daily newspaper in Britain gives the Luxembourg programme. The *Daily Worker* is now able to fill this gap." See the *Daily Worker*, November 29th, 1935.

[46] Compare the statement of Mr. Clifford J. Harrison, Publicity Manager for Horlicks Ltd. (a very large radio advertiser), in the *Advertisers' Weekly* for January 20th,

1944. ". . . the attitude of the British Press is the key to the situation. . . . All advertisers who used sponsored radio were handicapped by lack of means of announcing their programmes."

[47] See the *Newspaper World*, June 16th, 1934.

[48] See the *World's Press News*, June 29th, 1933.

[49] See the answer of the Postmaster-General, Sir Kingsley Wood, to a Parliamentary question. Parliamentary Debates, House of Commons, July 24th, 1933. See also P. P. Eckersley, *The Power Behind the Microphone*, p. 143.

[50] See John D. Tomlinson, *op. cit.*, pp. 159-160 and 208-209.

[51] See John D. Tomlinson, *op. cit.*, p. 224. Mr. Tomlinson is in no sense a supporter of the Luxembourg claims. He refers to the " specious technical and political arguments offered in support of its request " (p. 209) and states that it is " one of the most blatant cases of private commercial interests being supported by its government to the detriment of other countries, and European broadcasting in general " (footnote 4, p. 225).

[52] Information supplied by the British Broadcasting Corporation.

[53] Translation provided by the British Broadcasting Corporation.

[54] See the *Journal Télégraphique*, published by the Bureau International de l'Union Télégraphique, May 1933, p. 126.

[55] See answers to Parliamentary questions, Parliamentary Debates, House of Commons, July 24th, 1933, February 10th, 1936, July 6th, 1936, and March 3rd, 1937.

[56] See the *News Chronicle*, January 5th, 1938. See also P. P. Eckersley, *op. cit.*, p. 148.

[57] See John D. Tomlinson, *op. cit.*, pp. 224-225.

[58] See the report of the Ullswater Committee, pp. 34-35.

[59] See Parliamentary Debates, House of Commons, April 29th, 1936. A similar point of view was expressed in a letter to *The Times*, January 20th, 1932. Compare A. Morgan-Williams, *Points against radio advertising in any form* (March 1945), p. 12 : " If entry of goods is controlled, why should ideas that compete directly with our industries be imported free, simply because they are intangible and know no customs barriers ? "

[60] See Parliamentary Debates, House of Commons, July 6th, 1936.

[61] See Parliamentary Debates, House of Commons, April 30th, 1946.

[62] See Parliamentary Debates, House of Commons, July 10th, 1946.

[63] See Parliamentary Debates, House of Commons, July 16th, 1946. Mr. Morrison added that it would be a good use of Radio Luxembourg if it could broadcast to Germany and Austria on behalf of the British and French Governments. Later, Mr. Morrison indicated that negotiations were proceeding with the Luxembourg Government to obtain the use of Radio Luxembourg for this purpose. See Parliamentary Debates, House of Commons, July 29th, 1946. These negotiations do not appear to have been successful. A further indication of official policy towards foreign broadcasting (but not in this case necessarily commercial broadcasting) is furnished by Clause 37 (1) in the Representation of the People Act, 1948. This clause read : " No person shall, with intent to influence persons to give or refrain from giving their votes at a Parliamentary election, use, or aid, abet, counsel, or procure the use of, any wireless transmitting station outside the United Kingdom for the transmission of any matter having reference to the election otherwise than in pursuance of arrangements made with the British Broadcasting Corporation for it to be received and retransmitted by that Corporation." Some irritation with the Government's policy towards foreign commercial broadcasting was expressed in 1946. See, for example, the exchange between Mr. Morrison and Mr. Churchill, Parliamentary Debates, House of Commons, July 10th, 1946.

[64] See *The Times*, November 14th, 1935.

[65] See the speech of Captain F. L. Plugge, Parliamentary Debates, House of Commons, April 29th, 1936.

[66] See *The Spectator*, July 3rd, 1936. I should, perhaps, also mention an expression of mild disapproval by Eric Dunstan in *The Star* for March 17th, 1936.

[67] See the argument of Captain L. F. Plugge, who maintained that members " might consider that it would be a reasonable thing for the British Broadcasting Corporation to say : ' the listeners pay for our livelihood. We are the last body who would like to take something away from them which they are getting for nothing and which they enjoy. We want to give what we can and to see that they get as much as they can for their 10s.' " See Parliamentary Debates, House of Commons, April 29th, 1936.

[68] See the *Radio Times*, September 8th, 1933, p. 527.

[69] This definition is narrower than the one customarily used in the United States, since the broadcast is simply accompanied by an acknowledgment, without any other reference to the institution concerned, or its goods or services. But the definition given is the one relevant in a study of the early regulation of broadcasting in Great Britain.

[70] Since it does not appear to have been the intention that the broadcasting authority should charge for its facilities, the gain in revenue was indirect, through a fall in programme costs.

[71] See note [84] to Chapter 1 and note [34] to Chapter 2.

[72] See the report of the Crawford Committee, p. 14.

[73] See Clause 3 of the Licence and Agreement of 1926.

[74] See Clause 3 of the Licence and Agreement of 1936.

[75] Compare the statement of Mr. Herbert Morrison, after a reference to the memorandum issued by the Newspaper Proprietors' Association : " That is another contributing factor which does influence the minds of the Government, as we think the views of the newspapers are entitled to be taken into account." See Parliamentary Debates, House of Commons, July 16th, 1946.

PART III

PUBLIC DISCUSSION

CHAPTER SIX

PUBLIC DISCUSSION OF THE MONOPOLY, 1926—1936

1. INTRODUCTION

THE next two chapters consist of a survey of the views which have been expressed on the subject of the monopoly of broadcasting. Of course it has not been possible to make a complete survey. But use has been made of the large collection of Press cuttings made by the British Broadcasting Corporation and since this has been supplemented by additional research, the number of important references overlooked must be small. The relative amount of space given in this chapter to the different views in no way reflects the extent to which such views were held. An opinion widely expressed will certainly be noticed; but a viewpoint of great interest to be found in a single article might receive equal, or greater, attention.

This chapter will be concerned with the period 1926 to 1936. The next chapter will be concerned with the period 1937 to 1947.

2. SUPPORT FOR THE MONOPOLY

Apart from Mr. Reith's book, *Broadcast Over Britain,* which appeared in 1924 when the number of people interested in broadcasting policy was small, there has not been published, to my knowledge, any extended statement of the case for a monopoly of broadcasting in Great Britain.[1] None the less, the monopoly was strongly supported in public discussion. The arguments used in the Press and Parliament to defend the monopoly took three forms. The first was that British broadcasting was " the best in the world " ; and it was taken as axiomatic that the monopoly formed an essential feature of the British broadcasting system. This empirical argument, impressive though it was, had the weakness that it did not prove that there was not some other system which, if introduced in Great Britain, might be better. This weakness was not present in the second argument. This assumed that the only possible alternative to the British system was the American system ; and went on to assert that the American system achieved results which were very unsatisfactory. But for the individual who remained unconvinced by these two arguments there was the third. It was maintained that owing to the limitation in the number of wavelengths it was technically impossible (or undesirable) to have competing broadcasting systems in Great Britain. This was an *argument péremptoire* and could only be disputed by questioning the technical basis of the argument ; which very few had sufficient knowledge to do.

Let us consider these arguments in turn. The first was that the British Broadcasting system was " the best in the world." It was anticipated even in the early years that British broadcasting would be likely to occupy this position. Mr. C. A. Lewis, Deputy Director of Programmes in the British Broadcasting Company, writing in 1924, answered the question " Why was it that wireless telephony, whose possibilities were proved in late 1919 or early 1920, did not come into general use in the autumn of 1920, when things were just beginning to boom in America ? " in the following way : " The answer lies in a sentence, ' We are British.' Let others rush at the new inventions, and do the experimenting, spend the money, get the hard knocks, and buy their experience at a high price. We British sit tight and look before we leap. So it was in this case. We may often be behind in the early stages of a new science, but once under way we soon catch up and generally lead the field before long." [2] And later in his book, Mr. Lewis wrote : " Great Britain may now make a bid for the finest broadcasting system in the world. . . . The fact that we are also the first country in the world to solve the difficult problem of how broadcasting is to be paid for, gives us that financial backing on which all experiment and research must be based, and should enable us to establish a service which from all points of view should be second to none." [3] This was in 1924. In 1925, Lord Gainford, independent Chairman of the British Broadcasting Company, could say : " Authoritative and independent opinion is unanimous that the British broadcasting system is by a considerable margin the best in the world."[4] And in a memorandum to the Crawford Committee in 1925, submitted by the Wireless Association of Great Britain, it was stated : " It is an admitted fact that the British Broadcasting system is superior, both technically and in programme, to any other Broadcasting service in the world. . . ." In 1928, the Postmaster-General, Sir

William Mitchell-Thomson said in the House of Commons : " On the whole it can be said that we have established broadcasting in this country on a foundation which is not merely firm, but which is the envy of many other countries." [5] In 1935, Mr. Ivor Thomas, writing in the *Political Quarterly*, after a survey of the broadcasting systems of the world, came to the following conclusion : " When we consider what has happened in other lands, we may be eternally thankful that in this country broadcasting was from the start regarded as a public service, to be operated by a monopolistic institution, independent of direct Government control and existing only to serve the public, forbidden to indulge in commercial publicity and directed towards a high ideal. The B.B.C. is far from perfect. But . . . Britannia rules the ethereal waves." [6] In 1936, in the first debate in the House of Commons on the report of the Ullswater Committee, Mr. Clement Davies, a member of that Committee, said : " We were fortunate in hearing evidence from various countries, and were glad to know that other countries regarded our system on the whole as being the ideal system and the one which they desired now to copy and, in particular, it is the one, I understand, which the Dominions now desire." [7] And the Postmaster-General, Major Tryon, in opening the second debate following the Ullswater Committee's report, said : " Let those who criticise the B.B.C. look abroad and see what has happened under other systems and managements. I hope they will then be more ready to give credit where credit is due." [8]

It is possible for an institution to be " the best in the world " and yet capable of considerable improvement. But most supporters of the monopoly in Great Britain do not appear to have allowed even this possibility. They have tended to assume that the only alternatives to the British system were either to have a State-operated monopoly (which was ruled out on political grounds), or, if there were to be independent broadcasting systems, to organise the broadcasting service in the same way as in the United States. This was the choice put before Members of Parliament in 1929 by Sir William Mitchell-Thomson when he was Postmaster-General. [9] The same choice was put to Members very concisely by Sir Kingsley Wood, the Postmaster-General, in 1933 : " I put this final question. Is there any more promising alternative to our present British method as suitable and advantageous to this country ? There is the commercial system of America. Do we desire that ? There is direct

Government control. Is that advisable ? ''[10] And the same argument was repeated, at rather greater length, by a later Postmaster-General, Major Tryon, in 1936 : " There are only three things which you can do in this matter. You can have a broadcasting system conducted on purely commercial lines, as is the case in some other countries, where political parties buy so much time on the radio, where people holding the most extraordinary views buy time in which to advocate them, where advertisements are put on the radio and where the broadcasting, generally, is not, I think, on the high level of the B.B.C. programmes in this country. Alternatively, you can have the radio used as it is in some countries . . . where the people have to listen to what the Government tell them. Here we have the third method, which is something between the two and which is, I think, the right method." [11] This assumption that the only alternative to a monopoly is the American system comes out clearly in the report of the Crawford Committee, which was issued in 1926 : " It is agreed that the United States system of free and uncontrolled transmission and reception is unsuited to this country, and that Broadcasting must accordingly remain a monopoly—in other words that the whole organisation must be controlled by a single authority." [12]

There is no doubt that the unfavourable view generally taken of American broadcasting (which is identified with the commercial system) has been a potent factor leading to support for the monopoly. Early references to American broadcasting contrast the chaotic state of broadcasting in the United States with the order which prevailed in Great Britain. For example, in 1925, in the *Manchester Guardian*, the position is referred to in the following terms : " . . . it does seem we might congratulate ourselves for once on having in the matter of broadcasting, planned a new thing out pretty successfully from the beginning. The United States, the first large-scale experimenter in this entirely new form of public entertainment, managed to evolve a very considerable state of anarchy in the matter of distributing stations, and from that state America is even now unextricated." [13] There can be little doubt that it was this state of affairs that the *Economist* had in mind when it said in 1926 : " American experience has proved beyond a shadow of a doubt that broadcasting must be a monopoly." [14]

An interesting British view of American broadcasting in this early period was contained in a memorandum submitted by Mr.

Percy A. Scholes to the Crawford Committee. Mr. Scholes's memorandum was based on his observations during a lecture tour in the United States from September to early December, 1925. He wrote : " It might be thought that the existence of a spirit of competition between stations would produce a constantly rising standard in the type of programme and in the manner of performance but experience shows that this is not so. . . . Summing up my observations : (1) Broadcasting in the United States is at present in a state of chaos. (2) This appears to be the result of (a) the absence of any means of sound finance for Broadcasting Stations (b) the complete lack of unified control. Almost every American with whom I have discussed the subject, upon having our system explained to him, has admitted that it was far better than his own country's system—or, rather, complete lack of system." Mr. Scholes also explained that since the broadcasting stations had no direct revenue, " the musical performers and lecturers are, in almost every case, entirely unpaid." Performers were willing to broadcast because of the publicity. But because this motive " usually weakens after a certain number of unpaid performances," there is " a tendency towards a progressive decline in the standard of ability of artists available."

The early comment on the American system concentrated attention on the amount of interference which existed in the broadcasting service in the United States. But later, perhaps because the work of the Federal Radio Commission (set up in 1927), which allocated frequencies as between the various broadcasting stations, had led to a reduction in the amount of interference, it was the inferiority of the American programmes to those broadcast in Great Britain which attracted attention. Thus, in 1927, Mr. St. John Ervine wrote that his American friends had assured him that the British programmes were " neither surpassed nor matched by the American programmes."[15] In 1930, in the *Manchester Guardian*, in an article entitled " Poisoned Air," it was stated : " There are some things which we manage better than the Americans, and broadcasting is one of them . . . Some people over here have criticised the B.B.C. for lack of commercial enterprise. American experience suggests the danger of commercialising the air. It is worth while paying something to keep it clean." [16] And in 1931, Lord Crawford, who had been Chairman of the Committee the report of which led to the establishment of the British Broadcasting Corporation, could say of American broadcasting : " It is deplorable, it is grotesque, it is laughable, compared with the high state of efficiency here." [17] There is little reason to doubt that the following quotation from a leading article in *The Times* in 1934 represented the settled view of informed opinion in this period : " [profiting from experience in America] . . . it was wisely decided to entrust broadcasting in this country to a single organization with an independent monopoly and with public service as its primary motive. It is not perhaps too much to claim this decision as one further instance of the singularly skilful way in which the British race seems to manage its own affairs and to develop the art of government. Fears of the possible abuse of such a monopoly have proved largely groundless. . . ." [18]

The third argument used to support the monopoly of broadcasting in Great Britain was technical—that the limitation in the number of wavelengths made it necessary or desirable to have a monopoly. We have seen that certain statements made by the Postmaster-General, Mr. Kellaway, in 1922 might have created the impression that technical factors made a monopoly necessary and there were certainly some who believed this to be the case.[19] A similar conclusion, as we have seen in this section, was drawn from early American experience. In the debate which followed the report of the Crawford Committee in 1926, the Assistant Postmaster-General, Lord Wolmer, argued that a monopoly was essential for technical reasons. He explained that in " those countries where competition has been tried, the congestion in the ether has been found to be such that the programme of all listeners is interfered with—in other words, we have not yet arrived at a condition of affairs where the listeners can select their programmes with sufficient accuracy to enable that degree of competition to exist. That is the reason for monopoly." [20] This technical argument is of great significance, since if it is true, all other arguments are unnecessary. The part it played in the formation of opinion (and this was particularly important in the early days) was probably to create a feeling among those interested in broadcasting policy that a monopoly was inevitable and to silence those who were not or would not have been convinced by the other arguments for the monopoly. There is no evidence that it played a positive role in bringing about support for the monopoly ; so far as it had an effect, once the Corporation was established, it was to reinforce an opinion which was already made up on other grounds.

As was stated at the beginning of this section, the only extended statement of the case for a monopoly of broadcasting publicly available was that contained in the writings of Lord Reith. The form which support of the monopoly has taken in general discussion does not, of itself, imply assent to Lord Reith's views. It is possible to believe that the only alternative to the British system is the American and that the results it achieves are inferior to those of the British system without at the same time believing in the doctrine of the " programme monopoly." The fact that the American system involves listening to advertisements may be considered a sufficient disadvantage.

But there are good grounds for thinking that support for the British system and the opinion that it was " the best in the world," were based on reasoning similar to Lord Reith's, or, more probably, upon acceptance of the arguments which he had put forward. Statements in favour of the monopoly are often so short that it is not possible to be sure about the reasons which prompted them. But in those cases in which the reasons are given, the influence of Lord Reith is usually clear. The following quotation from an article by Mr. A. G. Gardiner is fairly typical : " It is one of the many advantages of the public ownership and control of the radio that certain standards have been maintained. We have kept out the advertiser of pills and corn-plasters and suchlike who holds the American radio in the hollow of his hand. . . . Let us be thankful for all this and set our faces like flint against any parcelling-out of the air for competitive services. . . ." [21] But a better reason for thinking that the general support for the British system was based on acceptance of Lord Reith's arguments can be found in the discussion on official policy towards wire broadcasting and foreign commercial broadcasting which was considered in chapters 4 and 5. Government policy in these cases was not determined by any technical difficulties but involved a straightforward application of Lord Reith's doctrine of the " programme monopoly "—and it met with general approval.

In this section I have confined my survey to the views expressed in the period of the first Charter of the British Broadcasting Corporation. The interest of this period is that support for the monopoly went almost unchallenged. In the debates on broadcasting policy in the House of Commons in 1933 and 1936, although there was criticism of certain of the policies of the British Broadcasting Corporation, the monopoly which it held was not questioned. When, at the end of this period, the Ullswater Committee was set up to consider broadcasting policy, it was able to report : " That the work of the B.B.C. has been widely approved may confidently be inferred from the remarkable absence of general criticism in the oral and written evidence which has been submitted to us." The Ullswater Committee added its own approval. It stated : " We feel that a great debt of gratitude is owed to the wisdom which founded the British Broadcasting Corporation in its present form, and to the prudence and idealism which have characterised its operations and enabled it to overcome the many difficulties which surround a novel and rapidly expanding public service." And later it was stated : " Our recommendations are directed towards the further strengthening and securing of the position which the broadcasting service in Great Britain has happily attained in the few years of its history." [22]

The Ullswater Committee expressed approval of the way in which British broadcasting was organised. But Lord Elton, a member of that Committee, has told us : " We examined almost every question except the great question, the fundamental question : Is a Government monopoly of broadcasting justified ? We went meticulously through detail after detail, but we took for granted the principle that there should be a Government monopoly in what is after all—whether intentionally or not—primarily a factory of opinion." [23] It is not an exaggeration to say that by 1936 the monopoly of broadcasting was accepted as a matter of course.

3. CRITICISM OF THE MONOPOLY

In the debate in the House of Commons on the proposal to establish the British Broadcasting Corporation, doubts were expressed by certain Liberals about the fact that it was a monopolistic organisation. Mr. E. A. Harvey maintained that " broadcasting is doing for the spoken word only what the printing press for four centuries has been doing for the written word, and no more. There is not a single argument that can be used in favour of the liberty of the Press that is not equally applicable to the liberty of the wireless." But, he added, " [we are told] it is impracticable here, because there are certain wavelengths, a limited range, and some of that range has to be given to the air service, and what is left is really the property of the nation, and it must be conserved. . . . If you have half a dozen companies all broadcasting, there will be jamming of waves and the whole thing will be chaos." He then commented : " Probably there is some truth in it ; but we find that in America, in Australia, and in the last two years in Canada, they do not find the clash of wavelengths to be an insuperable difficulty. There are competitive companies in all these countries struggling hard against each other." Mr. Harvey therefore proposed that there should be some temporary arrangement for another twelve months and " then it will be possible for us to set up in this country—as has been done in America, Australia and Canada—competitive broadcasting institutions. When we have done that we shall be on the road of real progress, and not until then. . . ."

Similar doubts were also expressed by Mr. L. Hore-Belisha. He said : " The House of Commons ought not lightly to establish a censorship over the free expression of opinion and the dissemination of knowledge. . . . We have no material whatever on which to reach a sound conclusion. . . . We are told by the Committee that there are four alternatives open to the House . . . not one of these alternatives is adequately argued. We are not given the reasons why they are produced as alternatives, nor are we adequately given the reasons why the last alternative is adopted. . . . It is not explained to us why the United States system of free and uncontrolled transmission, which I should have thought was more in accordance with the genius and spirit of the English people, is impracticable or impossible. It may be that it is. . . . I should like to know why. . . ." These speakers were answered by Lord Wolmer, the Assistant Postmaster-General, who said that " there is practically general agreement . . . that you have got to have a monopoly in broadcasting " and he argued that this was so for technical reasons. [24]

With the formation of the Corporation, criticism of the monopoly died away. In 1929, an agitation started which continued into the early 1930's for the introduction of sponsored programmes. [25] But this proposal did not involve any changes in the organisation of broadcasting and would have left the monopoly of the British Broadcasting Corporation unimpaired.* The main advantage seen

* Of course, if the sponsoring firms were allowed considerable independence in the choice of the programmes broadcast during their periods of radio time, it would introduce a competitive element into the situation.

K

by those advocating this change in policy would appear to have been that it would enable the Corporation to broadcast programmes which otherwise it would not have been able to afford.

But suggestions for the abolition of the monopoly began to be made in 1929. The early references which occurred in the popular Press were little more than statements that competition was desirable.[26] But there followed a number of suggestions for a reorganisation of British broadcasting to permit independent broadcasting systems to operate.[27] None involved the substitution of a commercial broadcasting system for the British Broadcasting Corporation. Only in one case was it suggested that commercial broadcasting should play a part. This was in an article written at the beginning of 1935 by Mr. J. B. Priestley.[28] He argued that the ideal broadcasting system would be a combination of the English and American systems. He suggested that the work of the British Broadcasting Corporation should be divided into two parts : cultural, which should continue to be under the control of the British Broadcasting Corporation ; and entertainment, which should be organised on commercial lines.

The other proposals did not involve any element of commercial broadcasting. The first was made by Major R. Raven-Hart in 1931.[29] His article appears to have been based on a study of the German broadcasting system, which he thought had advantages compared with the British system. The German broadcasting system was State-owned and administered by an officially privileged company. The difference between the two systems concerned the responsibility for the programmes. In Germany this was decentralised. There were nine regional companies plus one other (primarily educational) which ran a long-wave and a short-wave station. Major Raven-Hart thought that the system also had several " very serious disadvantages " : the higher cost of running the separate organisations ; lack of co-ordination between the various regional programme directors which might lead to a duplication of items or to simultaneous programmes of a very similar nature ; the possibility that the quality of the programmes in some of the smaller regions might be rather low. But the great advantage of the system was that it encouraged competition between the programme directors. It also meant that the " personal ideas, and even prejudices, of any director extend to one group only." The system had the advantage that authors and composers had more than one outlet for their work and broadcasting workers had more than one employer open to them. In applying the system to Great Britain, Major Raven-Hart thought that the two London stations could be treated as two unities, " each with its own organisation and direction." The results in this case might be " even more interesting than decentralisation by areas, since here the listeners would have a perfectly clear choice between the two programmes, purely as programmes, whereas in the case of decentralisation by regions the listener would always tend to prefer the nearest transmitter for purely technical reasons. . . ." And he added : " More especially would the experiment of decentralisation be of interest if each listener were able to give tangible proof of his preferences, which suggests a possible extension of the German system by allowing each listener, when taking out his licence, to allot the amount (less the Post Office deductions) to whatever station or group he preferred ; or, if this were considered too drastic, to allot thus perhaps one half of the amount, the other half going into a common fund for eventual division between the companies, as at present."

It does not seem that Major Raven-Hart's article attracted much attention. At all events, three years were to pass before another article was published making a similar suggestion.[30] In this article Mr. George E. A. Catlin vigorously criticised the monopoly. " For three hundred years the English people have fought to establish, and have prided themselves on having established, freedom of speech and the Press. In a little more than ten years they have, in principle, thrown that freedom away. In the case of the most important of all media for disseminating news and opinion, broadcasting, they merely retain the right to say such things as a censor, appointed by a government monopoly, approves beforehand, as expressing pleasant and unobjectionable sentiments." [31] But Mr. Catlin added that " if the very dangerous principles of a national monopoly be accepted, there is a strong case within this system for diversity. There is no reason why the conception of British Broadcasting under its new Charter should not be federal and why very different policies as to programmes should not be followed by the various stations." Later in the same year an article in the *Sunday Dispatch* advocated the establishment of a rival organisation to the British Broadcasting Corporation, which would not run on commercial lines but would share in the licence revenue.[32]

And in 1935, Dr. W. A. Robson, in an article on broadcasting policy, discussed whether it was necessary for broadcasting to be organised as a monopoly.[33] " The most serious question of all is whether the broadcasting service shall remain a monopoly. As between a competitive system run on commercial lines and socialised monopoly there can be no doubt whatever that the latter is infinitely to be preferred. . . . But the question does arise whether so immense a concentration of power and responsibility can safely be entrusted to any single organisation possessing an exclusive monopoly." He then outlined a scheme which would avoid this difficulty. " A possible alternative is to make the regional organs independent bodies. It is claimed that the regional directors have great freedom at present. Be that as it may, they are certainly overshadowed and dominated by the central organisation on all major questions. My proposal is that the five provincial Regions into which the country is divided should be made completely automonous broadcasting authorities for regional purposes. Each would be transformed into a miniature B.B.C., with its own board of governors appointed by the Government as the responsible body. Each regional corporation would organise its own programmes. Each region would be permitted to transmit on one wavelength only. A percentage of the licence fee would be allocated to each regional body based possibly on the number of listeners in its area." Dr. Robson justified his proposal in the following words : " There are, of course, numerous objections which can be urged against a scheme of this kind. Some of them are very weighty. But I do not think any of them would counterbalance the immense advantage of having several potential avenues of employment for artistes and speakers, of introducing an element of rivalry among the programme builders, of preventing as far as possible the exclusion from the ether of voices and views which ought not to be excluded. It cannot fairly be said that the B.B.C. is illiberal, but that does not meet the point. The *Manchester Guardian* is by universal agreement an exceptionally fair and liberal-minded newspaper, but would anyone be willing to make the *Manchester Guardian* the only daily newspaper organisation in the country ? Would it be desirable to place all the universities under a unified control so that if a teacher could not secure employment from the central organ no other opportunity would be open to him ? "

But these various suggestions for the establishment of independent broadcasting systems were hardly noticed in public discussion. No trace of their influence is to be found in the Ullswater Committee's report.[34] Mr. H. B. Lees-Smith may have had these proposals in mind when he suggested in the second debate on the Ullswater Committee's report that there should be greater regional autonomy within the framework of the Corporation. " What ought to be aimed at . . . is that the regional stations should be in the hands of men of quite independent minds who, within the general standard set by the Corporation, should be in competition with the national programme, trying to attract listeners away from the national programme on to regional programmes, and the national programme trying to attract them back. Thus there could be introduced into this wonderful experiment which we have initiated a new technique in public corporations, a technique of competition, or rather emulation, within a large national monopoly." [35] But it seems unlikely that Mr. Lees-Smith had in mind that degree of independence which these various proposals had envisaged. However that may be, this suggestion went unnoticed by other speakers in the debate.

The position as it existed at the time of the report of the Ullswater Committee was discussed in an article in the *Round Table*.[36] The section of the article which is relevant to the main theme of this book was entitled " A Plea for an Open Mind." The writer began by saying that the Ullswater Committee seemed " to have accepted the present organisation without adequately reviewing other possible systems." " The British Broadcasting Corporation has a monopoly of the most popular form of presenting knowledge, news, thought, and discussion. . . . Can the broadcasting service be properly monopolised by the State without endangering that freedom of thought and discussion which is a cardinal principle of any democracy that claims to be free. The first comparison that comes to mind is the Press. We could hardly reconcile a free democracy with a nationally owned Press—a British Newspaper Corporation created by charter and under the control of the Government of the day. Few of us would like to see a British Newspaper Corporation—with the sole monopoly of printing and distributing news—operating under licence from the Home Secretary. Freedom of the Press has grown up only by a continual process of less interference by the State and the gradual relaxation of restrictive legislation. . . . No one in this country would be satisfied with a State monopoly of the newspapers, whoever the Board of Governors might be ; and if we will not accept a State monopoly of the Press, why is it that we support the State control of broadcasting as established here, and as recommended by the Ullswater Committee to continue ? " The writer pointed out that the answer that there must be control of the number of broadcasting stations on technical grounds did not dispose of the question. " If the number of licences is to be limited, cannot the State give a licence to more than one body ? And need the body to whom the licence is given always be a public one ? If it is accepted that in matters of opinion there should be the fullest expression of ideas, it would seem unreasonable to give the monopoly of broadcasting to one corporation and not divide it among different groups on conditions that would provide sufficient scope for the presentation of all ideas. It is at least worth considering whether a system of many stations could not be established here, and whether that system would be a sufficient protection against the danger of monopoly."

The writer then considered the question of advertising. " The Ullswater Committee dismisses the introduction of advertising in so few lines as to lead one to suspect that its members did not approach the problem with open minds and with the determination to make the most of experience in other countries with different systems from our own. . . . People have a horror of introducing into England some of the systems of radio advertising to be found in certain foreign countries. But it is unreasonable to condemn all forms in all countries, and we might draw special benefit from experience in other parts of the Commonwealth. In Australia there is a combination of both systems. . . . The existence of this system does extend the range of subjects discussed and the type of programme given, and it does provide for the fullest expression of all shades of opinion. . . . Admittedly there are powerful and familiar arguments on the other side ; this is not a brief for radio advertising, but a plea for keeping an open mind. . . . It may be that the great majority of listeners in Great Britain would dislike above all other considerations the punctuation of programmes that they are hearing this or that by courtesy of some advertiser. But this has not yet been proved. . . . In these days, when freedom is on the defensive, it is surely unwise to reject, without much more profound consideration than seems yet to have been given, a system that is the bulwark of the present-day freedom of the Press." And this writer concluded : " If it is possible within the limited range of wavelengths at our disposal to have, say, seven stations in Great Britain, we would do well to consider with an open mind the possibility of a different system from that of a single corporation controlling all the broadcasting stations. . . . The stations could all be public corporations similar to the B.B.C. or alternatively some of them could be State-owned and controlled, like the B.B.C., and some privately owned. . . . These are only suggestions, necessarily inchoate in form. The trouble is not that they have been wrongly rejected but that they do not seem to have been considered at all."

Shortly after the debates in Parliament on the Ullswater Committee's report there appeared in the *Economist* an article entitled " How to run the Radio." [37] The writer argued that if it came to a choice between the American and the British systems, no doubt the British was the better. But he continued : " . . . is it really necessary to choose ? Could not the merits of both systems be combined ? . . . Let the State continue to collect the licence, let it, if you will, own the actual transmitting stations. But let the programmes be provided by two corporations, say the A.B.C. and the B.B.C., competing with each other. They should share the licence revenue and the listener might even be permitted to distribute some very small fraction of his ten shillings as a mark of favour to the corporation which he considers the better. . . ."

The amount of criticism of the monopoly of broadcasting was not large. But it is of interest to note its character. Criticism of the monopoly was largely based on the threat to freedom of speech and expression which was thought to be implicit in the monopoly ; the value of competition as a means of improving the programmes was not ignored, but it was a secondary matter compared with the maintenance of free speech. The second feature of the criticism was that it did not take the form of advocating commercial broadcasting in place of organisation by the British Broadcasting Corporation—although the possibility of mixed systems, in which part was organised on commercial lines, was envisaged. The situation was one in which the advocates of sponsored programmes (or commercial broadcasting) thought in terms of the maintenance of the monopoly. The advocates of competitive broadcasting thought in terms of the maintenance of non-commercial broadcasting or, at the least, a large area of non-commercial broadcasting. Critics therefore attempted to devise schemes—and they were all very similar—which would enable this to be done. The problem of finance was the obvious difficulty, but methods were suggested which, it was thought, would overcome it.

4. The monopoly and the staff

A discussion must now be interposed of a separate problem which, at first sight, may not appear to be connected with the question of the monopoly. In 1934 and 1935, accounts were published of staff troubles at the British Broadcasting Corporation.[38] And in 1936, the attitude of the Corporation to its employees became widely discussed, mainly as a result of the " talking mongoose " case, the name popularly given to the action for slander brought against Sir Cecil Levita by Mr. R. S. Lambert, editor of *The Listener*, a publication of the British Broadcasting Corporation.[39]

These difficulties with regard to the staff arose principally over what were alleged to be the military or semi-military procedures which were adopted by the Corporation and also to the control which it exercised over the private lives of its employees. In the Staff Regulations it was stated : " The only political activities permitted are those which may be defined as the minimum public duty of a private citizen. Any activity which may cause controversy or undue publicity is forbidden."[40] One example of the effect of the Corporation's policy was that Mr. P. P. Eckersley had to resign his position as Chief Engineer of the British Broadcasting Corporation because of his involvement in divorce proceedings.[41] In the case of Mr. R. S. Lambert, pressure was exerted on him by the Corporation not to bring an action for slander (which he ultimately won). The disclosures resulting from this case, as Dr. Robson has told us, " had the effect of riveting public attention on the personnel side of the B.B.C. in a way no abstract discussion could have done." [42]

These events are relevant to our main theme because the power of the British Broadcasting Corporation to exercise such a strict control over the actions of its employees in part derived from the fact that they had a monopoly. Those who wished to make broadcasting their career had to submit, or seek some other kind of occupation. It was not argued at the time that the solution to the staff problem was to be found in the abolition of the monopoly. Critics of the Corporation's policies suggested that trade unions should be allowed and Civil Service rules regarding staff should be applied.[43] But it is clear that this difficulty arose in its acute form because of the monopoly. Major Raven-Hart had earlier pointed out this aspect of the question. Dr. Robson wrote of the disadvantages of the monopoly to artists and speakers ; but the same disadvantages are suffered by employees of the Corporation.[44] And this has been pointed out on various occasions since then.[45] It is not easy to say how important the staff question has been in the formation of opinion on the monopoly. But there can be little doubt that these events brought out clearly the possible disadvantage of a monopoly not to the listener but to those engaged in broadcasting.

Notes on Chapter 6

[1] The memoranda presented by the Post Office and Mr. Reith to the Crawford Committee, both of which, from different standpoints, set out the case for the monopoly, were not published. Nor were the Minutes of Evidence of that Committee.

[2] C. A. Lewis, *Broadcasting from within*, p. 8.

[3] *Op. cit.*, p. 43.

[4] See *The Times*, July 17th, 1925.

[5] See Parliamentary Debates, House of Commons, July 12th, 1928.

[6] See the *Political Quarterly*, October 1935, p. 489.

[7] See Parliamentary Debates, House of Commons, April 29th, 1936.

[8] See Parliamentary Debates, House of Commons, July 6th, 1936.

[9] See Parliamentary Debates, House of Commons, March 4th, 1929.

[10] See Parliamentary Debates, House of Commons, February 22nd, 1933.

[11] See Parliamentary Debates, House of Commons, December 17th, 1936. The same argument had also been used by Mr. Herbert Morrison in an article, " Why bully the B.B.C. ? " in *The Star*, January 13th, 1933.

[12] P. 5.

[13] See the *Manchester Guardian*, November 28th, 1925.

[14] See the *Economist*, March 13th, 1926.

[15] See the *Daily Express*, November 22nd, 1927.

[16] See the *Manchester Guardian*, January 10th, 1930.

[17] See Parliamentary Debates, House of Lords, March 19th, 1931.

[18] See *The Times*, August 14th, 1934.

[19] See pp. [20]-[21] above.

[20] See Parliamentary Debates, House of Commons, November 15th, 1926.

[21] See *John Bull*, May 9th, 1936. It is of interest that this article was very critical of the Corporation's Sunday programme policy.

[22] All these quotations come from paragraph 7 on page 7 of the Ullswater Committee's report (Cmd. 5091, 1936).

[23] See Parliamentary Debates, House of Lords, June 26th, 1946.

[24] See Parliamentary Debates, House of Commons, November 15th, 1926. Lord Wolmer's argument is quoted at greater length on p. [132] above.

[25] This agitation started with an assertion that the British Broadcasting Corporation was contemplating " a sensational change in policy," the introduction of sponsored programmes. " No attempt will be made to imitate the American folly of a profusion

of conflicting stations and clashing programmes. It is proposed that the B.B.C. shall retain all its powers of control and censorship but grant facilities to commercial concerns to provide programmes on a competitive basis." See the *Sunday Express*, November 17th, 1929. This was followed by a denial. See the *Daily Herald*, November 18th, 1929. But the subject continued to be ventilated. See, for example, the *Manchester Guardian*, November 29th and December 4th, 1929, the *Advertising News*, December 2nd, 1929, the *Daily Telegraph*, January 17th, 21st and 25th, 1930, *Amateur Wireless*, October 25th, 1930, *The Times*, September 16th, 1931, and *Popular Wireless*, August 6th, 1932. The proposal has been mooted on various occasions since that time. See the *World's Press News*, April 25th, 1935. The question was again raised at the beginning of the war, see the *Newspaper World*, March 2nd, 1940, and the *World's Press News*, April 11th, 1940. Following these suggestions, the Corporation announced that it was not considering introducing sponsored programmes. See the *Daily Sketch*, April 23rd, 1940. A more recent proposal for sponsored programmes along these lines was contained in a pamphlet issued in 1946 by the Institute of Incorporated Practitioners in Advertising entitled *Broadcasting, a study of the case for and against commercial broadcasting under State control in the United Kingdom*. "It is not proposed that the B.B.C. should cease to be the chosen instrument for broadcasting or that official control should in any way be abandoned. What is suggested is rather that the B.B.C. should make use of those provisions in its legal structure which would allow commercial broadcasting to be carried on under certain conditions— in other words, not the creation of commercial competition for the B.B.C. but the expansion of officially controlled broadcasting with all the advantages of internal competition" (p. 27).

[26] See *John Bull*, April 13th, 1929, the *Sunday Pictorial*, May 26th, 1929, the *Sunday Sun*, June 16th, 1929, the *Wireless Magazine*, October 1929, the *Yorkshire Weekly Post*, July 19th, 1930, and *Popular Wireless*, August 1st, 1931.

[27] One early proposal which came close to this was that the British Broadcasting Corporation should have two separate programme organisations. See the *Wireless World*, September 25th, 1929.

[28] See *The Star*, January 16th, 1935.

[29] See " The Decentralisation of Broadcasting," *The Nineteenth Century*, July 1931.

[30] See " The Giant Air Monopoly," *The Fortnightly Review*, May 1934.

[31] But a similar point of view had been expressed by Sir Ernest Benn in 1932 in a broadcast discussion. See *The Listener*, November 23rd, 1932.

[32] See the *Sunday Dispatch*, September 30th, 1934, and October 7th, 1934. This suggestion was commented on by Mr. Alan Howland, who said : " The suggestion has been made recently, though not for the first time, that the Government should provide facilities for a broadcasting organisation to compete with the B.B.C. . . . However nebulous the scheme may be and however impossible of fulfilment, the temptation to toy with the idea as an idea is very nearly irresistible." But he concluded : " . . . there is not the slightest prospect of the B.B.C. monopoly being challenged and, if it were, there is no doubt in my mind that the B.B.C. is too jealous of its own power to allow a rival organisation to have a clear field. But it's a fascinating idea all the same." See the *Saturday Review*, October 14th, 1934.

[33] " The B.B.C. as an Institution," *The Political Quarterly*, October 1935. A revised version of this article was printed in 1936 in *Public Enterprise* (edited by Dr. W. A. Robson), pp. 73-104. Its reproduction in this form probably made this the most influential of the contributions critical of the monopoly published during the period of the first Charter of the British Broadcasting Corporation.

[34] Paragraph 21 of the Ullswater Committee's report dealt with the question of regional organisation. " The limitations, within which the Regional Directors have sole authority within their Regions, have been gradually relaxed during the existence of the Corporation. The position of the Regional Directors in relation to Broadcasting House has just been strengthened by the appointment of a Director of Regional Relations. We approve the gradual enlargement of their responsibilities, subject to the maintenance of a consistent policy for the service as a whole and to the ultimate control by the Corporation itself and a very small group of its highest officers whose duties are of national scope " (p. 10).

[35] See Parliamentary Debates, House of Commons, July 6th, 1936.

[36] See " Broadcasting in the Democratic State," by a correspondent, the *Round Table*, June 1936.

[37] See the *Economist*, August 22nd, 1936.

[38] The discussion was touched off in March 1934 as a result of a statement by Mr. Oliver Baldwin, then Film Critic of the Corporation. It was not confined to staff problems but embraced the whole question of the administration and methods of the Corporation. A motion was set down in the House of Commons for a Select Committee to inquire into the working of the British Broadcasting Corporation. See the *Daily Express*, the *Daily Telegraph*, the *Morning Post* and the *Evening Standard* for March 7th, 1934, the *Daily Herald* for March 8th, 1934, the *Birmingham Gazette* for March 9th, 1934, the *Daily Mail* for March 12th and 15th, 1934, and the *Daily Herald* and *Evening Standard* for March 17th, 1934. In consequence of this discussion, it was arranged for Sir John Reith to address a meeting of Conservative Members of Parliament. See the *Daily Express* and *Daily Mail* for March 16th, 1934. A comment on this meeting in the *Morning Post* for March 20th, 1934, was as follows : " The general impression among Members in the lobbies after the meeting was that Sir John Reith had performed a difficult task with complete frankness and that he had displayed a political ingenuity of which Cabinet Ministers might well be envious. The questions he had declined to answer were stated to have been few, and many Members confessed that he had inspired them with full confidence in the administration of the B.B.C. In consequence, it is unlikely that the demand for an inquiry before the granting of a new charter will be pressed."

[39] For an account of this case, see R. S. Lambert, *Ariel and All His Quality*, pp. 216-299.

[40] This regulation was quoted by Sir Stafford Cripps in the first debate on the Ullswater Committee's report. See Parliamentary Debates, House of Commons, April 29th, 1936.

[41] See *The Power Behind the Microphone*, p. 152.

[42] See W. A. Robson, " The British Broadcasting Corporation," in *Public Enterprise* (which Dr. Robson edited), pp. 91-92.

[43] See, for example, the speeches of Mr. H. B. Lees-Smith in the two debates on the Ullswater Committee's report and also his speech in the debate on the report of the Board of Inquiry set up to investigate the questions raised by Mr. Lambert's case. See Parliamentary Debates, House of Commons, December 17th, 1936.

[44] See Robson, *op. cit.*, pp. 82-83.

[45] See, for example, Sir Frederick Ogilvie's letter to *The Times*, June 26th, 1946, and " The B.B.C. Marks Time," the *Round Table*, September 1946.

CHAPTER SEVEN

PUBLIC DISCUSSION OF THE MONOPOLY, 1937—1947

1. PUBLIC DISCUSSION 1937 TO 1945

IN the years immediately following 1936, articles critical of the monopoly ceased to appear. The British Broadcasting Corporation, it was stated in 1938, " has reached port as an accepted British institution. The advantages of monopoly, so far as this country is concerned, have proved to outweigh the advantages of disseminated effort." [1] But interest in broadcasting policy was stirred to life by a correspondence in *The Times* which started on February 7th, 1939. A correspondent wrote to say that the news bulletins of the British Broadcasting Corporation did not promote a friendly feeling towards foreign countries and that this was inconsistent with Mr. Chamberlain's policy. There followed an immense correspondence which continued each day until February 25th. Few aspects of the news bulletins were left untouched. They were defended as being impartial ; they were attacked as being biased. Some advised switching off the news and reading *The Times* next day. One letter pointed out a danger in that while extremists were not allowed to broadcast, accounts of their speeches might be included in news bulletins. It was not until the last day of the correspondence that anyone raised the question of whether it was desirable that broadcasting should be a monopoly. Mr. David Rice wrote as follows : " If this is a country of free speech is it not strange that there should be centralised broadcasting ? . . . is it not high time for the revocation of the B.B.C. monopoly ? Free speech, as regards the wireless, is non-existent at present. . . . The revocation of the B.B.C. charter as far as monopoly is concerned would also bring a little much-needed competition ; advertising broadcasting, so popular in America, is often preferable to the Portland House output." But Mr. Rice was alone in raising this question. The leading article in *The Times* which accompanied the end of the correspondence opened as follows : " Let no one suppose that the letters of criticism which have lately been reaching *The Times* in scores represent any general public dissatisfaction with the conduct of the B.B.C. as a whole. The strong foundations on which that great institution was built by Sir John Reith and his staff have proved themselves impregnable to all assaults upon his high conception of its duties. . . . No informed body of opinion in this country surveying the experience of other countries would seek to diminish the powers or the standards of a system which is incomparably the best in the world."

But this opinion was not shared by everyone. Mr. Kingsley Martin commented : "Surveying this correspondence, my own first conclusion is that of Mr. Rice—that the B.B.C. monopoly is a mistake. I believe that American wireless, urged by competition, gives a better and less nationalistic news service than the British. The public demand for news is not seriously thwarted by the absurdities of advertising which were so much ridiculed in Britain when the question of the monopoly was under review some years ago. It may be that the Canadian method by which a government wireless must compete with those of private companies may be the right solution. . . ." [2]

The second World War concentrated attention on the future of Britain rather than on the future of British broadcasting. None the less, this subject was not entirely neglected. A number of books by ex-members of the staff of the British Broadcasting Corporation, all critical of the monopoly, appeared in the early years of the war. Mr. R. S. Lambert's *Ariel and all his Quality* appeared in 1940 ; Mr. P. P. Eckersley's *The Power behind the Microphone* and Mr. Paul Bloomfield's *B.B.C.* in 1941. And two pamphlets, both critical of the monopoly, also appeared. Sir Ernest Benn published his *B.B.C. Monopoly* in 1941 and Mr. A. C. Turner published his prize essay on *Broadcasting and Free Speech* in 1943. In all these works emphasis was laid on the threat to free speech which was involved in the maintenance of the monopoly.

And the subject continued to be discussed in the journals. The *Wireless World* revived its pre-war proposal for competitive broadcasting not by a "violently disruptive reorganisation of British broadcasting, such as commercialising it on American lines" but by the setting up of two separate programme boards for the British Broadcasting Corporation. [3] In the *Wireless World* in 1943, it was said : "The competitive principle seems at last to be more generally accepted, and if we agree it is desirable, the basic problem now seems to be the devising of means for putting the principle into practice. . . ." [4] This was in a comment on a " Plan for Post-War Broadcasting in Britain " which was evolved in the Cossor Research Laboratories and presented by Mr. K. I. Jones and Mr. D. A. Bell to the Wireless Section of the Institution of Electrical Engineers in November, 1943. [5] Mr. Jones and Mr. Bell did not propose any alteration in the arrangements for medium wave sound broadcasting and television, which would continue to be operated by the British Broadcasting Corporation as a monopoly. But they proposed that a large number of independent frequency modulation stations should be established. " While some of this large number of independent f.m. stations would be operated by commercial concerns and depend on advertising for their revenue, others might be operated by educational bodies, etc., and so the service need not necessarily be dominated by advertising considerations."

And in 1943 there appeared the first Ministerial proposal for a weakening of the monopoly. Mr. Brendan Bracken, when Minister of Information, in a speech at a luncheon held to mark the twenty-first anniversary of the B.B.C. discussed the future of British broadcasting. He referred to a rumour that the British Broadcasting Corporation had agreed to accept advertising and said that he " would be surprised if the British Government would approve of the introduction of commercial broadcasting. . . ." But he " saw no reason why healthy competition should not be developed within the structure of the B.B.C. . . . A measure of broadcasting home rule might be given to a number of regions. In that way the B.B.C. would become the mother of a number of really healthy competitive enterprises and it would thereby get rid of some of the stain of monopoly. The worst disaster that could befall the B.B.C. would be if it were to become a happy combination of negative virtues." [6] And in a debate in 1944 on the Ministry of Information, Captain L. D. Gammans suggested that in addition to the British Broadcasting Corporation there should also be some form of commercial broadcasting. He found support in the debate from Mr. R. Tree and Captain L. F. Plugge. Mr. Brendan Bracken, in his reply, said that he thought the time had come for an examination of the Charter of the British Broadcasting Corporation. " As a matter of fact the Reconstruction Committee are having a preliminary look at what can best be done for the B.B.C.'s future." [7]

Later in 1944 there appeared some of the most important articles that have ever been published on the organisation of

British broadcasting. They appeared in the *Economist* under the title " A Plan for Broadcasting." It is essential to examine in some detail the proposals made in these articles. [8] In the first, the *Economist* maintained that it was wrong to assume that the choice of the way in which broadcasting could be organised was limited to a State-owned monopoly or commercial broadcasting : " human ingenuity is not so barren nor the technique of social organisation so confined. . . . The aim should be to devise a system avoiding the manifest faults of both. . . . Must we really commit ourselves beyond recall to one or the other ? Why cannot we exercise our minds in trying to evolve a system that is better adapted than either to serve the purpose for which broadcasting exists." To place so much power in the hands of a monopoly " however high-minded and public-spirited " was " obviously and disastrously dangerous." " The only event in human history at all comparable with the invention of radio, from the social point of view, is that of printing. What would have happened to our liberties—indeed, to our intelligence—if the printing press had, from the start, been monopolised by a public corporation, be it never so well-intentioned and devoted to its duty ? For centuries now, it has been common form among the Western democratic peoples to look down upon any benighted country which reserved the power of the Press to Authority, and to pity it not only for its political captivity but also for its ignorance, the intellectual backwardness and the technical poverty that are the inevitable consequences of a censorship. So firmly is this doctrine held, that the smallest infraction of it, if it relates to printed matter, will be hotly resented and condemned. Yet a complete breach of the same doctrine, relating to an instrument that may yet prove to be still mightier than the pen, is looked upon with complete indifference." This article concluded with the following words : " If radio was to be the servant of a free society and not its assassin, it must follow in the printers' footsteps . . . there should not be a single Broadcasting Corporation. Variety is essential to interest, and competition is the necessary mechanism of variety. Whatever plan is chosen for the ownership and financing of broadcasting . . . the main essential is that there should be no monopoly."

The second article dealt with the technical aspects of the question. It was argued that broadcasting was not likely to continue to be based on a small number of stations in the medium waveband. Two means were available for overcoming this congestion of the ether. One was frequency modulation, which would mean a large number of stations, each with a restricted radius. The other was wire broadcasting, " a large number of programmes being diffused on a wire network, from which the listener's receiving set would select one. . . . In either case, something more like a network of local stations instead of the present national stations." In the third article a scheme was outlined for the reorganisation of British broadcasting. It was suggested that " there might be three broadcasting companies, A.B.C., the B.B.C. and the C.B.C., each receiving a fixed proportion, less than one-third (e.g. 1/4th or 1/6th) of the listener's licence fee, while each listener on paying his fee would nominate one of the three to receive the final proportion. In this way each company would be assured of a certain minimum income, in return for which it would be required to observe certain general stipulations about the number, type and length of its programmes. One of these being that during peak hours each company should provide three programmes—one of general entertainment, one of higher cultural value and one of an instructional nature. Furthermore, each company would have the incentive of doubling its income if it could please its listeners more than its rivals. Thus the listener would have the choice of not merely several different programmes, but also of several different sorts of programmes." In the fourth and last article it was argued that if the programmes were to be distributed by wire " the network could either be owned jointly by the programme companies, since it would carry the programmes of all three, or else by some independent body charging for its services." It was also suggested that the three companies should be constituted in different ways. One might be " a co-operative venture, its governing body elected by vote of its employees." The second one could be a commercial concern " giving scope to business men from the entertainment, publicity and Press industries." The third company could be modelled on the British Broadcasting Corporation. The cost of this scheme would be of the order of £15 million a year. This might be met by raising the licence fee to 30s., or, if this was politically inadvisable, the additional revenue might be provided by an excise duty on the sale of radio sets or by a limited amount of advertising " provided it were rigidly restricted in volume and confined to off-hours." But if these methods " were not sufficient or acceptable, there was no reason why a subsidy from the State might not be considered. A convenient way of applying it would be for the State to provide the transmitting facilities below cost, or even free of charge. This would avoid the necessity of actual cash payments to the programme companies." This article concluded : " The main purpose of these articles is less to win assent to the details of the scheme proposed than to attempt to widen the range of public discussion on the subject. . . . Radio is the newest art and the newest social phenomenon. Why should it become a conservative art while still so young ? Why should we believe that, without experience and without experiment, and almost without thought we should have hit, at first go, on the perfect system. . . . It is very important that the discussion which will arise before the B.B.C.'s present charter expires at the end of next year should be free and wide ranging. To conduct it on the basis that only minor modifications of the present system are admissible—because of some pretended, and wholly unproven, superiority of the present system—would be to make radio old before its time, to ignore the manifest dangers of State monopoly of any organ of information and discussion and to confess a bankruptcy of administrative ingenuity."

I have not been able to find any reaction to these articles, unless it be in a speech on Post-war Broadcasting by Sir William Haley, Director-General of the British Broadcasting Corporation, delivered to the Radio Industries Club ten days after the last of the *Economist* articles.[9] The first section of his speech which is relevant to our theme related to coverage : " There are many conceptions of broadcasting, but two are paramount. There is that which envisages broadcasting as something to be exploited, something to make money out of. For that kind of broadcasting you do not worry overmuch about coverage. In a country like ours you would just put a station here and there to skim the cream of the most thickly populated communities and let the rest go hang. In our British wisdom we decided on the other way of broadcasting, where broadcasting is a non-commercial service and in which every listener, no matter where he is in the United Kingdom, has an equal right with every other listener to the best service he can be given. It is the B.B.C.'s duty, within the limits of its technical resources and of the geographical difficulties to be overcome, to see the village has as good listening as the city dweller ; the family

L

in the provinces every bit as good entertainment as the people in the metropolis. Admittedly this is the hard way. Again, I do not have to tell this company that to cover even so small an area as the United Kingdom involves a great many transmitters. It is necessary to emphasise this because there is extraordinary ignorance on this point. I think I can state on your great authority, Mr. President, that there is no transmitter in existence anywhere in the world or likely to be built that will cover all the United Kingdom at one and the same time on the medium wave band. This is a simple fact which should never be forgotten." He then continued : "Every now and again hopelessly impractical ideas are put forward for a number of great independent stations competing with each other for all the listeners' attention. In such practical company as this I will stick to practicalities and say that only by the most careful and most highly co-ordinated planning are we ever going to ensure the right of each and every listener in this country to a service, let alone to a choice of services. It is only by using every wavelength it can reasonably expect to have at its disposal and by using every one of the great number of medium-wave transmitters that the B.B.C. possesses, that we have been able to evolve the following plan. As it is, we expect, working in step with yourselves, in due course to use frequency modulation to get it as near as we can to one hundred per cent. efficient." Sir William Haley referred to the question of the monopoly and suggested that its disadvantages could be overcome by internal competition. " The one drawback that is sometimes charged against the B.B.C. is that its monopoly robs the listener of the fruits of competition. We are going to attempt in typical British fashion to get the best of both worlds. All the power and strength that comes from the centralisation of resources in the B.B.C. will be at the listener's disposal ; all the competition we can engender in programme building and in the creation of new broadcasting ideas and conceptions will be there for his benefit, too."

Early in 1945, *The Times* surveyed the situation, in view of the approaching end of the second charter period.[10] The main theme of this article is indicated by the following quotation : " It is unlikely that the Parliament and people of this country will discard out of hand perhaps the most fruitful experiment yet attempted in the combination of national responsibility with professional independence and enterprise. The leading issue in the approaching discussion of the B.B.C. should be, not its abolition, but the permanent establishment of conditions to guarantee that independence and to serve that enterprise." This article also included a tribute to Lord Reith. " It is above all as a public service that the B.B.C. must be judged. It was as a national trust that Lord Reith regarded the monopoly which, mainly for technical reasons, had to be granted and was granted practically without challenge in the infancy of wireless broadcasting ; and it was an integral part of this conception of trusteeship that the stimulus of commercial competition should be replaced by the self-imposed duty to pursue a calculated policy of honest experiment aimed at the best and broadest objectives . . . it would be a disingenuous critic who ventured to contend that the errors of the B.B.C. have exceeded the familiar failures and failings of commercial and competitive broadcasting in other countries." But the case of those who were opposed to the monopoly was examined. " Admittedly important principles are involved, or at any rate invoked, on the other side. It is argued that broadcasting should not be monopolistically controlled, any more than the Press or the business of entertainment, and it is indeed the soundest of principles that monopoly should be invariably suspect, above all perhaps in the spheres of opinion and taste. But it is a complementary principle of no less validity that the sole form of monopoly which can or should be tolerated by a free community is that which is operated as an independent public service in the general interest, and unceasingly subject, as the B.B.C. has always been, to the direct and at times severe pressure of public opinion. This is the single but probably decisive test and justification for the B.B.C." The article also dealt with the critics who contend that " a single service cannot provide the variety of programmes that is required. They therefore demand competition between separate and rival broadcasting concerns. But the advocates of a dispersal of broadcasting, public or private, overlook the fact that, unless a considerably larger revenue could be extracted from the consumer, the competing concerns would be in the position of having to divide something like the present inadequate revenue among more purses, with several weak corporations taking the place of the present strong one. Nor would the introduction of commercial financing meet the need. British listeners have become accustomed to the conception of broadcasting as a public service, and to the disinterested and generally effective execution of its trust by the B.B.C. It can be said with some assurance that they would not readily accept a change which would involve an invasion of their listening-time and their firesides by the interested and persistent appeals of competing advertisers." The " temporary success " of stations such as Radio Luxembourg " offers no proof to the contrary. They were novelties, and their popularity was largely confined to Sundays, when, at that time, the B.B.C. felt itself bound not to attempt entertainment."

2. THE DEBATE ON BROADCASTING POLICY IN 1946

It was probably because the Charter of the British Broadcasting Corporation was due to expire at the end of 1946 that there appeared in the winter of 1945 various references to the possibility of introducing competitive broadcasting in Great Britain.[11] But the debate on broadcasting policy did not begin in earnest until February, 1946, when Mr. C. R. Attlee, the Prime Minister, stated that " His Majesty's Government have given the fullest consideration to this matter and have decided that no independent investigation is necessary before the Charter is renewed." [12] There followed a series of articles in the Press critical of this decision.[13] Not all of these suggested that the possibility of competition should be examined, although some did. Others pointed to the technical and other questions which it was thought needed to be considered. Towards the end of June, Lord Brabazon put down a motion in the House of Lords asking for an investigation before the Charter of the British Broadcasting Corporation was renewed. The morning of the debate, a letter appeared in *The Times* from Sir Frederick Ogilvie, the second Director-General of the British Broadcasting Corporation.[14] There is little doubt that this letter made a considerable impression. It contained the following passages : " What is at stake is not a matter of politics but of freedom. Is monopoly of broadcasting to be fastened on us for a further term ? Is the future of this great public service to be settled without public inquiry, by Royal Commission or otherwise, into the many technical and other changes which have taken place in the last ten years ?

" Freedom is choice. And monopoly of broadcasting is inevitably the negation of freedom, no matter how efficiently it is run, or how wise and kindly the board or committees in charge of it. It denies freedom of choice to listeners. It denies freedom of employment to speakers, musicians, writers, actors and all who seek their chance on the air. The dangers of monopoly have long been recognised in the film industry and the Press and the Theatre, and active steps have been taken to prevent it. In tolerating monopoly of broadcasting we are alone among the democratic countries of the world.

" I was Director-General of the B.B.C. from the autumn of 1938 to the beginning of 1942. At the time of leaving I set down some of my impressions and experiences in a memorandum which Sir Alan Powell and his colleagues on the B.B.C. Board of Governors have had in their possession since the end of the war. My chief impressions were two : the evils of the monopoly system and the gallant work of a very able and delightful executive staff in trying to overcome them. The B.B.C. itself, good as it is, would gain vastly by the abolition of monopoly and the introduction of competition. So would all the millions of listeners, who would still have the B.B.C. to listen to, but would have other programmes to enjoy as well. So would all would-be broadcasters gain. If rejected by the B.B.C. they would have other corporations to turn to.

" The only possible losers would be the various Governments of the day—Labour, Tory, Coalition, or what not. Governments are thoroughly suited by the charter as it stands. What better could any Government wish for than to have at the end of the street a powerful efficient instrument which has all the appearance of independence, but which by the existing provisions of the charter and licence it can control at will ? "

Lord Brabazon, in his opening speech in the House of Lords debate, said that there were many aspects of British broadcasting which required investigation particularly in view of the recent technical developments. But he also dealt with the question of sponsored programmes. Advertisements should not be introduced into the programmes of the British Broadcasting Corporation. But he thought a mixed commercial and non-commercial system, such as existed in Australia, had advantages. " I maintain that this is a possibility that . . . merits investigation." Lord Elton followed. His speech was largely confined to the problem of the monopoly. He pointed out that the Ullswater Committee (of which he had been a member) had failed to examine this fundamental question. He referred to the considerations which had been advanced in favour of some degree of competition in broadcasting and in particular to Sir Frederick Ogilvie's letter in *The Times*. He also said that many

who had heard " the broadcasts from the competitive systems of
the United States and Canada " had been very favourably impressed. One of the main reasons for this was that " under a competitive system enormously more generous fees are paid to the
artists than are paid under our monopoly." In Great Britain there
was no professional broadcasting as was the case with a competitive
system. It was also true that with the monopoly certain opinions
were almost entirely excluded from the microphone. " There can be
no doubt that some element of competition in the air would be
powerful in eliciting not only new artists but new ideas." Lord
Tweedsmuir paid a tribute to the work of the British Broadcasting
Corporation. But he added : " It has the vices that are inherent
in all monopolies, and they will come out in the long run. The
first is an arbitrary attitude towards the public, and the second is
that with the lack of competition a monopoly eventually sells to
the public an inferior product." He thought that if we studied the
mixed systems of Canada, New Zealand and Australia, " there
must be certain points which we can learn and which will redound
to our benefit." Other speakers stressed the advantages of competition. Lord Samuel said that the House of Lords were " not
being asked here and now to express whether the monopoly should
be maintained or whether it should be abandoned. We may hold
one view or the other. For my part, I do not feel that I have
sufficient information, or that I am sufficiently aware of the facts,
to arrive at any opinion on that point. It is for that reason that I
would press for an inquiry, in order that both Houses of Parliament,
and the public, should receive full information as to what the
situation is, and what future alternatives may be." The debate
was not, of course, primarily concerned with the monopoly,
although this question received considerable attention, but with
the demand for an inquiry. This was not opposed by any speaker
in the debate.

Lord Listowel, the Postmaster-General, devoted a great deal of
attention to the reasons (about which he could not be too explicit in
advance of a White Paper which the Government was soon to issue)
why it was undesirable to hold an inquiry. But he referred to those
speakers who had stressed " the advantage of competitive broadcasting as exemplified in the United States as compared with the
monopoly enjoyed by the B.B.C." Lord Listowel went on to outline
the reasons why it was desirable to retain the monopoly in Great

Britain : " There is, I am perfectly certain, a strong theoretical case that could be made out for competitive broadcasting, but this case ignores completely the peculiar practical difficulties which face us in this country. The main difficulty, expressed very simply, is a technical difficulty, the lack of a sufficient number of suitable wavelengths. This lack may possibly be overcome by frequency modulation, but I can assure noble Lords that if we were to switch over from monopoly broadcasting to competitive broadcasting in a short period of time, if we were to change our present system, there would immediately be an outcry from thousands of people all over the country because the programmes to which they listen would have deteriorated to such an extent. I am perfectly certain that any Government of any political complexion which might be in power at the time of such a decision would have to restore the *status quo* very soon after the attempt to set up a competitive broadcasting system for this country.

" I should like to emphasise that point because, owing to the ignorance of the general public about the technical problem of wavelengths it is generally ignored that it is this particular difficulty which makes a number of competing stations quite impracticable. The noble Lord is aware, as I am, that wavelengths are allocated by international agreement ; that no country has as many as it wants; that we are limited to a very small number. . . . So long as we are limited to this small number of wavelengths suitable for broadcasting programmes to home listeners it is essential that they should be planned for the country as a whole and allocated as they are at the moment by agreement between the different regions and for the different programmes of the B.B.C."

The Press did not find Lord Listowel's defence of the Government's decision very convincing. *The Times* thought the request for an inquiry " reasonable." [15] The *Spectator* commented : " It is almost impossible to find a single person who, on due consideration of the question, fails to see the need for a full and public discussion of the working of British broadcasting." [16] The *New Statesman* considered the case for an inquiry " overwhelming." [17] But the Government maintained its attitude and the *White Paper on Broadcasting Policy*,[18] issued early in July, 1946, set out the reasons which led the Government to reject the demand for an inquiry. They were " satisfied that the present system of broadcasting is the one best suited to the circumstances of the United Kingdom." None the less they agreed " that the problems of a body like the

British Broadcasting Corporation " needed to be ventilated and they were " not opposed in principle " to an inquiry. But it was not the right time. The war years were abnormal ; there had been important technical progress but it was " too early to foresee with any clarity its effect on peace-time broadcasting " ; the international agreements which allocated the wavelengths to the various countries would have to be revised. The Government therefore proposed that " in order to span the period of transition," the Charter should be renewed for five years.

One of the factors which weighed with the Government in coming to the decision not to hold an inquiry was that they were satisfied that broadcasting ought to remain a monopoly. The basis for this view was set out in the *White Paper*. It opened with an *Historical Retrospect* and the passages which dealt with the history of the monopoly were as follows : " The Sykes Committee, in recommending a single broadcasting service, had in mind not only the part which broadcasting would play in the life of the nation and in international relations, but also the need to use the limited number of wavelengths available for this purpose in the best interests of the community. The Crawford Committee, in endorsing this recommendation, considered and rejected the alternatives of continuing the British Broadcasting Company in its existing or in a modified form or of placing the service under direct Government control. It rejected the United States system of free and uncontrolled broadcasting as unsuited to this country. . . . After a thorough investigation, the Ullswater Committee . . . endorsed the general principles which had guided the Corporation in the conduct of the broadcasting service. . . ." [19]

These passages would appear to suggest that all the Committees on broadcasting policy had investigated the question of the monopoly and all had come to the conclusion that a monopoly was desirable. They would tend to lead readers of the *White Paper* to infer that the arguments in favour of independent broadcasting systems, however plausible they may appear at first sight, were not such as to survive a critical examination. It is therefore unfortunate that this account in the *White Paper* is historically inaccurate. The Sykes Committee did not recommend that there should be a monopoly. They left this question open. It follows that the Crawford Committee could not have endorsed a nonexistent recommendation. It is, however, true that the Crawford

Committee recommended that broadcasting should be organised on a monopolistic basis. But all the evidence presented to this Committee was in favour of the monopoly[20] and the members of the Committee appear to have considered its desirability to be self-evident.[21] The Ullswater Committee certainly upheld the monopoly. But this Committee accepted its desirability without question.[22] The position is that the assumptions on which the arguments in favour of the monopoly are based have never been questioned by any of the Committees on broadcasting ; nor have any of them undertaken a careful examination of possible alternative systems—a state of affairs which would not be apparent to the reader of the *White Paper*.

But what were the reasons given for the Government's support of the monopoly? They were set out in paragraph 14: "The Government think it proper, however, to set out at this stage their views on whether, in the present state of broadcasting technique, the B.B.C. should continue to be the only body licensed to originate broadcasts in this country, since, if it is agreed that a single national broadcasting organisation is desirable, there is no evidence of any widespread desire for a radically different type of organisation. It has been argued that the existing system places too much power in the hands of a single corporation, and deprives broadcasting of the advantages of healthy competition. The Government are, however, satisfied that the present system is best suited to the circumstances of the United Kingdom. Where only a limited number of suitable wavelengths is available to cover a comparatively small and densely populated area, an integrated broadcasting system operated by a public corporation is, in their opinion, the only satisfactory means of ensuring that the wavelengths available are used in the best interests of the community, and that, as far as possible, every listener has a properly balanced choice of programmes. Co-ordination and the planned application of resources, rather than their dissipation, is, moreover, in the opinion of the Government, likely to lead to the greatest advances both in technique and programmes. Finally, the Government are satisfied that the record of the British Broadcasting Corporation during the twenty years of its existence fully justifies its continuance. The Corporation has, no doubt, been open to fair criticism from time to time ; and, indeed, criticism and constructive suggestions from Parliament, the public and the Press are desirable. But, taken as a whole, the achievements of British broadcasting since 1926 will bear comparison with those of any other country." And in the next paragraph, they dealt with the problem of regional organisation and of internal competition : " Both the Government and the Corporation are fully alive to the advantages to be derived from the spirit of competition in broadcasting, and in order to encourage this, the Corporation is actively pursuing a policy of enhancing the status of its individual regional organisations, and fostering a spirit of emulation throughout the service, with the object of developing a number of vigorous regional bodies, each with a staff drawn largely from the region which it serves and each with a distinctive programme policy in keeping with the character of the region and the needs and wishes of its people. The Government welcomes this policy of regional devolution. The general standard of broadcasting cannot fail to be enriched by the encouragement of the cultural and entertainment resources of the several regions. They consider, however, that, in order to ensure that the regional directorates of the Corporation are in close touch with movements of thought and opinion in their regions, there should be established in each region a Regional Advisory Council for the purpose of advising the Corporation on all matters affecting the regional programme policy. The composition of these bodies should be broadly representative of the general public of the region and members should be chosen for their individual qualities and not as representatives of particular interests." [23]

The Times commented on the *White Paper* as follows:[24] " . . . the B.B.C. will go forward very much on existing lines, as it would indeed have done in any event ; for the purpose of most of those who have demanded, and demand, an inquiry, is not to bring about any fundamental change. The general desire, now crystallised by experience, is to retain broadcasting as a public service, ultimately supervised by Parliament, and on the other hand to free the executive of the Corporation as much as possible from political interference in the day-to-day conduct of its affairs. The proposals of the Government conform in the main to this well-defined trend of public opinion. . . .

" A necessary consequence of the conception of broadcasting as a public service is that it must remain a monopoly. The Government accept from the B.B.C. the unchallengeable advice ' that any attempt to use sponsored programmes would be resented by a large body of public opinion.' Nor are they misled by the specious plea that the benefits of the competitive spirit might be introduced by breaking up the B.B.C. into separate corporations. That way lies only the division of resources, the narrowing of outlook, and the reduction of efficiency, while there would be no true competition, for that depends upon a conflict of financial and other interests." The *Manchester Guardian* was outspoken not only in its defence of the monopoly but also of the Government's decision not to hold an inquiry[25] : " It is a little difficult to know why this sudden demand for an inquiry sprang up. . . . A constitution with which the country has been pretty well content for years all at once begins to grow hooves and a tail and a former Director-General stirs out of his Oxford repose to descry in his former charge the ' nationalisation of the infinitely precious things of the mind and the spirit.' It is hard not to suspect in all this the sulphurous smell of the political and commercial pit and not a disinterested attempt to secure the best possible broadcasting service. . . . But what do the critics want ? To judge by the Lords debate last week some people are merely curious and would like to take the system up by the roots and look at it.* Others are not really certain they can trust a publicly owned system. It is ' monopoly,' ' socialism.' They want some sort of ' corporation ' to provide ' competition.' Anyone who has given much study to the hybrid forms in some British Dominions or to the struggles of the American Federal Communications Commission to safeguard the public from the abuses of privately owned systems will be extremely sceptical of these pleas for ' competition.' . . . The Government is entirely right to stick to a system which in our small island at least has proved its worth and technical suitability."

But not all comments were as complimentary as this. In the *Spectator* it was stated that " The White Paper on broadcasting policy . . . is completely unacceptable as a reply to the growing demand for an early inquiry into the working of the B.B.C. and the possibility of alternative arrangements. . . . The arguments advanced—the abnormal conditions of the war years, the rapidity of technical advance and uncertainty about the international allocation of wavelengths—are completely inadequate and the passage of time will not make them adequate. The statements that only a monopoly can produce a ' properly balanced choice of

* Presumably a reference to the speech of Lord Samuel.

programmes ' (whatever that may be) and that the Government will try to prevent commercial broadcasts from abroad ignore the fact that the listener has the last word in these matters by turning a switch.   Equally surprising is the argument which represents the ' dissipation of resources ' as the alternative to the B.B.C. . . . There are many acceptable alternatives to monopoly in broadcasting. . . . It is the business of responsible inquiry to examine the alternatives but the *White Paper* does not do it." [26] And criticism continued until the debate in the House of Commons. [27]

Mr. Henderson Stewart opened the debate.[28] After paying a tribute to the work of the British Broadcasting Corporation, he pointed out that the broadcasting system in Great Britain was based on a Royal Charter. " The essence of that Charter is that broadcasting is operated by a single monopoly within Great Britain, subject to certain specified, and a good many unspecified, controls by the central Government." He thought that in the early days the monopoly was " inevitable and right " but even " nine or ten years ago men were beginning to express doubts as to the wisdom of continuing a service which precluded all competition in any form of broadcasting. . . ."   There were various matters that required investigation but " it is into the nature of the monopoly itself, out of which all these other defects spring, that I think a penetrating inquiry is most strongly required to-day." He referred to the Government's satisfaction with the existing system expressed in the *White Paper* but added " as Sir Frederick Ogilvie has said, from the point of view of the Government, it is an ideal system. No competition in programmes or engineering to offer troublesome comparisons. Not too much news about what happens inside the machine. A polite authoritative rule giving the people what it thinks they ought to have ; an arrangement whereby the B.B.C. do not trouble the Government too much, and take orders from them when necessary. It is a good system for the Government. But the question we have to ask ourselves is whether it is the ideal system for the people, our people, with their highly individualist and democratic character. The things of the body, such as food, clothes, fuel and light are controlled, and probably will be controlled for a lengthy period ; and it is for that very reason that I plead that the things of the spirit shall enjoy the fullest freedom we can give them."   Later Mr. Henderson Stewart said : " Surely, nobody seriously suggests that if, instead of one, we had two, three or four independent broadcasting corporations or organisations in this country, each vying with, competing with, challenging the others in engineering, technical production, and programmes, the standard of broadcasting in this country would not improve ? The establishment of these separate organisations need not have anything whatever to do with commercial broadcasting." He then referred to the desire of Welshmen and Scotsmen for independent broadcasting corporations.[29] Mr. Henderson Stewart did not advocate commercial broadcasting but he thought the arguments which had been advanced in its favour were worthy of re-examination.

Mr. Herbert Morrison followed. He referred to the British Broadcasting Corporation as " a most interesting example of the British national genius for finding workable solutions to the most intractable problems." He agreed that broadcasting was " at least as powerful a vehicle of ideas as the printing press. In broadcasting, however, the public's choice of listening matter is very narrowly limited by the number of wavelengths available. Clearly, therefore, the body which decides what goes into a broadcasting programme has an enormous power for good and evil over the minds of the nation, and that power must not fall into the wrong hands. I think that we are all agreed that this is the fundamental problem : To ensure that the microphone is controlled by some body in which the public can have confidence." Mr. Morrison then praised the method of organisation by means of a public corporation which prevented broadcasting " falling into the hands of private or sectional interests which might use it for their own private ends." It was also independent of the Government. There was no objection in principle to " subjecting the B.B.C. from time to time to a searching inquiry by an independent body. All great channels for the dissemination of information to the public would, the Government believe, benefit from having their state of health examined by an independent inquiry from time to time. . . ." Mr. Morrison then said that the Press, which had "vigorously demanded an inquiry into the B.B.C.," was not excluded from that consideration.* In justification of the Government's decision not to hold an inquiry into broadcasting, Mr. Morrison referred to the forthcoming international conferences on the allocation of wave-

* I do not propose to consider the discussion of this suggestion. But the assumption of some speakers that this foreshadowed an inquiry into the Press proved to be correct.

lengths. Mr. Morrison also answered the critics of the monopoly. " Let us look at the possible alternatives to this present State monopoly, the public service, which some people profess to find so distasteful. Private enterprise in the field of broadcasting fairly inevitably, perhaps not quite certainly, means commercial broadcasting. There are powerful and not always disinterested voices pressing the claims of commercial broadcasting in this country to-day and pointing to the United States system, or to the system which, in some British Dominions, permits commercial broadcasting services alongside those run by the State, as the models which we should adopt. It is not for us to criticise the internal broadcasting systems of other countries, but I must confess that nothing I have heard or read has convinced me that the American listener gets such consistently good entertainment as we do in this country.· . . . Personally, I find it repugnant to hear, as I have heard, a programme of beautifully sung children's hymns punctuated by an oily voice urging me to buy somebody's pills. . . . But I am quite prepared to admit freely that these are matters for individual judgment and opinion. What is not open to dispute is that, owing to our limited resources of wavelengths, the number of commercial programmes which could be made available to listeners in this country would be very limited indeed, and the power of the owners of the transmitting stations correspondingly great. I have a feeling that to mix up commercial advertising with this business introduces into it an element of unhealthiness which would not be for the good understanding and good of British broadcasting, or, in the end, for its quality either." He had no sympathy with the argument that commercial broadcasting would increase the revenues available to the broadcasting system. " The B.B.C. has never been short of money. . . . As for artistes' fees, I believe them to be adequate to anyone who is not suffering from megalomania. We should be on our guard against interests who want to see the B.B.C. unduly milked." About the second alternative of " the State running both our system and the commercial system side by side," Mr. Morrison said that this ignored the wavelength difficulty. " That does not mean that this unwillingness to split up the concern, which we feel would have unwise effects on its effectiveness, that the Government do not recognise the value of competition and emulation." The Government therefore welcomed the policy of regional devolution. In his final remarks, Mr. Morrison said : " I do not think in this

BRITISH BROADCASTING CORPORATION

Audience Research Department

PANEL MEMBER'S GUIDE

What the Listening Panel is for

One of the jobs of the Audience Research Department is to tell the BBC quickly and accurately what listeners think of the broadcasts which they hear. The method employed is to send questionnaires about different broadcasts to a cross-section of the listening public known as the Listening Panel. Those members of the Panel who happen to hear the broadcasts about which questions have been asked answer and return the questionnaires. A careful analysis of the replies received enables the Audience Research Department to compile a report on each broadcast showing what typical listeners have thought of it, for amongst the Panel's 3,600 members are listeners of widely varying interests and tastes, drawn from all parts of Great Britain.

How it works

Once a week, you, as a panel member, will receive an envelope from the BBC. It will contain (*a*) a covering note, (*b*) a gummed reply-paid addressed label and (*c*) five or six sheets of questions (two of which will be double). Most of the sheets of questions are divided by perforations into three parts. The first thing to do when you open your envelope is to tear along the perforations, thus dividing the sheets into separate slips. The slips carry questions about forthcoming broadcasts (some slips devote both sides to one broadcast, while others have questions about one broadcast on one side and another on the back).

Please keep the slips handy during the days to which they apply, so that whenever you hear a broadcast about which there is a questionnaire you can answer our questions about it. It is very important that panel members should not DUTY-LISTEN.

What DUTY-LISTENING is and why it is wrong

DUTY - LISTENING is what happens when a panel member, solely out of a (mistaken) sense of duty, listens to, and answers questions about, a broadcast which he wouldn't have dreamed of switching on if he only had himself to please. For example, a panel member who normally avoids thrillers because they make her nervous but who listened to one simply because she had received some questions about it, would be DUTY-LISTENING. So would the panel member be who listens to ' Chamber Music ' in order to answer the BBC's questions about it, despite the fact that he knows that to him ' Chamber Music ' never will seem worth listening to.

The principle underlying the listening panel scheme is that the way a broadcast has been received by its audience can be judged by finding out how a typical "sample" of that audience reacted to it. Panel members who have only listened to a broadcast out of a sense of duty are obviously not typical of that broadcast's audience. That is why DUTY-LISTENING is "against the rules".

Quality not Quantity

Panel members need not worry if, as a consequence of the NO DUTY-LISTENING rule, they find they are completing only a small proportion of the questionnaires they receive. What matters is not so much the number of slips completed and returned, but their reliability. To be frank, carelessly completed questionnaires are worse than useless. A few slips carefully completed are far more valuable to the BBC than a large number dashed off just before the post goes.

About the Questions

Most of the questions speak for themselves. Many are followed by a printed list of alternative answers. Such questions should be answered by *crossing out* the answers which do *not* apply. You may sometimes find this system a bit irritating because none of the answers expresses your views exactly. Nevertheless, the system has great advantages to us because it simplifies, and consequently speeds up, the job of analysis. Of course, if you feel very strongly that *none* of the alternative answers expresses your view, then by all means say so.

Many questions will invite you to add comments in your own words. This is where you can let yourself go. But please remember one thing: do *not* use these spaces just to repeat in different words the cross-out answers you have already chosen on that question.

Sometimes you may be asked questions which you have already answered, either in your detail form or on a previous questionnaire (*e.g.*, "Are you a **regular** listener to **this series**?"). This is only done when we want to simplify the work of analysis by bringing together on the same paper your answer to this and to certain other questions.

"Amount heard" and "Reaction summary"

At the foot of each questionnaire you will find "Amount heard: ALL $\frac{1}{2}+$ $\frac{1}{2}$ $\frac{1}{2}-$ ", and also "Reaction summary: A+ A B C C−". *As it is essential that this part of the questionnaire should always be completed, please read the following instructions with special care.*

The words "Amount heard" on the questionnaires are short for "Please indicate approximately how much of this broadcast you heard by putting a ring round either **ALL**, if you heard the whole of the

CHART

Wouldn't have missed this for anything **or** *Can't remember when I have enjoyed (liked) a programme so much* **or** *One of the most interesting broadcasts I have ever heard* **or** *One of the most amusing broadcasts I have ever heard* **or** *One of the most moving (impressive) broadcasts I have ever heard*	**A +**
Very glad indeed I didn't miss this **or** *Enjoyed (liked) it very much indeed* **or** *Very interesting indeed* **or** *Very amusing indeed* **or** *Most moving (impressive) broadcast*	**A**
Pleasant, satisfactory broadcast **or** *Enjoyed (liked) it* **or** *Interesting broadcast* **or** *Amusing broadcast* **or** *Rather moving (impressive)*	**B**
Felt listening was rather a waste of time **or** *Didn't care for it much* **or** *Rather dull (boring)* **or** *Rather feeble* **or** *Not very impressive*	**C**
Felt listening was a complete waste of time **or** *Disliked it very much* **or** *Very dull (boring)* **or** *Very feeble* **or** *Not at all impressed*	**C —**

broadcast, or $\frac{1}{2}+$, if you did not hear it all but you did hear most of it, or $\frac{1}{2}$, if you heard about half the broadcast, or $\frac{1}{2}-$ if you did not hear as much as half of it."

The words "Reaction summary" on the questionnaires are short for "Please sum up your feelings about this broadcast by ringing either **A +, A, B, C** or **C —**". The chart above will show you what these letters stand for. When in doubt look for the phrase which most nearly describes what, *on balance*, you feel about the broadcast, and the correct letter to ring will be found by its side.

B stands midway between **A +** (extreme enjoyment or pleasure) and **C −** (extreme dislike). **A** gives you a half-way house between **A +** and **B**, and **C** gives you a half-way house between **B** and **C −**. A lot of people—out of kindness of heart—give **A +** when they really mean **A**, or **A** when they mean **B**. Please *don't* do this, for if **A +** and **A** are used too freely it is unfair on really deserving broadcasts. Besides, a reference to the phrases opposite **B** in the chart shows that it is no discredit to a broadcast if most people give it this ruling.

Please be sure to complete both the "Amount heard" and "Reaction summary" on every questionnaire you answer, for unless this is done we cannot make use of the other answers.

Signing the Slips

Just above your name on the envelope which brings you these papers you will find your personal reference number. Please write this, together with your name and occupation, on the back of every slip bearing a completed questionnaire. We are sorry to have to trouble you to do this, but it will save us much time. If your name and number are only on one slip, it is impossible to identify any of the others once the slips are sorted according to programmes.

Replies can be in pencil or in ink, provided they are legible. Of course, if you can type your answers, so much the better.

Sending in your Slips and Covering Note

Please be sure to post completed questionnaires back to us promptly on SUNDAY. We have to get ahead quickly preparing our analyses, so slips returned late are in danger of being left out. Blank slips should *not* be returned—the salvage people will be glad of them.

Whenever you send back a batch of slips, please return the covering note which came with them, having filled in the particulars required. (You need not return it if you are unable to complete any of the questionnaires.) The envelope in which the slips reached you should be used for returning the completed ones. The gummed flap should be stuck down and the reply-paid label supplied should be stuck over the original address. If this is done no stamp is required.

Two last Points

If you want a personal reply to any point, mention this when writing your query or comment on the back of the covering note. But *please restrict such requests to a minimum* as our staff is limited.

Please treat our communications to you as confidential. We shall treat your answers as confidential, too.

News Letter

Once a month we shall be sending you a copy of the Audience Research News Letter, a confidential monthly sent free to all Audience Research workers. We hope you will find this interesting.

case that a public monopoly is a bad thing. It is a basic service. After all, there are other monopolies that have been established. Gas, electricity and water are local monopolies but they are monopolies. There is a telephone monopoly. . . . I believe that in some cities there are actual newspaper monopolies in local publications. It is not necessarily either right or wrong and we think that in this case it is right."

The next speaker was Mr. Brendan Bracken. He said that the question of the monopoly was the " most lively " issue. He had much to say that was good of American broadcasting. Its entertainment was " infinitely superior to that provided by the B.B.C." ; its " educational and other broadcasting features " were " truly brilliant " ; it was " far more courageous in dealing with controversial issues " ; it was " much less rigidly controlled " and therefore made " all sorts of rewarding experiments." But the American system also had defects. And Mr. Bracken illustrated this section of his speech by quotations from the report of the Federal Communications Commission, popularly known as the Blue Book.[30] The conclusion which Mr. Bracken drew was that " we should not accept sponsored radio without a thorough inquiry into its working." Mr. Bracken also referred to the proposal which had appeared in the *Economist* ; but this he did not favour. " At the present moment, the revenues of the B.B.C. are barely adequate, if television is included, to cover its cost. The probable result of the proposal to set up three competing stations or systems not taking advertising will result in three financially embarrassed broadcasting systems. I hardly think that that would be an acceptable substitute for the B.B.C." But Mr. Bracken urged that there should be an inquiry : " Our broadcasting standards and performances are of the highest consequence to all our people. It may be that, quite by accident, we have fixed upon the best system of broadcasting. Or, are we perpetuating a monopoly which will cramp the great potentialities of broadcasting ? This question can only be settled by setting up the strongest possible committee of inquiry the Government can appoint."

Later in the debate, a speech opposing the demand for an inquiry was made by Sir Ian Fraser, a member of the Crawford Committee and a former Governor of the British Broadcasting Corporation. He did not agree that there ought to be an inquiry every time the Charter was renewed. " There should be an inquiry into an important and powerful organisation like this, or any powerful cause of controversy, when a special case is made out. It should not become a regular feature of our life to disturb a well-run and deserving concern at intervals." He denied that the broadcasting service had become a monopoly " almost by mistake." The Crawford Committee " deliberately chose to recommend the setting up of this new type of public corporation. The men who set it up, the men who controlled it, the men who engineered it, and Parliament, which has supported and sustained it in many debates and by much thought—all of us—which means this country—may well be proud, not only of the service which has been rendered, but of this new type of public corporation which has been found capable of expressing our will, our thoughts, our ideals and our aims in this new medium so effectively and so well."

But in the course of Sir Ian Fraser's speech an interesting disclosure was made. He said that Mr. Bracken had asked for more controversy " as if it were the B.B.C. which was holding back. I can assure him that that is not so and with the exception of controversy at a time when a matter is coming up for debate in Parliament, there is no withholding save the view of the broad-caster as to the amount of that particular kind of programme that the listener will accept." This caused Mr. Bracken to interject : " I am sorry for interrupting the hon. Gentleman, but I really do think that he is not doing any great service to the B.B.C. by ignoring certain facts. For instance, before the war, when the then right hon. Member for Epping (Mr. Churchill) implored the Governors of the B.B.C. to give him an opportunity to state to the country the desperate dangers it was entering upon by the squalid policy of appeasement, the B.B.C. refused to give him an opportunity to speak." And Sir Ian Fraser replied : " That is unfortunately true, and since the matter has come out it is quite right that it should be ventilated. May I say that at that time the elder Statesmen, of whom Lloyd George was one, the right hon. Member for Woodford (Mr. Churchill) another and Sir Austen Chamberlain a third, all joined together in representing that there was too much sub-servience on the part of the B.B.C. to the Whips' Rooms in relation to party broadcasts. The B.B.C. was engaging in frank and fearless controversy, and it was putting on first one party and then the other, but it came to take advice from the Whips' Room as to who it should put on. The right hon. Member for Woodford, being

unhappily not a white-headed boy of the Whips at that time, was
frowned upon. It was very wrong that the Governors of that time—
I was one of them—should have taken that view, but things looked
so differently afterwards."

During the debate, strong attacks were made on the monopoly
by Mr. W. J. Brown and Mr. K. W. M. Pickthorn. Mr. Brown's
view was that all monopolies were dangerous ; that monopolies
which could mould public opinion were most dangerous ; that
" the wider the area of economic life that is controlled by the
Government," the more dangerous such a monopoly became ; and
that the cure for a monopoly was to destroy it. Mr. Pickthorn
argued that the contradictory views as to the technical possibilities
ought to be examined. He did not like a monopoly of broadcasting.
" The idea of two systems is an idea which an honest and intelligent
man may hold and for which there is much to be said. Into that
suggestion there has never been a full inquiry and it seems to me
quite nonsensical to pretend that it is now too late, and even more
nonsensical to pretend that it is now too soon." And he went
on to suggest that the possibility of sponsored programmes should be
examined.

The Assistant Postmaster-General, Mr. W. A. Burke, wound up
the debate. He said that Mr. Bracken had relieved him " of the
necessity of dealing with American broadcasts." He considered
that " the level of British programmes is equal to the level of
American programmes." As to the monopoly, he said : " All the
committees have either recommended or endorsed the recommendations of previous committees that there should be a single broadcasting authority in this country, and that is the position at the
present time." * He then continued : " Sponsored programmes
would mean that some rearrangement of the wavelengths that we
have at our disposal would be necessary. Whether or not we agree
with the conception of a single broadcasting authority, we shall have
to face up to the position that to introduce any other broadcasting
organisation into the country would mean giving up one or more
of the wavelengths we possess at present. . . . If we were to depart
from the single authority, we would have to destroy the balance in
our B.B.C. programmes which we are trying to set up. The B.B.C.
has set itself, as far as it can, with the wavelengths at its disposal,

* In making this statement, he had been misled by the *White Paper*.   See pp. 158-159
above.

M

to give a variety of essential programmes—a light programme and a serious programme, and then a programme for each of the six regions. To take one of the wavelengths away would mean that one of the regions would have to go, or else a single programme would have to be put in its place in the national programme for the whole of the country, and that in itself would destroy the balanced conception which the B.B.C. has of meeting the wishes of the community."

This debate did not lead to any review of broadcasting policy in the Press. Indeed, a number of newspapers seem to have been more concerned about Mr. Morrison's statement foreshadowing an inquiry into the Press than about what was said on broadcasting.[31] *The Times* commented on the question of the monopoly : " Mr. Morrison insisted firmly that the continuation of a public monopoly is at present compelled by paucity of available wavelengths. Mr. P. P. Eckersley's letter, published on this page yesterday and challenging this position, was cited by Mr. Henderson Stewart in his opening speech ; and it is plain that there is a technical debate of great importance still to be settled between the experts. But for the time being the view stated by Mr. Morrison has not been authoritatively reversed. In any case there is no serious dispute that the British system of entrusting its administration to a public corporation with a wide measure of autonomy, and the utmost devolution within it, is the most acceptable." [32] And the *Manchester Guardian*, which thought the debate was disappointing, considered that it " was not wholly wasted. It proved at least that there is no demand for commercial broadcasting in this country. Hardly a single speaker was prepared to champion the sponsored programme. It is therefore clear that if we are to have better broadcasting in this country, which is presumably the object, it must be done within the wide boundaries of the B.B.C. . . ." [33]

The situation as it existed after the debates in Parliament was reviewed in an article in the *Round Table*.[34] But the arguments used had by that time become very familiar. This article drew attention to the paradox of a " freedom-loving country " in which the broadcasting system, by being a monopoly, violated " the chief principles of freedom at every turn." Freedom of choice was denied to broadcasters ; " an enormous patronage " was placed in the hands of a single authority ; and broadcasting was deprived of "the stimulus of rival standards." The persistence of the monopoly was partly to be explained because it suited the Government but it was "mainly due to the confused thinking which lingers on, not least in high places, as between monopoly and public service on the one hand, and as between competitive and commercial or 'sponsored' broadcasting on the other." The article quoted *The Times*: "A necessary consequence of the conception of broadcasting as a public service is that it must remain a monopoly." This the *Round Table* article characterised as a resplendent *non sequitur* and continued: "Public service and monopoly have, of course, no necessary connection whatever. . . . Outworn aphorisms about monopoly are of no interest. The question to-day is: granted a public service, what is the most suitable size and type of unit or units for it? For British broadcasting, the broad answer is clear: one public body for the engineering side and several public bodies for programmes." On the question of commercial broadcasting, it was stated: "If sponsoring were to be introduced into British broadcasting, two absolute conditions should apply to it. First, it should be confined to programmes of entertainment and excluded altogether from programmes of opinion. . . . And secondly, there should be strict regulations regarding the balance of programmes as a whole and the ethics and artistry of advertising."

In contrast with the previous occasions when the Charter has been granted or renewed, interest this time did not die away after the debate in Parliament on the decision. In October, 1946, the Council of the British Actors' Equity Association unanimously accepted a recommendation by its broadcasting sub-committee that "some form of competitive organisation is desirable in addition to the present B.B.C." What they had in mind was the setting up of another Corporation, similar to the British Broadcasting Corporation, but independent of it.[35] In December, Mr. Benn Levy, a Member of Parliament, who was associated with the theatre, advocated a "system of genuine autonomy for stations or groups of stations. They would be federated, as it were, for all technical purposes under the Post Office, but otherwise as independent and free as competing publishing houses. . . ."[36] And in the same month the *Economist* once more asked the question: is a monopoly the best way of organising broadcasting?[37]

3. Two contributions

In July, 1946, in the midst of the debate, there appeared two most important contributions to thought on the subject of broadcasting policy. Neither appear to have attracted any attention. But they were both of great interest.

The first was an article by Sir Ernest Barker on " Broadcasting and Democracy." [38] I propose to set out Sir Ernest Barker's argument by means of extensive quotation. " There are many newspapers ; and different newspapers take different lines, express different trends and are engaged in disagreement and discussion with one another. . . . There is one system of broadcasting, and only one system ; and the world of broadcasting is in no sense a microcosm of the political world. Under these conditions broadcasting is necessarily a neutral thing. It is all things to all men. It does not expound any trend of opinion, it does not attack any trend of opinion. . . . Broadcasting, as it now exists among us, is a means, or a conduit, rather than an organ. It may be active, indeed, in providing information, or furnishing talks by experts which can be taken up into and made a part of discussion afterwards. But that, at best, is an ancillary function. The full activity of being an effective organ of discussion is denied to it.

" But it does not follow that broadcasting, under some other system, might not be an effective organ of discussion, and therefore an active part of democracy. Imagine for instance, that Great Britain had some half-dozen broadcasting systems, instead of one. They might be organised on a regional basis (one at Manchester, one at Edinburgh, and so forth) or they might be organised on a functional basis (one dealing with one sort of a programme or one type of subject, and the others with others) ; or—perhaps best of all—they might be organised on a mixed sort of basis, partly regional and partly functional. . . . If such a thing were possible, and if there were half-a-dozen different broadcasting systems—each with some local colour, or some mixture of both sorts of colour—then the world of broadcasting would begin to be a little more like the world of the newspaper, and thereby it would also become (in virtue of being immersed in debate and discussion) more of a microcosm of the political world of government by discussion. . . .

" Within the limits of its present system, British broadcasting has rendered the maximum service in its power to the whole system of national discussion.   The forum has been thrown open fairly : the exhibitions in the arena have been regulated fairly. . . . But at the end of the argument we are still left with the real riddle of the Sphinx.   Is the forum and the arena enough—the managed forum, the regulated arena ?   Or is there needed a system of broadcasting which is something more than the forum, the arena, the conduit—something which is itself discussion and itself democracy ? "

The next contribution was practical in character.   In the Final Report of the New Towns Committee,[39] the possibility of establishing municipal broadcasting stations was considered and the type of service which they might perform was described.   The discussion was, of course, directed to the functions which might be undertaken by the New Towns ; but the argument was general in character and very largely applied to any municipality.   I quote below the relevant parts of this report : " Whether or not large cities and towns may have a local broadcasting service of their own depends on considerations of national broadcasting policy. We understand that recent advances in radio technique make it possible, and this has led us to consider the part that broadcasting could play in developing a community sense in the new towns. We believe that the possibilities are very great ; the whole issue is at any rate worthy of serious consideration.

" Such a service could provide a forum for the free and open discussion of many of the problems which will arise in the course of the town's development, it could keep the citizens in regular touch with the activities of the agency and the local authority ; and it could become an effective channel for constructive criticism on every subject from the policy and rate of building to the planting of flowers in the public gardens.   It could co-operate with the local education authority ; it could create and maintain a regular and lively interest in the field of theatre, music and the arts.

" The service might be run in various ways.   It could be done by high or low frequency, based on the use of existing or specially installed lines ; with high frequency it would be possible to send several programmes along the lines in addition to the local one. The simplest method for a local programme would be by ultra-short wave broadcasting in which the frequencies available are many times greater than in the long or medium wave bands. Ultra-short wave broadcasting is developing rapidly in the United States of America and to a lesser extent in some Scandinavian countries ; if the new towns were to have their own stations they might well be anticipating a national development whereby the number of available programmes increased.

" The range of ultra-short waves can vary from a mile or two to a little beyond the horizon according to the height and power of the transmitter. For a new town a ten-watt transmitter would cover the area. The capital and maintenance costs of transmission would not be onerous ; sets capable of receiving these waves as well as the normal waves would cost relatively little more than those now in use.

" We recommend that the installation of an ultra-short-wave broadcasting service in one of the first of the new towns should be examined as a matter of urgency. A Postmaster-General's Licence would, of course, be required, and the question as to what body should establish and operate the service would have to be settled. Experience gained in this way might be of considerable value when national policy is reviewed." [40]

The Chairman of the New Towns Committee was Lord Reith.*

4. THE SILVER JUBILEE

A silver jubilee is an occasion on which critics may be expected to remain decently silent. Supporters of the institution demonstrate their loyalty and reaffirm their faith. The comments made on the occasion of the silver jubilee of the B.B.C. (Company and Corporation) in November, 1947, are therefore likely to be most useful for their disclosure of the reasons why it was considered that the policies of the British Broadcasting Corporation deserve to be supported. Our particular interest is, of course, in the monopoly, but since this is basic in the organisation and policies of the British Broadcasting Corporation it is not to be expected that it would be ignored.

Let us turn first to those comments in the Press which related to the monopoly. The following extracts are from the *Scotsman*, the *Manchester Guardian* and *The Times* ; a selection representative of the most responsible section of the British Press.

The *Scotsman* commented : " Any alternative system would

* This should not be taken to mean that there has been any radical change in Lord Reith's basic views ; the content of the programmes broadcast could be controlled by a new supervisory body on which the British Broadcasting Corporation was represented.

probably have been open to manifold abuses. The present position
of the B.B.C. as a responsible public body, holding the balance
carefully between political parties, while allowing an increasing
measure of controversial discussion, trusted both at home and
abroad for its scrupulous accuracy, moderation, and devotion to
truth, is one which is hard to challenge. Whether it would be good
for it to have to face some commercial competition is
arguable. . . ." [41]

The *Manchester Guardian* spoke of " the enormous moral, political
and artistic influence which the B.B.C. has power to wield." To
the question : " Is it good that the B.B.C. should enjoy a
monopoly ? " it gave the following answer : " Though critics of the
Right and of the Left assail it, there is no real doubt that it comes
well out of such inquiries. The alternative to monopoly would be a
commercial system subject to abuses and a general lowering of
standards which could never be desirable. The Corporation
is responsible to Parliament, it holds the scales carefully between
political parties and now more than ever ventilates political discussion freely . . . it is trusted, both by us and by other peoples;
it is addicted to truth and honesty. Its record in the war showed how
wide was this trust." [42]

The Times, faithful supporter of the monopoly from the early
days, considered " how well national needs are being met under
this British system " and in a short and well-managed campaign
routed the opponents of the monopoly : " Inquiry may well begin
by asking whether monopoly is inevitable. If more than one
authority were allowed, then each would be faced with problems of
wavelengths and of finance. The number of wavelengths available
for broadcasting in this country is limited. An international conference is to meet next year to reallocate European wavelengths,
and such is the congestion and confusion now prevailing that
Great Britain has little or no chance of improving her position.
The setting-up of rivals to the B.B.C. would mean an operation on
wavelengths such as Solomon proposed for the baby. A revolution
may, one day, be brought about by the engineers who are actively
experimenting to extend the channels available by the use of
ultra-short waves. The possibilities opened up are fascinating but
somewhat remote, for, apart from other difficulties, all sets would
need alteration before listeners benefited. The financing of rivals
could be done either by sharing the licence revenue of the B.B.C.

or by allowing advertisers to sponsor programmes. If the first
choice were adopted there would not be enough money for any
one full service. The advertising alternative would be a remedy
worse than any disease to which the B.B.C. is likely to fall victim.
The case for retaining the monopoly on practical grounds is
clear. . . ." [43]

I now turn to the talk on " The Place of Broadcasting " given
by Sir William Haley, Director-General of the British Broadcasting
Corporation in connection with the silver jubilee celebrations. [44]
This talk contained a tribute to Lord Reith and to the part he
played as architect and builder of the British broadcasting service.
But perhaps an even greater tribute to the influence of Lord Reith
is to be found in the content of Sir William Haley's talk. The
ideas contained in it are Lord Reith's ; and this even applies to
many of the phrases in which these ideas were expressed. It would
be difficult to find a better example of the dominance of Lord
Reith's views among those responsible for broadcasting policy than
in this talk given by the Director-General of the Corporation some
nine years after Lord Reith had ceased to have any official
connection with it.

Sir William Haley did not deal directly with the monopoly
question. But early in his talk he referred to Lord Reith's conception of broadcasting " run in the public interest as a public
service." And he added : " But this could not have come about
if the decision had not been taken that it should be a unified
service," that is to say, a monopoly. Sir William Haley did not
explain why he considered this to be the case, but it is clear from the
rest of his talk that the reason is the same as that which led Lord
Reith to the same conclusion—to make it possible for standards
to be maintained. That, at any rate, is the conclusion I draw
from the following passages in this talk : " Broadcasting's place
within any community is largely decided by the constitution it is
given. A commercial service run for profit can do one kind of
thing. But it has to forgo a host of others. A government-controlled
system can, at the other end of the scale, do a completely different
kind of thing. Whether it is to the community's ultimate good
depends on the government. In Great Britain broadcasting has been
established as a public service run by an independent corporation.
Let us examine the responsibilities of this rôle. First, it can conceive
that its highest duty is to the disinterested search for truth. This is

a stern concept. Absolute impartiality in all matters of controversy must be its golden rule. . . . Secondly, where broadcasting is independent and a public service, it can be used as a means of education in the broadest sense. What does this mean ? It means to use the microphone to inform and interest listeners in all things that matter. It means to inculcate citizenship, to pay proper attention to public affairs, to encourage tolerant discussion, and to seek to widen as far as possible the range of debate over the whole field of human interest. . . . Finally, within this sphere of broadcasting and the community there is the responsibility which a unified public service has to raise standards. There are many people who believe this task is better done if it is not talked about. To a great extent this is true. It should certainly be avowed as little as possible in the actual process. No one wishes to feel perpetually at school. But on an occasion such as this, when one is taking stock of British broadcasting as a whole, it should be frankly stated that to raise standards is one of the purposes for which the B.B.C. exists." But Sir William Haley went on to say that this work " will never be successful unless it is done within the broad contract that the listener must be entertained. The B.B.C. is a means of entertainment, as well as of education and information. It will rightly lose its listeners if it disregards that part of its triple function. It is not a function to be lightly dismissed or despised. To be a source of companionship, of recreation, of good humour, of escape, and of fun to millions of people is something of which to be proud. We must strive to do better in this field as eagerly as in any other. . . . The B.B.C. is not violating its part of the contract if, while giving him the best of what he wants, it tries to lead him to want something better. Broadcasting should not fear to assume leadership. But an essential part of leadership is not to get out of touch." Later, Sir William Haley dealt with broadcasting and the individual. " Here the public service has an exactly opposite aim to the commercial or the government service. It does not want people to be listening all the time. . . . For broadcasting will not be a social asset if it produces a nation of listeners. Whether broadcasting is an art is a point for sophists. What is important is that it is not an end in itself. Broadcasting will bring about a musically minded nation only in so far as it gets people to play and to fill the concert halls. Its greatest contribution to culture would be to cause theatres and opera houses to multiply throughout the land. If it cannot give to literature more readers than it withholds, it will have failed in what should be its true purpose. Its aim must be to make people active, not passive, both in the fields of recreation and public affairs."

5. THE STATE OF OPINION ON THE MONOPOLY

In 1936 there was general agreement among those writing or making speeches on broadcasting policy that a monopoly was desirable. What was the position in 1947? There can be little doubt, judging both from comment in Parliament and Press, that the view that a monopoly is desirable still commanded a substantial majority. But there was a difference. In 1946 and 1947 there was considerable criticism of the monopoly, whereas in 1936 there was virtually none. The emphasis laid on the value of internal competition is an indication of the change in attitude. But there is no reason to suppose that those anxious for the abolition of the monopoly represented more than a small minority. The difference between the position in 1936 and that ten years later was that the monopoly was no longer taken for granted. The monopoly was something to be discussed and justified ; but among informed opinion the dominant view was that it should be retained.

The views which I have considered in the previous paragraph are those held by people who write or make speeches on broadcasting policy. What of the opinions of the population at large ? Polls on the question of the monopoly were conducted by the British Institute of Public Opinion in 1942 and 1946.* The results in both years were substantially the same. The results of such polls must be treated with caution but they indicated that for the population at large there was no overwhelming support for the monopoly nor an overwhelming opposition to the introduction of commercial broadcasting. Indeed, among the working classes the sample actually showed a small majority in favour of introducing commercial broadcasting presumably because they thought the programmes provided would be more to their taste. But for the upper and middle classes the position was different. For these, in which the great bulk of the educated classes are to be found, there was a clear majority in favour of retaining the monopoly. The reasons for

* The results of these polls and some comments on them will be found in Appendix III of this book.

this difference in attitude are not hard to find. In general, the arguments by which the monopoly is justified are unlikely to be read, understood or appreciated except by those with some education. It is also possible that some of the members of the upper social classes who preferred the programmes of the commercial stations may have been less willing to admit it. But there is more to it than this. Though the programme policy of the Corporation gave the lower social classes what they ought to have, it gave the educated classes what they wanted; or, at any rate, more of what they wanted than they thought they would obtain with what was believed to be the only alternative—commercial broadcasting.

NOTES ON CHAPTER 7

[1] See E. Liveing, " British Broadcasting and its Role," the *Fortnightly Review*, May 1938, p. 545.

[2] See Kingsley Martin, " Public Opinion and the Wireless," the *Political Quarterly*, April-June 1939.

[3] See the *Wireless World*, October 1942.

[4] See the *Wireless World*, December 1943.

[5] See the *Journal of the Institution of Electrical Engineers*, March 1944.

[6] See *The Times*, December 9th, 1943.

[7] See Parliamentary Debates, House of Commons, June 29th, 1944.

[8] See the *Economist* for October 28th, November 4th, November 11th and November 18th, 1944.

[9] See the *Relay Association Journal*, December 1944, p. 1561.

[10] See *The Times*, February 12th, 1945.

[11] See *Time and Tide*, October 6th and 13th, 1945, *Everybody's*, November 10th, 1945, the *Sunday Times*, December 9th and 16th, 1945, and the *Economist*, January 5th, 1946.

[12] See Parliamentary Debates, House of Commons, February 19th, 1946.

[13] See, for example, the *New Statesman*, March 2nd, 1946, the *New English Weekly*, April 25th, 1946, the *Spectator*, May 3rd, 1946, the *News Chronicle*, June 1st, 1946, *The Times*, June 22nd, 1946, and the *Sunday Times*, June 23rd, 1946.

[14] See *The Times*, June 26th, 1946.

[15] See *The Times*, June 27th, 1946. In this article it was stated : " In defending its existing rights and duties against that body of opinion which professes to favour ' freedom of the air,' the B.B.C. need have no substantial fears, and the Corporation could derive no greater support and inspiration in the future development of both programmes and technical methods than from the findings of such an inquest."

[16] See the *Spectator*, June 28th, 1946.

[17] See the *New Statesman*, June 29th, 1946.

[18] Cmd. 6852 (1946).

[19] These quotations are taken from paragraphs 3, 4 and 9 of the *White Paper*, pp. 3-4.

[20] Except, perhaps, for a memorandum by Mr. G. S. Hans Hamilton. But his main proposal was one for internal competition.

[21] For the evidence presented to the Crawford Committee, see pp. 55-59 above.

[22] See Lord Elton's statement, p. 134 above.

[23] These quotations come from p. 6 of the *White Paper*.

[24] See *The Times*, July 3rd, 1946.

[25] See the *Manchester Guardian*, July 3rd, 1946.

[26] See the *Spectator*, July 5th, 1946.

[27] See *Time and Tide*, July 6th, 1946, *Picture Post*, July 13th, 1946, the *Sunday Dispatch*, July 14th, 1946.   On July 16th letters appeared in *The Times* critical of the Government's policy from Mr. Arthur Mann, a former Governor of the British Broadcasting Corporation, Mr. E. Searle Austin, the editor of *Advertisers' Weekly*, and Mr. P. P. Eckersley.

[28] See Parliamentary Debates, House of Commons, July 16th, 1946.

[29] Suggestions have been made on various occasions that there should be separate broadcasting corporations for Wales and Scotland.   Evidence asking for such a corporation for Wales was presented to the Ullswater Committee.   See the report of the Ullswater Committee, pp. 11-12.   For proposals of a similar character for Scotland, see two reports of the Saltire Society : *Broadcasting : a policy for development in Scotland*, December 1944, and *Broadcasting*, July 1946.   See also Parliamentary Debates, House of Commons, April 9th, 1946.   For expressions of similar views in the House of Commons debate of July 16th, see the speeches of Lady Megan Lloyd-George and Mr. M. MacMillan.

[30] This report, *Public Service Responsibility of Broadcast Licensees*, was issued by the Federal Communications Commission in March 1946.   Mr. Bracken said : " My slight knowledge of broadcasting in the United States would hardly justify me in making didactic criticisms of sponsored radio, but, if the Committee wish to obtain the best of all information about some of the defects of that system, they should read the most recent report of the Federal Communications Committee (*sic*), the United States Government instrument for dealing with broadcasting matters.   It has been reprinted by the National Association of Broadcasters, the representative body of the industry, who, presumably, concur in most of its recommendations and strictures.   There are some astonishing passages in this report."   Although this report was reprinted by the National Association of Broadcasters, Mr. Bracken's presumption that the Association concurred in the report was the opposite of the truth.   See *The Blue Book ; an analysis*, by Justin Miller, president of the National Association of Broadcasters.   I quote two passages : " Most of the broadcasters disapproved, very decidedly, because the Blue Book, after presenting a few instances of alleged poor performance, gave, to the people of the country, the impression that *all American broadcasting was as bad as the worst* " (p. 4).   " The Blue Book was accepted by American people, generally, as a truthful, objective, impartial description of American broadcasting ; when it was, instead, a highly biassed, partial presentation of the case for the prosecution " (p. 20).

[31] See the *Daily Telegraph*, the *Daily Mail* and the *Evening Standard* for July 17th, 1946.

[32] See *The Times*, July 17th, 1946.   *The Times* devoted a large part of its article to the question of an inquiry into the Press.

[33] See the *Manchester Guardian*, July 18th, 1946.

[34] " The B.B.C. Marks Time," the *Round Table*, September 1946.

[35] See the *Manchester Guardian*, October 31st, 1946.

[36] See the *Daily Herald*, December 11th, 1946.

[37] See the *Economist*, December 14th, 1946.

[38] See the *B.B.C. Quarterly*, July 1946.

[39] Cmd. 6876 (1946).

[40] P. 54.

[41] See the *Scotsman*, November 14th, 1947.

[42] See the *Manchester Guardian*, November 13th, 1947.

[43] See *The Times*, November 10th, 1947.

[44] See *The Listener*, November 20th, 1947.   Compare, also, Sir William Haley's article in the *Radio Times*, November 7th, 1947.

CHAPTER EIGHT

A COMMENTARY

1. INTRODUCTION

IN this chapter I wish first to examine the logic of the arguments which have been used to justify the monopoly, to discover the assumptions underlying them and to discuss how far they are well-founded. It is, of course, a severe handicap that the question of the monopoly has never been authoritatively examined.[1] And, in one important respect, that will limit the scope of my discussion. The lack of any authoritative examination of the question has meant that the alternative methods of organisation have never been set out and their advantages and disadvantages appraised—at any rate, in any publicly available document. It is therefore almost impossible for anyone who has not himself undertaken a study of the probable results of alternative arrangements to come to any definite conclusion as to whether a monopoly is desirable. None the less, it is possible to examine the logic of the arguments used and to consider whether, taking into account the criticisms which can be made, the case for the monopoly is so overwhelming as to make it inconceivable that any alternative arrangement could be better. And this is what I propose to do.

I divide the arguments which have been used to support the monopoly into two groups :

(1) Those which are based on technical and financial factors and on grounds of efficiency and

(2) Those which are based on the advantages possessed by a monopoly from the standpoint of programme policy.

2. ARGUMENTS BASED ON TECHNICAL AND FINANCIAL FACTORS AND ON GROUNDS OF EFFICIENCY

The most authoritative statement of the case for the monopoly based on technical and financial factors and on grounds of efficiency is that contained in the memorandum presented by the Post Office to the Crawford Committee. Although this memorandum was written in 1925 it cannot be said that later statements of the case for the monopoly from this standpoint have added very much to it. But I shall, of course, include in my examination such new arguments as have been advanced since 1925.

I start with the technical arguments. A great deal of stress has been laid by those defending the monopoly on the limitation in the number of wavelengths available for use in Great Britain.* It has never been seriously argued that this fact makes it impossible to have independent broadcasting systems, although in the early days of broadcasting some may have believed this to be the case.† But it has been strongly urged that the limitation in the number of wavelengths makes it very desirable that broadcasting should be organised as a monopoly. This is because it is considered that the determination of the number, the location, the power and the wavelengths of the broadcasting stations (a function that I shall in future call the allocation of wavelengths) ought to be in the hands of a central authority in order to prevent interference and to secure adequate coverage. This was the contention of the first and third points in that section of the memorandum which the Post Office presented to the Crawford Committee which set out the case for continuing the monopoly. The first point was that the locating of stations to reach " the maximum population . . . with the minimum number of wavelengths . . . can be done most effectively by a single authority." And as its third point the Post Office stated : " If separate authorities, and in particular municipalities, were licensed, it would be difficult to prevent the establishment of numerous separate stations in adjacent towns with the consequent overlapping of services and risk of interference."

But there is one aspect of the public discussion of this technical argument which reveals its indecisive character : it has never, so far as I am aware, been denied by opponents of the monopoly. Critics have been concerned with the monopoly in the operation of broadcasting stations and more particularly in the production

* According to the *White Paper* on broadcasting policy, 1946, the number of wavelengths available at that date in the medium and long wavebands was twelve (p. 12). In addition, some eighty-six wavelengths were available in the short waveband. Information on the short wavelengths was furnished to me by the British Broadcasting Corporation.

† It should also be noted that, although the number of available wavelengths limits the number of programmes that can be transmitted at one time, the number of programming organisations can be greater than the number of wavelengths, since time on a station can be shared.

of programmes.   If the technical argument is to be used in a form relevant to the question of the monopoly, it is not enough to show that the allocation of wavelengths should be carried out by a central authority.   It must also be shown that because this function has to be performed by a central authority it is necessarily desirable that this authority should also undertake the operation of the broadcasting stations and the production of the programmes. But the technical argument has never, so far as I know, been developed in this way.

It does not appear to have been realised that the allocation of wavelengths, the operation of broadcasting stations and the production of programmes are separate and separable functions. For example, in the United States, wavelengths are allocated by the Federal Communications Commission but the stations are independently operated and the production of the programmes is to a considerable extent in the hands of other organisations.   If this technical argument for a monopoly were to be applied to the United States it would be necessary to show, *not* that there ought to be a Federal Communications Commission, but that because it undertakes the allocation of wavelengths it ought also to operate the broadcasting stations and produce the programmes.

The limitation in the number of wavelengths has also been used as the basis for an argument, independent of technical considerations, which leads to the conclusion that the production of programmes ought to be in the hands of a monopoly ; but this will be examined later.   An argument which is more nearly related to this technical argument was that put forward as the second point in the case for the monopoly in the Crawford Committee memorandum of the Post Office.   It was stated that a single broadcasting authority " would consider itself bound to cover the widest possible area ; a number of separate authorities would tend to concentrate upon the populous centres, yielding the largest revenue, and none of them would be under an obligation to cater for the less remunerative districts." This is a very obscure argument. It was apparently assumed that if there were separate broadcasting authorities there would be no control over the location of broadcasting stations, so that operators would be free to set them up wherever they wished.   As an abstract proposition, it is incontrovertible that, in these circumstances, stations would tend to be established where the revenue was highest.   Unfortunately, we are not told what assumptions the Post Office was making about how

the revenue which would accrue to each station would be determined.   Since, apparently, stations which a central authority
would consider it undesirable to set up would none the less be able
to obtain an income, the Post Office would appear to assume that
the stations would not be financed by a division of the revenue
obtained from licence fees and would therefore not be subject to
Government control. Perhaps it was assumed that the broadcasting
service would be financed by revenue obtained from advertisements.
But all this argument tells us is that if there were no control of the
location of broadcasting stations and the service were financed by
means of revenue from advertisements, broadcasting stations would
not necessarily be set up in the right places. This argument, which
purported to justify the monopoly, in fact has little connection
with it.

The argument of the Post Office which was discussed in the
previous paragraph appeared to imply that independent broadcasting authorities could be financed only by means of revenue from
advertisements.   And this is consistent with a later point made
in the Post Office memorandum to the Crawford Committee (the
fifth point in the case for the monopoly).   The Post Office foresaw
considerable difficulty in financing the broadcasting service by
means of licence fees unless there was a monopoly.   They argued
that it would not be fair to the station which provided expensive
programmes which were listened to in other regions if all the licence
revenue went to the local station. [2] It has, of course, been one of
the main defences of the monopoly that any alternative system in
which there were independent broadcasting systems would imply
the introduction of commercial broadcasting.   " The alternative to
monopoly would be a commercial system subject to abuses and a
general lowering of standards which could never be desirable." [3]
I do not here wish to discuss the merits and demerits of commercial
broadcasting.   But the assumption that independent broadcasting
systems would have to be financed by means of revenue from
advertisements is by no means self-evident.   The question of the
monopoly is a problem of organisation ; the question whether there
should be sponsored programmes is a problem of finance.   The
problems of organisation and finance may be inter-connected ; but
they are separate problems.   It is possible to imagine a broadcasting
monopoly which was wholly financed by means of revenue from
advertisements.   And, conversely, there is no obvious reason why

independent broadcasting systems should not be financed by a division of the revenue from licence fees. In fact, a number of schemes have been devised which would allow independent broadcasting systems but which would not involve commercial broadcasting. [4] No doubt there would be difficulties in carrying out these schemes but there is no reason to assume without investigation that they are insuperable. It would also be incorrect to assume that a division of the revenue from licence fees is the only alternative to finance by means of revenue from advertisements. A broadcasting station can be financed by a municipality, as is the case with the New York City station, and as was proposed for Great Britain by the New Towns Committee; or it may be financed and run by a university, as is done by the University of Wisconsin and other universities in the United States.

Another argument based on financial considerations has been advanced by *The Times*.[5] It pointed out that " advocates of a dispersal of broadcasting, public or private, overlook the fact that, unless a considerably larger revenue could be extracted from the consumer, the competing concerns would be in the position of having to divide something like the present inadequate revenue among more purses, with several weak corporations taking the place of the present strong one." But this does not constitute a very strong argument in favour of the monopoly. It is true that if the present broadcasting organisation were split into several separate organisations and the present revenue of the British Broadcasting Corporation were divided between them, each would receive less than the Corporation. But each would require less. I will illustrate my point from another field. Let us suppose that all the universities in Great Britain were run as part of a single organisation and that someone then suggested that there might be advantages if there were independent universities such as Oxford and Cambridge and London and Manchester and Birmingham. It would not be considered a convincing counter-argument to suggest that under this plan Oxford would receive a smaller income than was previously made available to the combined University and that therefore it would constitute a weak University. But it may be that *The Times* was thinking not of the division of the existing broadcasting organisation but of the utilisation of certain recent technical advances such as frequency modulation or wire broadcasting to enable new broadcasting systems to be set up

N

alongside the British Broadcasting Corporation. This would certainly require additional revenue. But this does not, of itself, decide the question. There is not a fixed sum set aside to be spent on the products of each industry irrespective of the state of technology. If it becomes possible to have additional broadcasting systems in Great Britain as the result of technical advances, the question which has to be asked is : would the additional benefits which would flow from their operation be worth the additional cost ? Such a question can be answered only by an examination of the facts ; it is not one for dogmatic assertion.

Another group of arguments relates to the advantages which a monopoly is said to possess from the point of view of costs and efficiency. Two of the points in the Post Office memorandum fall into this category. The first was that by means of simultaneous broadcasting " the London programme can be distributed over the whole country and London can get the advantage of any item of special interest transmitted from a provincial station. To carry this out effectively and systematically all stations need to be under a single control." This was written in 1925. Since that date, the experience of the American networks, the members of which consist almost entirely of independent stations in a country in which distances run into thousands of miles and which operate in different time zones, has clearly demonstrated that it is possible to have simultaneous broadcasting carried out " effectively and systematically " without a monopoly. Of course, this does not prove that a monopoly might not have been even more efficient. Simultaneous broadcasting with independent stations involves a mass of contractual arrangements which must be costly to negotiate. On the other hand, the substitution of a monopoly would involve additional management costs for the co-ordination of the work of the various stations which otherwise would not be required. It is difficult to say where the balance of advantage rests or to appraise the significance of this factor without a detailed knowledge of the working of the alternative systems. All that it is possible to say is that the argument advanced by the Post Office is not conclusive.

The same may also be said of the other arguments which are based on the claim that a monopoly would be more efficient than separate broadcasting authorities. The Post Office argued (its sixth point) that a single broadcasting authority could probably employ a better technical staff and provide better programmes

than could separate authorities spending the same amount of money.
" There would be a saving in administrative and overhead charges
and the multiplication of fees for news copyright royalties, etc.,
would be avoided. The difficulty of providing facilities for several
organisations to broadcast important functions, speeches, would not
arise." [6] There is little difficulty in agreeing that a larger organisation *might* be more efficient ; the difficulty is to agree that it would
necessarily be so. We are prone in our present age to exaggerate
the advantages which accrue to large-scale organisation and to
minimise the disadvantages. [7] And one would expect the disadvantages to be particularly noticeable in such creative work as
that involved in the production of broadcast programmes. Of
course, it is not possible to assert that a splitting up of the British
Broadcasting Corporation would not bring some loss of efficiency ;
but it is also possible that there might be a gain in efficiency. Quite
apart from other considerations, it is reasonable to assume that the
force of competition would operate as a stimulus to improvements
of all kinds. A similar argument can be applied to the Press. It
might be the case, if *The Times*, the *Daily Telegraph*, the *Daily Express*
and the *Daily Mail* were all placed under the same management,
that all these papers would be improved and become more satisfying
to their readers; but this is not certain, and powerful arguments
could, no doubt, be advanced to suggest the contrary. The position
appears to me to have been well stated in the *Round Table* : " Outworn aphorisms about monopoly are of no interest. The question
to-day is : granted a public service, what is the most suitable size
and type of unit or units for it ? " [8] It is not inconceivable that the
answer to this question might be, if it were investigated, that there
should be more than one broadcasting organisation.

3. ARGUMENTS BASED ON THE NEED FOR A UNIFIED PROGRAMME
POLICY

The most potent of the arguments used in support of the
monopoly was not based on technical factors or on considerations
of finance or efficiency ; it was based on the need for a monopoly
in order to carry out a unified programme policy. Lord Reith's
influence has been dominant in the formation of broadcasting
policy in Great Britain and the need for a unified programme
policy was central in his views on the conduct of a broadcasting

service. He considered that a monopoly was " essential ethically, in order that one general policy may be maintained throughout the country and definite standards promulgated." [9] There developed the doctrine of the " programme monopoly." [10] It led the Corporation to attempt to hinder the development of wire broadcasting and foreign commercial broadcasting. In neither of these cases was there any question of the Corporation being deprived of a wavelength or of its financial position or efficiency being impaired. The aim was to prevent British listeners from hearing programmes which did not conform to the programme policy of the British Broadcasting Corporation.

The simplest argument in favour of the monopoly from the point of view of programme policy is similar to that used for the control of the location of broadcasting stations. Without control of location, all broadcasting stations might, for example, be located in Birmingham and the rest of the country be left unserved. The same argument applies to the programmes : without control over programmes, might it not happen that the broadcasting stations would devote themselves to Bible readings, or talks on gardening or on Communism, or to the performances of dance bands, leaving listeners who preferred some other type of programme unserved ? This is an aspect of the question which cannot be ignored. But the question remains : is it necessary to exercise detailed control over the programmes in order to avoid this difficulty ? Is it not enough for the regulating body to give general directions to those running the independent stations, deciding by their anticipated performance whether to grant a licence and by their actual performance whether to renew it ? Mr. Reith thought that this would not be enough. In his evidence to the Sykes Committee, he argued that such general control would be inefficient as compared with control through a monopoly. [11]

Such an argument might be considered decisive, were it not for the grave dangers which are implicit in a monopoly in this field. I need not enlarge on them. Mr. Catlin, Dr. Robson, Sir Frederick Ogilvie, the writers in the *Economist* and the *Round Table* and others have emphasised not merely that the programmes may suffer from the absence of competition but that such a concentration of power imperils freedom of speech. To those who believe this to be so, the question whether it would be possible, without establishing a broadcasting monopoly, to secure the degree of control which may be needed over programme content is therefore a vital one.

But these considerations do not appear to have troubled those supporting the monopoly of broadcasting because they do not seem to have thought that it constituted a threat to freedom of speech. Mr. Herbert Morrison, in his speech in the House of Commons in 1946, seems to have thought that a broadcasting monopoly was not essentially different from other public monopolies, such as gas, electricity and water.[12] The real danger, as was explained by the Assistant Postmaster-General, Mr. Burke, later in the debate, came from independent operation. " To take one of the wavelengths away would mean that one of the regions would have to go, or else a single programme would have to be put in its place in the national programme for the whole of the country, and that in itself would destroy the balanced conception which the B.B.C. has of meeting the wishes of the community." [13] This is a far-reaching claim. A wavelength in independent hands is a wavelength lost. If the Birmingham broadcasting station were operated by the Birmingham City Council, if the Light Programme were transmitted by a commercial broadcasting station, if the Third Programme were under the direction of a Board appointed by the leading British universities, the programmes would inevitably suffer because it would " destroy the balanced conception which the B.B.C. has of meeting the wishes of the community." While others see the concentration of power in the hands of the broadcasting monopoly as a threat to freedom of speech, supporters of the monopoly see in any dispersal of this power a threat to the programme policy of the Corporation. This attitude came out clearly in the discussion of Government policy in the case of wire broadcasting and foreign commercial broadcasting.

How is this attitude, with its brusque rejection of the appeal to freedom of speech and thought justified in detail ? The appeal to the principle of freedom of speech has been met by arguments which stressed the need for impartiality, the maintenance of standards and a balance of programmes.

The part which impartiality should play in the programme policy of the British Broadcasting Corporation has often been emphasised but probably the most concise expression of this point of view was that of Lord Mount Temple. He stated that " however controversial the matter broadcast, in whatever realm of thought, a fair and independent neutral balance should be struck between opposing lines of thought." [14] This argument has an immediate appeal : is not fairness to be preferred to unfairness ? But the question remains : why is fairness to be achieved only through a monopoly ?

But first let us examine what the policy of impartiality means. It implies that those running the broadcasting stations should not be allowed to express their own point of view through broadcasts. There should be no editorials. But it is not enough that there should be no expression of station opinion : the managers of the station should not have a point of view which they express through the choice of programmes broadcast.

I do not wish to discuss the question of whether if there were independent broadcasting stations, they ought or ought not to have an editorial policy. What I wish to consider is why it is maintained that it is necessary to have a monopoly if impartiality is to be the rule for broadcasting stations. The strength of this argument as part of the case for a monopoly is a practical one. This policy requires such high-mindedness on the part of those running the broadcasting stations that it is difficult to think of alternative institutions to which the broadcasting stations could be entrusted. If the stations were run by municipalities, these would obviously have a bias ; the same would be true if the stations were run by private enterprise. Newspapers and the political parties are ruled out for the same reason. Even entrusting the stations to the universities would involve a risk of bias. Indeed, it is unlikely that any group outside the British Broadcasting Corporation has been thought capable of matching up to the rigorous standards required. But, of course, even this practical consideration would not exclude independent broadcasting systems brought about by the splitting up of the existing Corporation.

Yet it is open to doubt whether this policy of impartiality is possible even for the British Broadcasting Corporation. I will quote from an article which appeared in the *Spectator* in 1936.[15] It said that the Ullswater Committee had assumed " too easily that impartiality is an ideal which can be realised by human beings. It is, strictly, impossible that the B.B.C. should approach impartially the problems it must face. Like everyone else, they must make decisions of policy and of attitude. . . . The B.B.C. has a personality of its own, pervasive and unmistakable, and it affects its reactions to public events, to education, to entertainment, and to the arts : it is the foundation of its policy." And when Sir William Haley, Director-General of the British Broadcasting Corporation, tells us that it is necessary " for those responsible for the conduct of broadcasting continually to be examining their bases of decision, to be reassessing questions, controversies, rival convictions and what the majority may at any moment call cranks, in order to ensure that citizens have what, within a democratic society, reasonable people would consider their fair rights at the microphone," [16] it is difficult to see how it is possible to do this unless those in charge of the British Broadcasting Corporation decide which are the important and which the unimportant issues and which views merit attention and which do not. The fact that the Corporation has been criticised by the Right and the Left hardly proves, as many of its supporters contend, that it is impartial ; of itself it merely shows that the Corporation has not been consistently at one of the extremes. What the general tendency of the programme policy of the British Broadcasting Corporation has been on controversial questions it is impossible to say, because the programme policy of the Corporation has never been examined.

We know that one of the effects of the Corporation's policy was that Mr. Winston Churchill was denied broadcasting facilities in the period before World War II.* It is now, of course, admitted by those connected with the British Broadcasting Corporation that this was a mistake.[17] But it is clear that it was a mistake which would have been less likely to occur had there been some other broadcasting system to which Mr. Churchill could have appealed for facilities to broadcast. It is not enough to compare what would happen if broadcasting were administered perfectly by a single organisation with what would happen if there were a number of independent organisations with various kinds of bias ; a single organisation will also have a bias, but made more dangerous because it may not be easy to discover.

The second reason used to explain why the achievement of a proper programme policy depended on having a monopoly was that it was necessary to maintain standards. This argument would appear to be composed of three strands of thought. The first is that

* See pp. 166-167 above for a discussion of this action when Mr. Churchill wished to criticise the policy of appeasement. Mr. Churchill had been denied facilities on an earlier occasion when he wished to talk on India. See his speech, Parliamentary Debates, House of Commons, February 22nd, 1936.

the ordinary laws against slander, obscenity and blasphemy are not appropriate to broadcast matter. The second is that the demands of some people, although not of themselves objectionable or harmful, are unworthy of being met.* As it was expressed by the reviewer of Mr. Reith's book in *The Times Literary Supplement*, to employ broadcasting for " the dissemination of the shoddy, the vulgar and the sensational would be blasphemy against human nature." [18] The third is that a monopoly is needed in order to raise standards—in this context the standards of taste of the listeners. The first reason appears to assume that a code for broadcast matter could not be devised which could be applied if there were independent broadcasting systems. It is perhaps true, as Lord Reith has argued, that a monopoly would be more efficient in enforcing a uniform policy[19] but a highly efficient application of such a code contains within itself a threat to liberty of thought and expression and to artistic development. The second argument—that certain demands are unworthy of being met—implies a philosophy which we now call totalitarian. It implies a State with ends other than the welfare of the citizens as they conceive it. The third argument is that a monopoly is required to raise the standard of taste of listeners. The argument is simple. It would nullify the policy if some stations provided the programmes which raised standards of taste but on others programmes were available which many listeners preferred but which did not contribute to the raising of their standards of taste. The logic of this argument is admirable ; doubts emerge only when one considers its assumptions and its implications. It assumes that a central body can distinguish between good and bad taste and will continue to do so as our notions of what constitutes good and bad taste change through time. It also assumes that control of individual activities is desirable in order to raise standards of taste. Its implications are far-reaching. This argument would justify and may in fact require a monopoly in a far wider field than broadcasting if its purpose is to be fulfilled. For example, some of those who did not find a programme being broadcast which they liked, instead of listening to the improving programme might read a book or newspaper or go to a cinema. But even if this argument in favour of the monopoly is accepted in its entirety, such improvement as occurred in our taste in music, literature and

* The Sunday programme policy of the British Broadcasting Corporation in the period before World War II was probably the expression of such a view.

the arts would have to be weighed against the threat inherent in such a monopoly to our freedom of speech and ultimately even to the springs of artistic activity.

The third reason for supporting a monopoly on grounds of programme policy was that it was necessary to bring about a balance of programmes. This could be taken to mean that programmes should not be all of one kind (an argument we have already discussed). In the early days of broadcasting it may have been interpreted in this sense. But later it acquired a new meaning. The balance of programmes became the right amount of different kinds of programme which the listener should hear. Wire broadcasting and foreign commercial broadcasting threatened the balance of programmes because they provided something which some listeners preferred to hear—and which the British Broadcasting Corporation thought they either should not have or already had in sufficient quantity. This argument involves a claim to determine on behalf of the listener which broadcast material he should hear.

At the beginning of this chapter I said that my aim was not to come to a conclusion as to whether a monopoly was desirable but to consider whether the arguments for a monopoly were so overwhelming as to make it inconceivable that any alternative arrangement could be better. I have shown that the technical arguments are incorrect, the arguments on grounds of finance unproven and those on grounds of efficiency inconclusive. But, of course, the really important argument has been that a monopoly was required in order that there should be a unified programme policy. This argument is powerful and on its assumptions it is no doubt logical. Its main disadvantage is that to accept its assumptions it is necessary first to adopt a totalitarian philosophy or at any rate something verging on it.

4. FORCES IN SOCIETY FAVOURING THE MONOPOLY

If it is true, as the analysis of the last section suggested, that the arguments used to support the monopoly have grave weaknesses ; if it is true that some of the most influential arguments were totalitarian in character and could also be used to support a State-controlled monopoly of the Press ; then one question demands an answer—Why is it that the monopoly of broadcasting has enjoyed such widespread support ? This is the question I shall attempt to answer in this section.

It is my view that the solution of this paradox can in part be found in certain institutional forces which contributed greatly to the general acceptance of the monopoly. And I now wish to consider the influence of the political parties, the Press, the Post Office and the British Broadcasting Corporation.

It might have been thought that the opposition of the political parties would have led to a division of opinion concerning the way in which broadcasting should be organised. But this was not so. It was a Conservative Government which was responsible for the formation of the British Broadcasting Corporation. But the formation of the Corporation was not opposed by the Labour Party. On the contrary, they welcomed it as a piece of socialistic legislation. The Liberal Party (or some of its members) had expressed doubts about the monopolistic character of the broadcasting organisation in the early days. But this attitude was not maintained. On the Ullswater Committee, representatives of all three political parties were in agreement that the monopoly ought to continue. The fact is that the question of the form which the broadcasting organisation should take has never, up to the present time, been a matter of serious political controversy.* There has been considerable criticism in Parliament of the policies followed by the Corporation but the monopoly has been accepted as basic in the organisation.

But what of the Press, the watchdog of our liberties ? Did it not see in the policy adopted towards broadcasting a threat to freedom of speech and expression and ultimately to the foundations of a free Press itself? It must be recorded that it did not. The Press, particularly the daily newspapers, has, on the whole, strongly supported the monopolistic organisation of broadcasting in Great Britain. Partly no doubt this was due to the fact that the question was not subject to political controversy ; partly also it was a reflection of the views generally held on broadcasting policy. But it may also have been affected by what were conceived to be the economic interests of the Press. The only alternative to the monopolistic organisation of broadcasting by the British Broadcasting Corporation was commonly thought to be commercial

* The more critical attitude towards the monopoly shown by the Conservative Party in the 1946 debate, when they were in opposition, was no doubt due to the fact that they felt themselves free to oppose " a piece of socialistic legislation " ; even though the Corporation had in fact been the creation of a Conservative Government.

broadcasting as in the United States, with the service financed by means of revenue from advertisements. Evidence was given to the Sykes Committee and to the Crawford Committee (and, no doubt, to the Ullswater Committee) by the Newspaper Proprietors' Association and by other associations representing the Press. They objected to the finance of broadcasting by means of advertisements, largely, it would seem, because it was thought that it would injure the newspapers. And when this method of finance made its appearance in the form of broadcasting from abroad, the Press, as we have seen, attempted to hinder its development. What I have described is, of course, the action of the newspaper associations. What the effect of this attitude of the Press has been on editorial policy and through this on the formation of public opinion on broadcasting, it is difficult, if not impossible, to say. To do it, we would have to decide whether editorial policy would have remained unchanged if the position had been reversed and advertising had been possible only with a monopolistic broadcasting organisation and not with competitive broadcasting systems. I can only express my own belief that in these circumstances, the representatives of the Press in their evidence to the various Broadcasting Committees would have adopted a more sympathetic attitude towards competitive broadcasting systems. This may or may not have affected the reports of these Committees, although it is probable that it would, but I believe that this difference in attitude would not have been without its effect on editorial policy and through this on the formation of public opinion on broadcasting.

The Post Office was the department primarily responsible for Government policy towards broadcasting. Now it so happened that the Post Office itself operated the postal, telegraph and telephone services as monopolies. Post Office tradition would be one in which the disadvantages of competition and the advantages of monopolistic operation were stressed or assumed. This does not mean that the Post Office would inevitably favour a monopoly in all industries with which they dealt. But they would be likely to have a bias in favour of a monopoly. And in the case of broadcasting, a monopoly was administratively more convenient.[20] The Post Office from the first exerted such influence as it possessed (and this was considerable) in order to bring about a monopolistic organisation. And when the Post Office presented its evidence to the Crawford Committee, it acted as an advocate. In the memorandum which Sir Evelyn

Murray, Secretary of the Post Office, presented to the Crawford Committee, he summarised the case for a single authority.[21] And that was all. In this memorandum there was no setting out of the issues, of the various alternatives, with their advantages and disadvantages ; there was the presentation of a case. The Post Office was the body to which a Committee would look for advice on broadcasting policy. In the case of the Crawford Committee, we know the advice they were given was that a monopoly of broadcasting was desirable. And there is no reason to suppose that at any date after the formation of the Corporation, the Post Office ever took any action other than that which would further the maintenance of the monopoly. Certainly, in the case of the two most important threats to the monopoly of the Corporation, wire broadcasting and foreign commercial broadcasting, the Post Office took such action as lay within its power to protect the monopoly.

The radio manufacturers who associated together to form the British Broadcasting Company had no strong convictions about the desirability of a broadcasting monopoly ; that a single company was established may be largely ascribed to the action of the Post Office.[22] But after the decision to form a single company was made, Mr. Reith was appointed to be General Manager. There is no reason to suppose that his views on the organisation of broadcasting played any part in causing him to be selected. But, by chance, the Directors of the Company had appointed someone who believed strongly in centralised control and whose philosophy led him to the conclusion that the broadcasting service should be organised as a monopoly.[23] Mr. Reith was active in spreading his views, and very convincing not simply because of his ability to express them, but also because of his evident sincerity. Under his guidance, both the Company and the Corporation, through their public relations departments and in other ways, endeavoured to gain support for the view that broadcasting should be organised as a monopoly. It was very largely due to Mr. Reith's influence that in 1926 the British Broadcasting Corporation was established and the idea that broadcasting should be organised as a monopoly was generally accepted. And this work on behalf of the monopoly continued after the Corporation was formed. It is my view that Mr. Reith's activities when he was head of the British Broadcasting Company and later of the Corporation represented the most important single factor responsible for the widespread support which the monopoly enjoyed.

The influence of the political parties, the Press, the Post Office and the British Broadcasting Corporation all exerted in favour of a monopoly of broadcasting could hardly have failed to result in widespread support. Yet it is interesting to observe that this combination of circumstances was quite accidental. Had the Labour Party been in power at the time of the formation of the British Broadcasting Corporation ; had independent broadcasting systems not been associated in the minds of the Press with commercial broadcasting and finance by means of advertisements ; had another department, say the Board of Trade, been responsible for broadcasting policy ; had the views of the first chief executive of the British Broadcasting authority been like those of the second ; with this combination of circumstances, there would be no reason to suppose that such a formidable body of support for a monopoly of broadcasting would ever have arisen.

But there would not have been this support in high and influential quarters nor would there have been this general acceptance of the monopoly among the educated classes if it had not been possible to give compelling reasons for adopting a single organisation. The arguments used were in fact very persuasive. I have set out in previous sections my reasons for thinking that these arguments have grave weaknesses. But they were believed by those who were experts in the field of broadcasting and there was no investigation which would cast doubt on their validity.

To the layman interested in broadcasting policy, the case for the monopoly must have appeared overwhelming. The technical arguments suggested that a monopoly was inevitable or, at the least, highly desirable ; and the arguments on grounds of programme policy were powerful. They were aided by an appeal to patriotism ; for was not the British system " the best in the world " and the British Broadcasting Corporation a typically British institution ? The alternative was thought to be commercial broadcasting as in the United States, a horror against which the monopoly was a shield. Furthermore, the educated classes appear, on the whole, to have been well satisfied with the programmes of the British Broadcasting Corporation.

But this support for the monopoly also reflects the spirit of the age. According to our temperament, we welcome or acquiesce in the extension of central planning, even, it would appear, when it relates to a source of news and opinion. A monopoly is still regarded with disquiet ; but only if it is a private monopoly. A monopoly held by a public authority, as in the case of British broadcasting, is considered to be free from the vices of private monopolies and to possess virtues of its own.

Notes on Chapter 8

[1] Compare pp. 158-159 above.

[2] See p. 56-57 above.

[3] See the *Manchester Guardian*, November 13th, 1947.

[4] See pp. 136-138 and pp. 149-151 above.

[5] See *The Times*, February 12th, 1945, from which the quotation is taken. This argument was repeated in *The Times* of November 10th, 1947, and by Mr. Bracken in the House of Commons in the 1946 debate.

[6] See p. 57 above.

[7] See S. R. Dennison, "The Problem of Bigness," *Cambridge Journal*, November 1947.

[8] See p. 169 above.

[9] See p. 49 above.

[10] A term which, I believe, was first used by Mr. P. P. Eckersley. See p. 71 above.

[11] See pp. 51-52 above.

[12] See p. 164-165 above.

[13] See p. 168 above.

[14] See p. 81 above.

[15] See the *Spectator*, March 20th, 1936.

[16] See *The Responsibilities of Broadcasting*, p. 5, the Lewis Fry Memorial Lectures delivered in the University of Bristol, May 11th and 12th, 1948.

[17] See *The Responsibilities of Broadcasting*, p. 7. Sir William Haley indicated that there were others besides Mr. Churchill who were " kept . . . off the air."

[18] See p. 53 above.

[19] See pp. 51-52 above.

[22] See pp. 21-22 above.

[21] See pp. 55-58 above.

[22] See pp. 18-23 above.

[23] See pp. 46-55 above.

APPENDICES

APPENDICES

APPENDIX I
GREAT BRITAIN AND NORTHERN IRELAND
Number of Radio Receiving Licences Current

	Thousands			*Thousands*
March 31st, 1922	8	December 31st, 1932 ..	5,263
October 31st, 1922 ..	18	December 31st, 1933 ..	5,974
December 31st, 1922 ..	36	December 31st, 1934 ..	6,781
March 31st, 1923	122	December 31st, 1935 ..	7,403
June 30th, 1923	163	December 31st, 1936 ..	7,961
September 30th, 1923 ..	180	December 31st, 1937 ..	8,480
December 31st, 1923 ..	597	December 31st, 1938 ..	8,909
		December 31st, 1939 ..	8,948
December 31st, 1924 ..	1,130	December 31st, 1940 ..	8,904
December 31st, 1925 ..	1,645	December 31st, 1941 ..	8,626
December 31st, 1926 ..	2,178	December 31st, 1942 ..	9,139
December 31st, 1927 ..	2,395	December 31st, 1943 ..	9,436
December 31st, 1928 ..	2,628	December 31st, 1944 ..	9,649
December 31st, 1929 ..	2,957	December 31st, 1945 ..	9,987
December 31st, 1930 ..	3,412	December 31st, 1946 ..	10,770
December 31st, 1931 ..	4,331	December 31st, 1947 ..	11,054

Source : The statistics up to December 31st, 1923, are taken from the Report of the Broadcasting Committee 1925 (the Crawford Committee), Appendix III, p. 22 (Cmd. 2599, 1926) ; the statistics from December 31st, 1924, to December 31st, 1945, are taken from the White Paper on Broadcasting Policy, Appendix 2 (Cmd. 6852, 1946) ; the statistics for December 31st, 1946, and December 31st, 1947, were provided by the Post Office.

APPENDIX II
COMPOSITION OF THE COMMITTEES ON BROADCASTING
The Sykes Committee of 1923

Major-General Sir Frederick Sykes (Chairman).
> Unionist Member of Parliament.
> Chief of Air Staff 1918-1919 and Controller-General of Civil Aviation 1919-1922.

Major the Hon. J. J. Astor.
> Unionist Member of Parliament.

F. J. Brown, Esq.
> Assistant Secretary, General Post Office.
> Representative of Post Office on Imperial Communications Committee.

Sir Henry Bunbury.
> Comptroller and Accountant-General, General Post Office.

Viscount Burnham.
> Member of the General Post Office Business Advisory Committee.
> Chairman, Newspaper Proprietors' Association.

W. H. Eccles, Esq.
> Professor of Applied Physics and Electrical Engineering at the City and Guilds of London Technical College.
> President, Radio Society of Great Britain.

The Right Hon. Sir Henry Norman.
> Liberal Member of Parliament.
> Vice-Chairman of Imperial Communications Committee and Chairman of Wireless Sub-Committee.

J. C. W. Reith, Esq.
> General Manager, British Broadcasting Company.

Field-Marshal Sir William Robertson.
> Chief of the Imperial General Staff 1915-1918.

Charles Trevelyan, Esq.
> Labour Member of Parliament.

The Crawford Committee of 1925

The Right Hon. Earl of Crawford and Balcarres (Chairman).
> President, Board of Agriculture and Fisheries 1916.
> Lord Privy Seal 1916-1918.
> Minister of Transport 1922.
> Member of the Cabinet 1916 and 1922.

The Right Hon. Lord Blanesburgh.
> Judge High Court of Justice 1915-1919.
> Lord Justice of Appeal 1919-1923.
> Lord of Appeal in Ordinary from 1923.

Captain Ian Fraser.
> Unionist Member of Parliament.
> Chairman of the Executive Council of St. Dunstans.

The Right Hon. William Graham.
> Labour Member of Parliament.
> Financial Secretary to the Treasury 1924.

Rudyard Kipling, Esq.
> Author.
> Mr. Kipling resigned from the Committee at an early period in the inquiry.

Sir William Henry Hadow.
> Musician and author of books on music.
> Vice-Chancellor of Sheffield University from 1919.
> Chairman of Consultative Committee of the Board of Education.

The Right Hon. Ian Macpherson.
> Liberal Member of Parliament.

The Right Hon. Lord Rayleigh.
> Emeritus Professor of Physics, Imperial College of Science.

Sir Thomas Royden.
> Chairman of the Cunard Steamship Company and Anchor Line.
> President of the Chamber of Shipping of the United Kingdom.

Dame Meriel Talbot.
> Secretary of the Victoria League 1901-1916.
> Director of Women's Branch of Food Production Department, Board of Agriculture 1917-1920.
> Member of the Government Overseas Settlement Committee from 1919.

The Ullswater Committee of 1935

The Right Hon. the Viscount Ullswater (Chairman).
    Speaker of the House of Commons 1905-1921.
    Member of the Royal Commission on London Government 1921-1922.
    Member of Lords and Commons Committee on Electoral Reform 1929-1930.
Major the Hon. J. J. Astor.
    Unionist Member of Parliament.
    Member of the Post Office Advisory Council.
    President, Empire Press Union.
    Chairman of Times Publishing Company.
Major the Right Hon. C. R. Attlee.
    Labour Member of Parliament.
    Postmaster-General 1931.
E. Clement Davies, Esq.
    Liberal National Member of Parliament.
The Lord Elton.
    Fellow of Queen's College, Oxford, and Lecturer in Modern History.
Sir William McLintock.
    Senior partner of Thomas McLintock and Company (Chartered
        Accountants).
    Financial Adviser to Imperial Wireless and Cables Conferences.
The Marchioness of Reading.
    Chairman, Personal Service League.
The Right Hon. the Lord Selsdon.
    Formerly Sir William Mitchell-Thomson.
    Postmaster-General 1924-1929.
H. Graham White, Esq.
    Liberal Member of Parliament.

APPENDIX III

PUBLIC OPINION POLLS AND THE MONOPOLY OF BROADCASTING

The results of two polls conducted by the British Institute of Public Opinion on the subject of the monopoly of broadcasting are set out below.   The first was conducted in October, 1942, and the second in January, 1946.

POLL 1

Question : Would you approve or disapprove of allowing commercial broadcasting in this country, including advertising programmes ?

Answers :   *All figures are percentages.*

	Disapprove	Approve	No opinion
TOTAL	42	40	18
By social classes :			
Higher	63	35	2
Middle	55	35	10
Lower	37	42	21

POLL 2

Question : Should the B.B.C. continue to be the only radio in this country, or would you also like to have commercial broadcasting, paid for by advertising ?

Answers :   *All figures are percentages.*

	Maintain monopoly	Should also have commercial broadcasting	No opinion
TOTAL	47	40	13
By social classes :			
Higher	63	31	6
Middle	63	34	3
Lower	40	44	16

	Maintain monopoly	Should have commercial broadcasting only	Should have both commercial and non-commercial broadcasting	No opinion
TOTAL	42	4	45	9
By social classes :				
Higher	56	3	36	5
Middle	46	1	50	3
Lower	39	5	45	11

Note.—In Poll 2 the sample was divided into two and the answers obtained in different forms in order to make certain that the people questioned understood the implications of their replies.

It will be seen that the results of these two polls are broadly consistent with one another. Perhaps the most striking feature disclosed is the difference in the attitude of the different social classes. The upper and middle social classes approve of the monopoly and would disapprove of the introduction of commercial broadcasting. But among the lower social class, the majority of those who hold an opinion would approve of the introduction of commercial broadcasting.

It may be that some of those supporting the introduction of commercial broadcasting did not realise that this would also lead to a reduction in the programmes broadcast by the British Broadcasting Corporation, because wavelengths used for commercial broadcasting would no longer be available for use by the Corporation. Some of these might have expressed their approval of the proposal to introduce commercial broadcasting but would have been opposed to it had they realised its practical implications. None the less, it is improbable that their number was so great as to alter the general picture presented by these tables.

For the statistics included in this appendix I am indebted to the British Institute of Public Opinion.

INDEX

Advertising, 35-6, 140, 150, 155, 167, 168, 169; restrictions on, 11, 17, 41-2, 62, 118-19; and relay exchanges, 78, 89, 90. *See also* Foreign commercial broadcasting

Allighan, G., 109-10

America, influence of, on early broadcasting, 20

American broadcasting system, 128, 129, 130-2, 133, 141, 147, 156, 165, 167, 183; stimulus of, 8-9

American Marconi Company, 4

American Westinghouse Company, 12n.

Antwerp, Press Conference of 1934 at, 108-9

Astor, Major J. J., 86

Attlee, C. R., 90, 154

Australian broadcasting system, 140, 155, 156

Barker, Sir Ernest, on " Broadcasting and Democracy," 170-1

Bell, D. A., 148

Benn, Sir Ernest : *B.B.C. Monopoly*, 147

Birmingham, first broadcast from, 15 ; Post Office plans for relay system in, 93

Blake, E., 5-6

Bloomfield, Paul : *B.B.C.*, 147

Brabazon, Lord, 154, 155

Bracken, Brendan, 148, 165, 166

Brentford, Lord, 31

Brightside Divisional Labour Party, 114

British Actors' Equity Association, 169

British broadcasting, superiority of, 128-9 ;. suggested reorganisation of, 150-1

British Broadcasting Commission, 59, 119

British Broadcasting Company, registration of, 14 ; beginnings of, 15ff. ; agreement between members of, 30 ; difficulties with Post Office, 30-1 ; revision of Articles of Association, 37 ; agreement with Press over news, 103-5

British Broadcasting Company and Corporation, Silver Jubilee of, 172-6

British Broadcasting Corporation, formation of, 60-3 ; and sponsored programmes, 119 ; Charter of, 154, 162

B.B.C. Year Book, 78, 80

British Institute of Adult Education, 58

British Insulated Cables Ltd., 79

British Thomson-Houston Company, 12

Broadcasting, early experiments in, 4 ; amateur, 5

Brown, F. J., 20, 22

Brown, H. H., 10

Brown, W. J., 167

Burke, W. A., 167, 187

Burnham, Lord, 21

Burrows, A. R., 5

Cairo, I.T.U. conference at, 112

Canadian broadcasting system, 147, 156

Cardiff Corporation Bill, 82

Catlin, George E. A., 137, 186

Central News Agency, 17

Chamberlain, Sir Austen, 166

Chamberlain, Neville, 30

Chelmsford transmitting station, 4

Churchill, Winston, 166-7, 189 and n.

Clarendon, Lord, 61

Commercial broadcasting. *See* Advertising

Constructor, home, of receiving sets, 32-4

Controversial material, broadcasting of, 62

Cossor Research Laboratories, 148

Crawford and Balcarres, Earl of, 55, 131-2

Crawford Committee on Broadcasting, 46, 49, 50, 53, 54, 55ff., 106, 119, 128, 131, 132, 158-9, 165, 179-85, 193-4

Customs and Excise Department, 35

Daily Express, application for broadcasting licence by, 22 ; articles against monopoly, 30

Daily Mail, 4 ; proposed broadcasting service, 12

Davies, Clement, 129

Denville, A., 81-2 and n.

Donald, Sir Robert, 108

Dubilier Condenser Company, 79

Eccles, Dr. W. H., 50-1

Eckersley, P. P., 5, 8, 74, 87, 90-1, 142,

203